THE
BIZARRE
TRUTH

Andrew Zimmern

Broadway Books • New York

Culinary Misadventures
Around the Globe

THE
BIZARRE
TRUTH

BROADWAY

Copyright © 2009 by Andrew Zimmern

Published in the United States by Broadway Books, an imprint of the
Crown Publishing Group, a division of Random House, Inc., New York.
www.crownpublishing.com

BROADWAY BOOKS and the Broadway Books colophon are trademarks of
Random House, Inc.

Originally published in hardcover in the United States by Broadway Books,
an imprint of the Crown Publishing Group, a division of Random House, Inc.,
New York, in 2009.

All photographs courtesy of The Travel Channel, L.L.C.

Library of Congress Cataloging-in-Publication Data
Zimmern, Andrew.
The bizarre truth : culinary misadventures around the globe / Andrew Zimmern.
1. Food—Cross-cultural studies. 2. Food habits—Cross-cultural studies. I. Title.

GT2850.Z56 2009
394.1'2—dc22

2009027566

ISBN 978-0-7679-3130-4

Printed in the United States of America

Design by Ralph Fowler/rlf design

10 9 8 7 6 5 4 3 2

First Paperback Edition

To Rishia and Noah,

someday the luggage might actually

stay in the basement.

Contents

Contents

Introduction

Bizarre Truth? I can give you several, but one that comes to me in my dreams is the idea of writing or talking, which I do for a living, about a subject that I strongly believe is one that must be experienced up close and personally in order to be completely felt or understood. Not the most ringing endorsement for a great read or a good night spent in front of the telly. And let's face it, empirical, experiential, immersive travel always trumps reading about it. But we all can't be everywhere at once, can we? And what about music? Or sports? I guess I don't need to play in a World Series to appreciate baseball. Do you need to handle a guitar with the virtuosity of Frank Zappa or Prince to enjoy listening to music? No, you don't. And it is a fairly selfish conceit to try to keep all this goodness for myself. So I am committed to tell the tales and hopefully accomplish several goals in the act of doing so.

Educate, entertain, inspire.

There are lots of lessons to be learned by getting out and experiencing our planet. I think we live in a world where we are all motivated by self. We live in a world that has lost touch with its ancestry because we have grown more in every sense of the word in the last generation than in practically all the other ones combined. Gratification is instant or worthless, culture is disposable, literature and the arts are seemingly at the bottom of an all-time low when it comes to popularity. But this doesn't depress me. Frankly, I think we are simply at a pivotal swing point in our global evolution, and when tradition, culture, and ways of thinking are in flux they seem scary when analyzed under a microscope. But step back and take a view from up high, peek at the big picture, and you can see that what is happening is simply the "ebb and flow" of civilization. Things seemed awfully bad at the fall of the Roman Empire, didn't they? Well, I am not in the business of predicting a new Dark Ages, but I do know this for sure. I want everyone to take a deep breath, head out the door and see the world, spend time with people, not stand in line at a museum. Because in sharing ourselves with others we can learn a different way of looking at who we are and how we think and act, and maybe we can change in ways that would not be possible otherwise.

I was sitting at lunch one day in Sicily, and the thirteen-year-old son of the fisherman in whose home I was sitting and eating got up from the table. Potty break, I figured. Nope, he was headed off to work. On his own boat. That's the way it still works in the teeny town of Marzamemi on the southern coast of Sicily, near Pachino, far from the madding crowd. The town grew around its fishing industry, with the *tonneria* being the guiding force in the culture of the town. Tuna canneries in Sicily are a thing of the past; the industry is dead and the two remaining (out of nearly fifty a generation ago) operations are doing what they can to survive. Tuna are scarce. Men wanting to spend their lives on the water are even scarcer. But if you spent a day with this family you could learn more about Sicilian history and the human capacities for passion, dedication, pride, and good old-fashioned earnestness than you could in any other way I can think of. You can see how differently people live (in my country you can get arrested for child-labor-law violation), and yet how similar we all are under the surface circumstances of our lives. You can learn to appreciate life and be grateful. I want my son to know these stories, meet these people, see the world as it really is in African villages, European capitals, and Asian markets, because the way you learn how to live your life is by sharing it with others. You don't get anything out of life by living it based on self.

So education is important, but who wants to be beat over the head by the "pay attention" stick? Not me. I want to entertain. This is not intended to be revelatory in the classic sense. This is not a textbook, nor did I intend to write a serious tome. I am not half the writer or thinker you would need to be to accomplish that, but I do have experiences. And that's all it takes, quite frankly, which is why I believe so strongly in seeing the world for one's self. One of the most respected anthropologists in America, the chair of the department at a major university, once referred to me in casual conversation as a colleague and I corrected him, saying I was anything but. He rebuked me immediately, insisting that I had shared more real time, on the ground, with indigenous tribes than most tenured professors he knew. That was a wake-up call. I quickly realized that I viewed myself one way, and that others might see me as something else, and I could take advantage of that, becoming an agent of change to a certain degree, perhaps an awareness raiser for the global cultures I come in contact with. Education comes in many forms; I am always looking for an easier way than doing homework, but I am good at showing up for class. That means going places and seeing what's out there. I consider this book a way to engage a part of ourselves that remains fascinated by the human condition around the world. And I wanted it to make you think, laugh, and be hungry when you were done reading it. I am all about the food.

Which brings me to my thematic material. I am indeed primarily focused on experiencing food and sharing culture. Why? Because I know beyond a shadow of a doubt that everyone loves a good meal. And that food is the easiest way to bridge gaps, build friendships, and become family . . . all in one day. I consistently prove it again and again as I visit country after country, eating my way around the world. I also believe you can taste a culture and its people in their food. I swear to you I have tasted struggle and love, war and death, in a good bowl of stew. I wanted people to taste it also, and you can't do that eating at an Italian restaurant in Beijing. That's not to say that you can't find good veal Milanese in China, it's just I think you should be eating that dish in Milan if you want to really understand a cuisine and the folks who eat it. I wanted to give readers a sense of how I do that, not just what I find when I do. I give tips, like eating at the last stop on the subway, or investigating dying breeds, or perusing unique and arcane ingredients, or doing some hero worship at the altar of some great chef. Trust me; you'll learn a lot following some of these rules of the road. Most important, I also like to check out spiritual systems, and as a matter of course I regularly check out rituals wherever I can.

So why food and ritualistic traditions? Because the food always leads to conversations, and I am always asking people what they believe in, and why. The Greatest Questions, and ones we have been asking ourselves for thousands of years, are what do you believe in, why do you believe it, and what is your relationship to that belief? The next greatest question is, of course, "rare or medium rare?"

In all seriousness, you learn things in the oddest ways. When I was in the Kalahari, I spent some time with a local tribe outside of Xai Xai in Botswana, and we were hunting with snap snares, one of the trickiest ways to trap game, especially birds. We ended up checking our snares one afternoon, and lo and behold we had a bird in the small loop of string that the hunters had made the day before explicitly for that purpose. They made their own string! And they made it from stripping small plants of their fibers and winding them by hand. Anyway, when I found the teeny bird in the trap I grabbed my knife to cut the bird down, and was stopped immediately by one of the senior men in the group. "Why," he wondered, "would you waste the rope by cutting it?" I was floored. I hadn't even thought about it and yet it was obviously the most wantonly wasteful act I could imagine. I was stunned and had learned a valuable lesson on several fronts, but the real surprise was when we got back to camp I was told we wouldn't eat the bird 'til the next day because the tribe believed that the bird's soul would alert other birds to the traps unless we waited. And we needed those traps to keep snaring birds. My point is that belief systems and food are intertwined, sometimes directly, sometimes not, but you need to pay attention. I always try to learn everything I can about a culture, you never know.

The majority of my travel takes place with my family and workmates. And most of the working experiences are the lion's share of my traveling, and have taken place during the taping of *Bizarre Foods* and *Bizarre World*. Many years ago I took a meeting with the head of a production company here in Minnesota at the urging of a mutual friend (thanks, Robin!), and the resulting relationship between Colleen Steward and myself birthed both of our TV shows and several specials. The idea for our show was created at Tremendous Entertainment and was the collective result of a lot of smart and talented people over the years as we incubated, tested, and tried to sell the idea of sending me around the world mouth first. It took several years, but finally the amazing Pat Younge and his team at Travel Channel took a chance on an unknown talent and green-lit our show.

Shannon, Mike, Chris, Patrick, Tasha, Johanna, Scott, Steve, Gary, Luke, Joel, Tacy, Jane, Pam, Dave, Nina, Carrie, Laurel, Ellen, Ladonna, Erik, Troy, Steve, Darrin, Kel, Libby, Nicole, Tye, Debbie, and dozens of others worked very hard and put up with a lot of crap from me to make this show what it is. Here is essentially how it works.

We find locations and set the shooting schedule for the year, we rotate teams, researching and preproducing several shows at a time, enlisting the help of many local producers, writers, researchers, and videographers on the ground in each country to help us find the most compelling stories. We do not seek out strange enclaves or outrageous foods for the sake of shocking people. If we wanted to do that, we would shoot the whole thing at the town landfill here in Minneapolis and save a lot of travel costs. We find stories about real people and their cultural tradition. That's first and foremost on our minds. Then we try to tell the stories from the fringes, and that is ultimately where there are not only bizarre habits and customs, but also the greatest number of untold stories. It works for us. I always travel with a field producer and two videographers. We pick up sound techs, fixers, drivers, security folks, and PAs along the way. We typically travel seven to nine people as a crew, and we usually take seven to nine days to shoot a show in its entirety. Primary shooting usually takes six or seven days.

I spend more time on the road with my team than I spend time at home with my family. We are very close and have endured a lot together, shared life and death, and faced down some pretty hairy situations. I was in a small town in Morocco, outside a *madrasa* as luck would have it, on the day that Abu Musab al-Zarqawi was killed. My producer, cameraman, and I had to run for it, scrambling into the van and racing out of town. There was a lot of fear and misunderstanding on the street that day and we got caught up in it. That is not atypical.

My crew deserves more love and applause than I can ever throw their way, and I am eternally grateful for their ability to work seventeen hour days, day after day, and of course, they have to watch me eat. Never pretty. And we try to tell stories that help inform our audience about aspects of a place or a culture that they won't find elsewhere. Iceland had become a playpen for the Europeans up until the time of their economic collapse last year. It still is a place filled with incredible restaurants and a great lifestyle. The first stop on the subway, Reykjavík, bustles twenty-four hours a day. But for the handful of people brave enough to take on the assignment, curious enough to see what other people don't, Iceland offers adventurous experiences well off the beaten path—for example, snacking on freshly cured rotting shark meat at the Hildebrandur Farm in Bjarnhofn, a four-hour drive across a lunar landscape from Reykjavík. The farm is so far off the beaten path that on the day I went there we didn't see another car on the country's main ring road for the last half of the journey in and the first half back.

It's the same with the Philippines, where almost no one outside of the country, and very few native Filipinos, can comprehend the natural beauty of the southern province Palawan. A three-hour, hell-raising bus ride across the island brings you from Puerto Princesa, the island's only real town, to beaches reminiscent of Defoe's Robinson Crusoe tales, complete with wild komodo dragons and mischievous monkeys roaming the beaches. That's the type of experience that makes real travelers salivate. And even the crew and I knew it was special when we were there.

Now, the crew and I know we have it pretty good. We get to do some pretty cool stuff, but we also believe that you have choices when you travel and hope you try it our way at least once. For example, you can board some insanely overcrowded cruise ship and sail up into Anchorage, the Kenai Peninsula, and just about every other seaside deep-water harbor, where you'll avail yourself of whatever day trip the ship's staff recommends. You'll see Alaska, but it will be the same Alaska that 5,000 people saw the week before, and 5,000 more saw the week before that. Or you can call my pal Andy, drive three or four hours out past Girdwood, hop into a whirly-bird and get dropped on an ice field, or get onto a couple of snow machines and head to the top of a glacier in the Chugach Range. In fact, you can even get picked up on the side of the highway, if helicopter rides scare you, and ride all the way up the side of Carpathian Mountain. That's where you get the real backwoods adventure that is yours alone. Push your limits and you will learn things about yourself that you never imagined. When you're snowmobiling across an endless expanse of ice, knowing that you'll never lay eyes on another human being no matter how many times you do it—that's life at the last stop on the subway, traveling, not touring. No jet contrails, no streetlights, no safety net.

If glacial exploration is not your thing, try Samoa. Not American Samoa, but Samoa: a Pacific island nation composed of two large islands and a few small ones, all absolutely stunning. In the spring of 2008, I arrived in Upolu, a somewhat larger island in the Samoan chain, and spent a few days in the main town of Apia. Our crew caught wind of an interesting hunting expedition on the uninhabited island of Nu'utele. Intent on seeking out every "last stop" and "dying breed" experience we could, we packed up our gear, said a prayer, and boarded a dilapidated tin can of a boat and headed out to sea. Some would say, *Why bother?* Others might find this type of thing a little dangerous. They have a point, but I would say that an immersive, authentic experience is always worth the hassle, and in a world where statistics tell us that driving to work is the most dangerous voyage we ever take, some of the crazy stuff I have found myself doing doesn't seem very macho at all. So if this all sounds like your idea of a good time, you'll love this book. If you do it enough times, you might have the experience I had last year in Nicaragua. I am at the municipal airport in Managua, boarding an ancient World War II vintage plane to fly into the bush country on the Mosquito Coast. I had a witch doctor appointment at noon. On the plane, we met a couple of local fans who informed me that they called me El Pelon in Nicaragua, "the bald one." We all laughed, but our fixer Josh Berman was continuing the chat and I was curious, since I don't speak Spanish, what our new friends were saying. Josh was reticent to share, but I kept the pressure on and he confessed that the locals had told him they also call me El Chamboavaca. That means "he who eats like a pig, lurks like a snake, and shits like a cow." Someday that privilege may be yours.

So read on, and hopefully we can all take something from reading this volume, and I hope you are entertained by it. I will have been successful if just one person out there will be inspired to see the world, one human story at a time. One of the great lessons I have learned in my travels is that the most important thing we can ever share with each other are our stories. These are mine.

LAST STOPS
ON THE SUBWAY

[**Going to Extremes**]

Andrew arrives at Iceland's Alsey Island after a treacherous voyage through the freezing cold, raging sea.

Modern Day Vikings

Puffin Hunting in the Land of Fire and Ice

Iceland looks and feels like no other place on earth. As our plane touched down just outside Reykjavík, I was almost convinced we'd landed on the moon. Not surprising, given that NASA astronauts trained in Iceland prior to the first moon landing. In much of the country, the barren, rocky topography looks otherworldly. Iceland is roughly the size of Ohio, a moss-covered, glacial, rocky expanse born of the volcanic womb. Treeless mountains, sweeping fields of arctic grasses waving out to the horizon, awe-inspiring geysers, raging rivers, spectacular ocean vistas, and therapeutic hot springs fueled by boiling, underwater volcanoes are stunning but make much of the island uninhabitable. Iceland is called the land of fire and ice, yet despite its staggering natural beauty, the overwhelming majority of the population lives in the capital city of Rekyjavík. Everyone else is a farmer, or works in either the thermal energy business (booming) or the greenhouse gardening industry (emerging).

The country is changing and growing all the time—literally. In 1963, a volcanic explosion just off the southern coast of Iceland created an island one square mile in size. This landmass, named Surtsey after Iceland's mythological god of fire, grew to official landmass status in only three and a half years. I was fortunate enough to travel to Surtsey by boat one day. It's a phenomenal thing to see, an island that is as big as it is, that is as new as it is, and freakishly almost exactly as old as I am.

I knew the food in Iceland would be wonderful. As a chef in New York and Minneapolis, I'd always been floored by the quality of Icelandic lamb, dairy products, and seafood I'd run across from time to time. Icelandic animals drink the cleanest water on earth, eat the freshest grass, and breathe the purest air. Everything, from the horses to the sheep and cows, is genetically pristine and raised not only for their meat but for their milk and cheese products. Skyr, for example, the addictively cheesy yogurt product you see everywhere in Iceland, comes from cows that eat sweet grass for such a brief period of time, then silage for most of the year, which gives them a unique flavor profile that is distinctly their own. Sweet and white, devoid of the yellowed and grassy notes that conventionally raised cow's milk contains for much of the milking year.

I spent much of my time in Rekyjavík, puttering around town and enjoying the beautiful summer weather. Summer temperatures climb into the forties during the day, maybe fifties in the sun. We got a lot accomplished thanks to the globally famous amphetamine effect of the short nightfall. Occurring between 12 A.M. and 5 A.M., the mid hours of the night are mostly dusky blue and never really deep black.

The food scene in Iceland is vibrant. Small cafés like the Sea Baron serve up steamy bowls of chowder and lobster bisque, elegant eateries like Vox and Siggi Hall would be great restaurants with huge followings in any city in the world, and the local seaport boasts a lamb hot-dog shack that is a must for any food lover's Icelandic itinerary. I swam and spa-ed at the geothermal hot spring the Blue Lagoon. I availed myself of the local public bathhouses in town, which are very popular, and made a host of new friends courtesy of our larger-than-life host, Svein Sveinson. Svein, a filmmaker, bon vivant, and legendary lover of the good life, introduced himself to me online by sending me a picture of himself, stripped to the skin, after he'd stuffed his enormous six-foot-five-inch frame into the teeniest hot spring he could find.

After four or five days of cruising around town, I was itching for a change of pace. I was also looking forward to my first taste of puffin, those cute little black and white birds with big orange beaks. Before you get yourself all worked up about me eating this cute 'n' cuddly creature, consider the fact that only 300,000 people call Iceland home. The puffin population, on the other hand, runs between 8 and 10 million. Icelanders could eat puffin at every meal for now until eternity and they would never make a dent in that region's population. As a matter of fact, they urge people to eat them as a point of civic duty because there are just so many of them. The country even hosts giant puffin-centric food festivals, where everyone eats smoked puffins and grilled puffins and drinks to the wee hours of the morning. It's a strange food concept that few people outside Iceland really understand.

But to eat the best puffins, and to hunt them where they live, you need to head south of Reykjavik. There, you'll find the Vestmannaeyjarare Islands, a cluster of smaller islands that make up one of the region's most famous fishing communities. This area's other claim to fame is the 1973 volcanic eruption on Heimaey, the largest island in the chain. It's Iceland's version of Pompeii, but only a few decades old. Lava flows crushed half of the town, and when you see the end results of something that destructive and realize that it happened within your lifetime, it gives you great pause. You see homes buried, and cars half frozen in black, porous rock. Luckily, everyone was able to get off the island in time to save themselves, but my fantastically negative, cynical mind kept telling me I was trapped on an island without much of an escape route.

Millions of puffins call the Vestmannaeyjarare Islands home, and the local restaurateurs take advantage of this ample source of food. The rest of the citizenry are devoted puffin eaters or hunters, or both. Once our six-seat puddle jumper landed on Heimaey, we tried to negotiate our way over to the far side of Vestmannaeyjarare, tooling through the small town, lunching at a teeny fish house on steamed cod and brown bread. With its simple harbor, occasional spouting orca, seals and numerous birds, it was perfect for shooting a little b-roll. Along the way, we ended up running into a guy who claimed he could arrange to have us picked up by boat on the far side of the island and taken to an uninhabited island to experience a puffin hunt firsthand. Without hesitation, we piled the crew into our van and headed over to the far side of the island.

It's a bright, beautiful summer's day in Iceland, and in the sun it feels like it's in the low fifties. Perfect sweatshirt weather. We pass alongside a huge half-moon bay, complete with breathtaking views of the ocean and the outer isles, which include Surtsey, and start unloading our gear onto the mile-long black sand beach. There isn't a trace of human imprint as far as you can see. Not a jet contrail in the sky, not a footprint in the sand, not a boat at sea . . . it's just empty and desolate. You know for sure you're at one of the ends of the earth, a feeling I find so satisfying I could have sat at that beach all day.

We lock our vehicles, thank our new friends, and wait for our guide by a giant piece of driftwood that had washed up on the beach. After 20 minutes, we see a Zodiac boat puttering over to us. It lands on the beach and off steps Pall. He's a modern-day Viking: six feet tall, blond hair, 175 pounds, and shakes your hand with a grip that could crush pecans. Not big and muscley or long-haired with a horned Helga helmet, but he was clearly the kind of guy you just know can repair his own engines, build his own house, fight his way out of a bar brawl, and shoot the wings off a butterfly. He's the kind of guy who would travel alone in a Zodiac, a fourteen-foot flat-bottom rubber boat, across five miles of open ocean from an uninhabited island to pick me up. Hot on Pall's heels is a closed-cabin, twenty-foot cruiser with an inboard engine that will ferry the crew as they capture Pall and me having the "authentic" experience of taking the Zodiac to the island of Alsey, where his family has hunted for years.

I was glad I put on my knee-high rubber boots that morning as I piled into his boat from the surf side. The crew has already headed out into the channel on the cruiser, headed toward a giant boulder looming in the distance. I've been in a Zodiac plenty of times, so I plopped down on the edge of the craft on the gunwale, just as I did as a little kid puttering around the inner harbors of the South Fork of Long Island. It's the perfect vehicle for flat, calm water. Easy in, easy out. But today Pall instructs me to sit down on the floor of the boat itself, explaining that's how it's done in Iceland. I'm all confused—*What do you mean, sit on the flat bottom? In the water, no less?* And in his stern, Vikingly way, he says it again: Sit on the flat bottom. Next, he instructs me to wrap my arms around the ropes attached to the gunwales. *What do you mean, wrap my arms around the ropes?* He explains that I have to hang on tight unless I want to get thrown out of the boat. It is then that I begin to get a brief idea of what the afternoon will hold for me. He turns toward me, sees the look on my face, and a huge grin spreads across his, because he can clearly see I'm fucking shit-face petrified. After a moment of pure self-satisfaction, he tells me, "Today will be a great test of your manhood." And he goes back to staring out at the horizon as he guides the boat out of the quiet water and into the rolling seas.

When you're in a fourteen-foot flat-bottom Zodiac in rolling waves, maybe about eight or ten feet high, it's like being stuck on the longest roller-coaster ride of your life. No life preservers. No radios. Just me and Pall the Viking, cranking down the engine as hard as it could go in this little rubber dinghy. Oh, and in case you forgot, we're in Iceland. The water is just a degree above freezing. We are miles and miles from civilization as the crow flies, at least ten miles from the nearest town. If you fall into that water, you're a goner. You can't survive; it's just too cold. I say a prayer in my head.

Out of nowhere, an entire pod of killer whales pops up next to us. All those friendly, Sea World—inspired killer whale images go right out the window when you see this thirty-foot monstrosity cresting the waves adjacent to your itty-bitty keel-less Zodiac. I am sitting so low in that boat that I am almost eye level with the water. The killer whales are right there. The immediacy of the situation was oddly thrilling, and I am not a ballsy guy by any stretch of the imagination. The fear that was on my face became more and more evident to Pall, who just kept smiling at me. I know he thought it was just hysterical that I was almost peeing my pants.

We finally arrive at our destination after about a half an hour at sea, up the side of a wave and down the other side, repeat. The island looks like a giant round cylinder of granite rising straight up out of the water, topped with a grassy Kid 'n Play haircut. As we got closer, I could see a wooden cabin built on stilts on the side of the cliff. And I think I can see Pall's family waving at us. It turns out that every year in puffin-hunting season, which is about two weeks long, three generations of Pall's family—father, brothers, kids—head to Alsey and spend a few days hunting as many puffin as they can. I'm talking thousands of birds. They've done it every year since Pall's father, the patriarch of the family, was a kid. This is their ancestral family tradition.

We cruise into some softer water about a quarter mile offshore and idle beside a giant, two-inch-thick wire coming from the house and disappearing into the water beside us. I learn that the only way to unload the gear is through a pulley system. Several years earlier, the family sank a giant anchor into the water, attached a two-inch-thick wire cable about 500 feet off the cliff, and then pulled the wire up to the house, securing it with block and tackle to a landing about fifty feet below the house's platform. They lower the block and tackle down toward the water hooked up with a giant cargo net and we load up all our gear from the two boats. I watch it disappear as six or seven guys yank all the equipment to the top of the hill.

I assumed that while it looked tricky, that's how we were going to be getting on the island.

Nope.

Even these latter-day Vikings find that method a tad dangerous. If the equipment disappears, you're out the equipment. But people disappearing from that height, that's another story. Here is the safer method of hopping onto Alsey: You run the little Zodiac boat at top speed, straight toward the rock face of the cliff. A split second before you smash the boat's nose into the granite wall, Pall guns it into reverse. The boat freezes and you jump out at the last possible moment of sweet inertia, grasping, struggling to clutch the flimsy climbing rope dangling from some pitons high atop the cliff. As the boat pulls away, you hold yourself there, balance your feet on the slippery, wet rocks, and essentially pull yourself up, Batman Bat-rope style. Foot over foot, hand over hand, while other kind people (if you are lucky) who've arrived before you attempt to pull on the rope to make it a little easier for you. In comparison, getting back was a piece of cake: You just hang on to the rope, and when the boat comes in, you let go and fall (indelicately, I might add) into the Zodiac with a big thud. But leaping out of that boat onto the rock wall, aiming for this little piece of climbing rope about the width of your pinky, is one of those experiences that I will never forget. A literal leap of faith.

I knew that this great test of my manhood was not going to get any easier. Fortunately, Pall was a great coach and talked us through the whole thing. Our crew was wet, bruised, and scraped, but without Pall's expertise, we didn't have a prayer. Our success was directly related to the skill set of our leader, and he had gotten us all on the island.

We reconned on the top of the granite cliff and climbed our way to the top of the crest of the upper hillside, walking carefully along the cut-in path to the stone path at the highest part of the bluff, then up and over the last ridge to their hunting cabin. We walked about a quarter mile from the landing point to the house itself, where we changed into our puffin-hunting clothes, sturdier shoes, tough mackinaw jackets, hats, and hunting equipment.

Now, puffin hunting is done in a very specific way. You hide your-self in the rocks, holding on to a long and extremely unwieldy, twenty-foot-long, thick wooden pole that weighs at least forty pounds. At the end, they've attached a big net. I must admit that puffin, while beautiful to look at, are some of the stupidest ani-mals known to man. When feeding time comes, millions of them are just flying around their nests, so scooping a few into your net is as simple as swatting mosquitoes at the Friday-night family picnic. You time it precisely, however. When you see a puffin flit-ting past you, you swing this massively heavy net at it and attempt to guide the net toward the puffin's flight path. It's an ungainly process; the stick is so heavy and awkwardly long, it's like netting extremely speedy butterflies but on a much larger scale. The birds are so dumb that they don't really know how to move out of the way. Once you get a feel for how the puffins react, you can be very successful, starting your long slow arcing swing, aiming at an imagined point where the bird's flight path will intersect with the future position of your net. When you see someone with a lot of experience do it, it almost seems like they can will the bird into the basket. Pall's eight-year-old nephew netted about four of them while I was just getting comfy in my spider hole burrow. Pall, his brother, and their kids are just whooping it up—everyone has their puffin net in full extension, swinging it around, going gang-busters on these birds. Pall's youngest son nabs an additional two or three birds. His twelve-year-old son did the same, as did Pall and his brother. In an hour and a half, I netted one. It is literally as easy as shooting fish in a barrel, but only if you know how the puffins fly and aren't completely preoccupied by the thought of slipping and plummeting to your untimely demise. I almost fell off the hill the couple of times I summoned the courage to stand and swing my pole. The hill is nearly vertical, pitted with puffin nests, covered in thick matted grass so you can't see the rocks and ridges. That, in addition to the steepness, makes the terrain prac-tically unmanageable to do anything other than squat on. In fact,

Gordon Ramsey, the famous English chef, went hunting with Pall's family about three years after we did and fell into the water and almost died. It was horrendously scary sitting up there.

There was a charming aspect to it. You see, if you leaned out over the edge of the cliff just enough and looked down, you could see all the wild seals basking on the rocks, swimming to and fro and making cute seal noises. Perhaps waiting for someone to fall? Who knows. You could see the orcas blasting through their blowholes, rounding up krill, and all the seabirds diving into the water for their evening meal. It was glorious.

As the weather began to cool off, we started extracting the live birds from the net, snapped their necks, and breasted them out. Puffin meat looks a lot like wild Buffle Head duck: very dark and very purplish, with a small breast size. I'm accustomed to eating wild ducks and I've sampled sea ducks, which have some of the worst-tasting meat in the whole world—chewy, fishy, dry, and oppressively oily. I was expecting puffin to fall into this category, but the grilled puffin I ate on the deck outside the Alsey cabin was one of the most delicious meats ever to pass over my lips. It tasted like a delicately mild, finely grained piece of elk (or ostrich even) that had been waved over a pot of clam juice. The salty and sea life–intense diet these puffins have makes them naturally seasoned in a sense. Their musculature is such that they have a fairly small breast. You'd think it would be very tough from all the flying they do, but it's actually quite tender. Not grilling them past medium rare helps. Pall and the lads sprinkled the meat with salt, pepper, and a dash of their favorite grilling spice from the local supermarket and we devoured the entire platter before we even got inside the cabin.

Our hosts served up some smoked puffin once we got indoors. Smoked puffin is the most popular preparation you will find in Icelandic restaurants, mostly because it is so stable at that point and can sit in the fridge for weeks at a time without degrading in quality. We sliced it paper thin, pairing the meat with sweet Galia

melon. Here is yet another oddity of Iceland: They have no growing season. Sure, they have some hydroponic stuff that is coming
out of local greenhouses, but not much of it. A bag of carrots in
Iceland costs $10, but a pound of lamb or a pound of crayfish costs
next to nothing. It's the exact reverse of the way it is in the rest of
the world. Imagine a culture with plentiful meat and fish that are
very cheap, but where all the vegetables are very expensive because it's all shipped in from other places. So while I was all gaga
about the puffin, Pall's family swooned over this melon.

As we wrapped up dinner, I took a moment to explore the cabin
and was completely fascinated with the setup. It was a shack
without central heating, just a few electric heaters used only on
especially cold nights. Pall's family engineered a water system,
securing a PVC pipe 200 feet up the cliff from the cabin, topped
with a large 100-gallon drum so they could collect the rainwater
and glacial runoff. The pressure feed that resulted allowed them
to shower and wash up with rainwater, which they also drank.
Now, where in the world can you do that? It was one of the most
inspiring, self-sustaining environments I've ever experienced.
In a world where green living and sustainability is something
we try to force into our lives in dribbles and drabs, this family
was living in almost perfect harmony with their surroundings, despite the fact that it is only a place where, once a year, these
guys get together for the family hunting experience. Over the
decades, it's grown from a lean shack to more of a modern lodge,
now outfitted with two big community rooms, a living room, a
couple of bunk-bed-filled bedrooms, and a bathroom, complete
with slickly engineered, gravity-fed plumbing. They built a deck
around the outside of the house, and they primarily cook and eat
outdoors on the grill. It's a very macho, manly experience, and to
be perfectly frank, it's a little unsettling spending time with people whose eight-year-old kid can kick your ass. I've never felt
wimpier in my life.

Despite the fact that I could have been hung out to dry by the smallest of these guys, the camaraderie of it all was very familiar. I've spent a lot of time with friends and family duck hunting in New York and Minnesota, and the easygoing vibe of sitting quietly with the people you love in the great outdoors, with a gun on your shoulder or just a camera, is a contentment-inducing experience in the extreme.

The puddle jumper we'd chartered was leaving the airport in a few hours, and we knew that if we didn't get off the island fast, we'd miss the flight. We said our good-byes, scampered down the path we'd arrived on, climbed down the ropes, and dropped ourselves into the Zodiac, falling into the wet bottom of the dinghy. We ferried the crew out to the big boat and took our equipment off the zip line as Pall's brother and his kids sent it hurtling down from the house platform. Before heading back to the cruiser to drop me off, Pall took the Zodiac around to some of the caves where we had spotted some seals. He held the boat steady while huge waves broke on the rocks just in front of us, and I got a chance to stand a foot or so away from the wild seals before he took me back to the crew on the cabin cruiser, where we continued back to the main island.

Pall orchestrated a nice send-off for us, popping wheelies with his Zodiac against these giant rolling waves as his whole family gave us the Alsey cheer from the deck. They shouted, "Alsey, Alsey, Ah-Ah-Ah!" as we puttered off into the sunset, killer whales trailing us, cresting the surface of the water around our boat. It was probably the most exhilarating day of travel that I'd ever had in my life up to that point, the charm of the simplicity of another way of life quickly squashed by the immediacy of the modern-day fact that we had to race to catch a plane. We arrived at the harbor in the darkness and had to hijack several locals, begging them for a lift to the airstrip to catch our plane, almost leaving our guide, Svein, behind in the chaos.

The sense of accomplishment I felt after that day was incredible. The food was singularly fantastic; I have never had any eating experience like that. It's the type of eating that, as a collector of these moments in life, I find so unique. It's hard to measure it against anything else. I have yet to bump into any other group of people in my world that have hunted wild puffins and eaten them. I know there are some out there, non-Icelanders, but we are a rather small bunch.

There is a postscript to all this. The little boat that took us home, the cabin cruiser—well, the morning after he drove us home, it hit a rock and sank. Because of all the volcanic activity in the area, and the shaley nature of the rock in that part of Iceland, the rocky bottom of the ocean is always in flux. Say you are 100 yards offshore—you could be in 100 feet of water one day and in five feet of water the next. A rock can come up from the bottom of the sea or rocks can fall off the sides of the mountains into the water, which makes depth charts in that part of the world about as useless as the *Random House Dictionary* is at Harpo Marx's house. We were very upset the next day to find out that the boat sank, but looking back, I realized that at the point and time that I felt the most safe and secure was, ironically, the time that we were actually the least. Funny world.

The Most Dangerous Game

How I Almost Lost My Life Tracking Down Samoa's Elusive Giant Fruit Bat

Traveling from American Samoa to Samoa is a shot in the arm. It's like driving from Newark, New Jersey, to East Hampton, Long Island. Yes, it's the same part of the world, and to many observers there may not seem to be any difference between the two, but nothing could be further from the case. American Samoa is an overgrown military installation of an island with a modicum of beach tourism: a gorgeous island once, now wiped clean and free of accessible native culture. Land in American Samoa and you come face-to-face with the least appealing aspects of America's greatest contribution to world culture, the miles-long strip of Kentucky Fried Chicken outlets, McDonald's, and Hampton Inns. The local culture has been bulldozed underneath the tidal wave of mud that the modern-day developing world has sent their way.

Just a white-knuckled puddle jump away lies the stunningly beautiful, relatively unvisited islands of Samoa. A multi-island chain of inhabited and empty atolls of unmatched beauty, this just might be the last great unspoiled deep-Pacific country in which to find your own Robinson Crusoe experience. Just keep your hat low and your expectations lower, since you'll probably be spending one night in American Samoa anyway. After shooting for a week in Hawaii, I flew to American Samoa, landed, and spent the night in the glorious Quality Inn: Two hundred rooms of unmatched luxury, with a twelve-inch television chain bolted to the ceiling. Mold and mildew spewing from the ancient wobbly and rattling window

air-conditioning unit. Bedding stained from the endless proces-
sion of local call girls, short-haul truckers, military contractors,
and traveling salesmen who call these types of hotels home away
from home. I couldn't sleep. Food, save the five-dollar minibar
offering of Pringles, was nonexistent, so the crew and I headed out
into the night in search of dinner. We commandeered a local cab
and interrogated the driver mercilessly as to where to find the best
eats in town. Cabdriver interrogation (sans waterboarding!) is an
advanced research technique that field operatives like myself
have long since mastered. Growing up in New York City helped put
me at ease while sitting in the back of a beaten-down old Chrysler
with a shameless grafter slouched behind the wheel. A lifetime of
getting lost in cities all around the world has made me an expert at
extracting information from willing and less-than-willing locals,
and cabbies are a great resource for food tips. The driver in the
pimped-out 1987 Pontiac Coupe de Ville who shuttled us from the
airport to our hotel seemed like an okay sort of chap, so I gave him
ten bucks to park outside and wait for me in case I needed to pull
the plug on the hellhole we had been scheduled to sleep in that
night. I grabbed the team and off we went, piling in with Farid,
ducking the fourteen air fresheners he had dangling all over
the interior of his jalopy. A short while later, we emerged from the
cramped confines of his velour-encrusted love-mobile into the
parking lot of some dive serving some of the worst Chinese food I
have ever eaten. If Howard Johnson decided to make chicken chow
mein, it would taste better than the swill that passed for food at
the Quality Inn.

I was crushed, and on several levels. I hate wasting a meal, but
frankly it filled me with a dread that I fear more than any other.
Could the misery of AmSam be an accurate predictor of what the
next week's shoot would look like? I dread the Lost Week. That's
when you have your expectations for excellence dashed by a sixth-
sense premonition that the country you're about to step into simply won't measure up. Don't give in! Negative future fantasizing is

a game I play all too regularly, but ignore everything you see in American Samoa and remember, as little Orphan Annie says, tomorrow is only a day away. So I headed back to the hotel, crawled inside my silk sleep sack to avoid the humiliation and degradation of the not-so-Quality Inn, and set the alarm for 5 A.M.

Six of us were on the twin-prop heading into Samoa that next morning, and the plane was full. It takes only a half hour or so to head into Upolu, the most populated of the Samoan Island chain. We hopped into our van after a gentle landing and were off to the Aggie Grey's Hotel in the heart of Appia, the capital city of Samoa. You've probably seen this Samoa in your dreams: quaint city streets speckled with old colonial-style bungalows surrounded by brilliant tropical gardens, interspersed with marine shops and small local banks. Welcome to Samoa. We rounded the main harbor, snug with luxury sailcraft, industrial rust buckets, and professionally outfitted fishing boats with loud *Charter Me!* signs all bobbing in the early-morning sun. We pulled into the turnaround of Aggie's and fled the van for the friendly confines of the elegant lobby replete with a cozy coffee and tea lounge, a kitschy, open-air dining room with a few ukulele players, a guitarist and piano player pounding out Polynesian-style music at all three meal periods for the guests willing to endure the agony. Aggie Grey's is the Samoa of Somerset Maugham and Robert Louis Stevenson, an ancient hotel with luxurious gardens and a pedigree that most hotels would kill for. Ignore the fact that most services (like Internet or phones) are offered but don't function, and focus on the fact that hotels like Aggie Grey's simply don't exist anymore, holdovers from an era when traveling to Samoa meant staying for several months until the next tramp steamer left the harbor. Of course, traveling is different now, so Hotel Management has undertaken the massive (and, for the most part, completely unnecessary) task of creating a hotel that they believe appeals to international travelers.

Rather than cooking local fish (with an occasional grilled pork shoulder thrown into the mix), Aggie Grey's feels it necessary to do a themed dinner seven days a week, 365 days a year. When we arrived, the billboard in the lobby proudly hailed Chef Jaime's bold proclamations that tonight was "Mexican Night!" O-fucking-le. If you think the worst Mexican food in the world is served exclusively on domestic airline flights, you're wrong. Try going halfway around the world to the South Pacific to find a Samoan chef who thinks throwing salsa and a pinch of cumin into a dish equals Mexican food. Steamer trays filled with gallons of ground taco meat, piles of overly ripe avocados, platters of sickingly overcooked adobo chicken . . . my God, it was horrible. And in an effort to fill out the buffet we were subjected to the same sort of island-style poke salad (basically, a raw tuna salad with coconut milk and lime juice that was superb in its basic form), gussied up with whatever single ingredient they felt was most emblematic of the culture they were mimicking. Just horrendous.

We unpacked and headed out to shoot the little village of Tafagamanu, where the local government, in partnership with several nature conservancies, had established an underwater protection site for the study and propagation of the giant Pacific clam, a behemoth of a mollusk that can grow to the size of a Volkwagen Beetle if it has the time. Before we crept into the water to shoot our story, we met with the local villagers and their mattai, or chieftain. He greeted us at the large open *fale* that the tribe gathers in for important meetings and served us some homemade cocoa, and we made small talk for a few hours, much to the upset of my field producer, who was anxious to start shooting. In Samoa, every shoot each day begins with a business deal. Every story is shot in a different location, and each location is controlled in every sense of the word by the local tribes who received the islands back from the New Zealand government several decades ago. The Kiwis know how to leave a country, and after their colonial experiment tanked they ceded the country back to the tribes themselves, hundreds of them, so while there is a government in Samoa, the tribes and extended families own the land and the waterfront, another reason why there is so little development here. But to shoot each day means sitting and getting the blessing of the local people who control your every move. Want to shoot a sunset shot from the beach? Ask the tribe. Want to tape a stand-up walking down the road next to a banana farm? Ask the tribe. And they better like you, so sucking up and kissing ass is important. That being said, bringing each mattai a five-pound can of Hormel corned beef hash is de rigueur and goes a long way toward getting permission to shoot anything. The Samoans are addicted to the cheapest processed meats in the world. Canned hash, canned Dinty Moore stew, SPAM, they can't get enough of it, so doing business in Samoa required a constant shuttle back and forth to the local supermarket with Fitu, our fixer, piling can after can of the vile stuff into the back of the minivan. Irony of ironies—as we perambulated around the island, dosing out canned meat products with all the insouciance of a riverboat gambler, we ate very well. Oranges, grapefruits, dozens of banana varietals, and every other tropical fruit you can imagine grows extremely well here and can be had for pennies. Tuna is sold on the side of the roads for about a dollar a kilo, and that's the rip-off tourist rate. Every day, hundreds of local fishermen head out into the surf in teeny little canoes fitted with an outrigger to pull in the local yellowfin and blackfin tuna on hand lines. You heard me right. Sometimes as small as a few kilos, oftentimes as big as a man, the local tuna is traded around the island like a commodity, and with it you can pay bills, sell it from the side of the road, deliver it to the back door of a restaurant kitchen by foot, or bring it to the local market. It's a tuna economy here unlike anything I have ever seen before or since.

So we ate and drank with the mattai, shot our giant clam piece, and headed back to Aggie's for Mexican Night, swearing to never eat there again, and with justifiable cause. We awoke the next day and headed out to sea, traveling four hours into the South Pacific Ocean, where the big tuna run fast and thick. Deep-sea fishing is a passion of mine, and buckled into the fighting chair with several monsters hooked on the multiple lines we were running was thrilling in the extreme. Reeling a huge tuna into the boat is a challenge, but the motivation provided by the groan of the outriggers and the movement of the crew, sweeping fish out of the water with their gaffs, lashing the outrigger lines to my rod, and starting the whole process over and over until the coolers were full and we headed back to shore made for an easy day of work. Of course, eating the catch is what it's all about, and while clichéd, slicing and scarfing huge chunks of fresh tuna, raw, in the high hot Pacific sun is about as good a food day as one can have. The captain came down from the uppermost deck to show me the joys of true poke, mixing tuna with lime and coconut, cracking open the eyes of the fish and filling them with lime and soy sauce, and arguing over who would eat the still-beating hearts of the fish. Truly wonderful. We even got to try palolo, a rarity even in this part of the world, where these tiny little coral worms are eaten, seasonally, when they swim out of the coral to propagate twice a year. Sautéed in butter, they look like blue cream cheese and taste like rotten eggs mixed with anchovies, but spread on toast they are an addictive snack.

We skipped Italian night in the dining room that evening, headed out to the Appia Yacht Club, a generous description for a small Quonset hut on the beach with a postage stamp of a bar and restaurant with six tables on a twenty-square-foot deck built on the beach about five miles out of town. Drunken expats who long ago chucked in their cards in England, heading south with romantic notions of remaking their lives, these are the characters we found at the yacht club. Rumpled cashmere sweaters tossed around their shoulders, pathetically in their cups, arguing about the weekend's sailboat races and drinking cheap beer and rum, burning through the stipend provided by grandpa's trust, the people-watching was almost as superb as the food. Simply turned on a wood grill, the platters of true raw-fish salads and slabs of perfectly grilled local fin fish made the AYC our regular dinner stop every night for the rest of our trip. And as the Southern Cross revealed itself in the night sky turning from blue to black, I thought to myself, *Well, tomorrow should be another easy day in Paradise. How tough could a bat hunt really be?*

We woke at dawn and traveled to the Southeastern Coast, to the little town of Aleipat. On the horizon, as gazed at from the town's public dock, lies a small cluster of uninhabited volcanic islands, the largest one being Nu'utele, which is known for its pristine flora and fauna and is home to a rare and delicious breed of giant fruit bats. Ten-pound giant fruit bats, often referred to as flying foxes. Furry, large brown and black bats. Yumm-o!

It was on the beaches of Aleipat that I met the man who would eventually save my life. Afele Faiilagi, an environmental scientist with the Samoan Forestry Department, is inarguably the closest thing I have ever met to Lenny Kravits's doppelgänger, sans jewelry and a guitar. Buff in the extreme, he has a huge toothy infectious smile and sports baggy basketball shorts, a tank top, and flip-flops. He is that good-looking islander who is schtupping every hot South African and Swedish botanist coming through town doing research for their PhD. I was buoyed by his confident swagger and the easy way he carried himself. He was nervous about the TV part of the equation, but this guy spends his life prowling the jungles of Nu'utele and I wanted what he had, so off we went.

Afele commissioned a boat to take us out to Nu'utele. I use the term "boat" loosely; it was more like a tiny tin can, an ancient pontoon boat with an ailing 1960s Evinrude outboard on the back end, strapped to the transom with picture-hanging wire. We piled on the crew, our guests, and 500 pounds of gear, and pulled off from the dock in a warm and light morning rain. As soon as our voyage was under way, I got the feeling that the humble amount of money we had offered up for our five-mile voyage was probably more money than our anxious captain and mate had seen in months. It occurred to me that they probably said yes to the job not thinking of whether or not they could get us there safely with all our gear, or whether their boat was up to the task based on the day's weather forecast, but instead had seen the visions of sugarplums that our currency represented. Oftentimes on the road, the small sum of money we see only as a token payment is in reality a gargantuan sum to the person staring down at the stipend—so they take risks, stupid unfathomable risks.

The last thing you want to do when crossing a channel in the deep Pacific is put your life in the hands of a couple of old drunks whose vessel is actually a glorified soda can with a plywood storage bin affixed to the top. But we were on a tight schedule and our field producer needed to shoot. Well, the bay outside the harbor dock there is flat as glass, it's ten feet deep, and the boat is gliding out of her slip. We get out in the middle of the channel, and it's only five miles across to Nu'utele, but a half mile from shore all of a sudden we are in ocean several hundred feet dip in fourteen- or fifteen-foot seas, big rolling waves coming under the pontoons, and this little tin can of a boat is being pushed sideways. I'm petrified. I look around—there are no life jackets . . . there is no radio. The vintage forty-horsepower engine that is trying to push us over to this island is failing miserably. The guy who's driving the boat looks like the kid who carried my bags at the hotel but doesn't seem half as confident about making it to his destination, and he's got this worried look on his face. And all of a sudden, what had started as a "wow, this is sort of scary and thrilling" thing became scarier and scarier and scarier as the waves got bigger and the boat began to get pushed around more and more. The overcast sky swirled around us, the wind rose and fell, and my producer starts singing the theme from *Gilligan's Island*: "Well, sit right back and you'll hear a tale, a tale of a fateful trip, that started from this tiny port aboard this tiny ship." It was funny. The first time it was funny. The second go-round was less funny. On the third go-round, I turned to Chris and said, "If you sing one more bar of that thing, I'm going to punch your fucking lights out." THAT was pretty funny. Chris volunteered that when he's really scared he does that to calm himself, and I looked over at Joel, one of our videographers, and he looked really scared. I felt really scared, and I realized in a flash that we all truly felt somewhat doomed, in the middle of the ocean, on the boat ride to nowhere. After much nail biting and hair pulling, we finally got within the bosomy and calm natural harbor of Nu'utele, the sun came out, the waters were tranquil, and all we had to do was navigate through a maze of car- and bus-size rocks in this bay and try to beach the boat on the rocky shoreline. We did, and ran two lines, one to either end of the pontoon boat, then up and around the massive palm trees that stand vigil on the shoreline. Then, for about an hour, in waist-deep water, we ferried all our gear off the boat and made a temporary base camp in the trees.

Afele does a fantastic job helping us get situated under a little lean-to that is hidden in a small glade about a hundred yards up and off the beach. Dense tropical rain forest is all around you and at times you can't see five feet in front of your face, so the clearing and the corrugated steel topper on the old tent poles is a nice resting spot. No one lives on the island, but a lot of visiting biologists and other scientists venture out to Nu'utele to aid their studies, and the shelter is a constant on everyone's trip there. You can see the odd Danish cigarette butt or the Russian chocolate bar wrapper, and since no one spruces up and everyone uses the same area to build a little fire and stands in the same spot when it gets rainy, this uninhabited island has a little personal global village type of history that is oddly warming, and so we stow our gear and head out into the jungle and begin our botany lesson, led by this young Euell Gibbons of the rain forest.

He shows me water vines and edible snakes, we hack apart rotting palms looking for bugs and grubs, and he shows me sleeping snakes. We hack away with our machetes almost every few steps, looking for coconut grubs, and can't find any at all. In fact, we spend all morning looking for coconut grubs—after all, it was supposed to be an important throughline of our story—and we finally get to the point where Afele, exhausted and dejected but keeping it all close to the vest, suggests we start to climb the mountain. There is only one mountain, rising up out of the center of this island, and remember—the whole island chain is essentially volcanic, so the general topographic vibe is like you are walking on a giant inverted ice-cream cone squished on top of a small pancake, and since Nu'utele's soil is clay-based on this one side of the mountain, we are having an incredibly tough time making any headway. Vertically challenged, we press on. The rainstorm that had come through the night before and earlier in the morning kept threatening rain again, but it burned off every time the sun appeared ready to peek out. It was a bright but cloudy afternoon, but the ground was so wet and slick that you couldn't get any traction on it even with sturdy hiking shoes. The slopes were almost a full forty-five degrees steep, but it felt worse as we slipped and slid, and one by one our crew gave up, something that had never happened before, forced to turn back, unable to climb this mountain. Everybody is carrying tripods, cameras, and equipment, so it takes us a while on the narrow path we are cutting to actually turn around. Afele sends us back on our own as he continues to scamper up the incline in his flip-flops, cruising up the mountain in pursuit of a few weevils or grubs, and we go back to the little shelter to wait for the arrival of the second group of intrepid locals coming to meet us for part two of our island experience. The mood is sour. Half the day is gone and we still have no story in the can, Afele is up on the mountain and we don't know what he is doing or when he is coming back, and we roll into our base camp to meet the Samoan Bat Hunting Club, come to take us on a bat hunt.

The Samoan Bat Hunting Club sounds very elegant, but kind of like the Tobago Iguana Hunting Club that I spent an afternoon with one day the year before when I was scatter-gunning iguanas down in Tobago, the SBHC guys seemed an odd mix to me. They were a group of about six or seven guys, all of whom really dug going out into the woods and blasting away at bats with their guns, but they were also divided into two cliques. The first was made up of their self-appointed leader, named Paul, and the four guys who were his personal lackeys, enjoying life seemingly at his pleasure. They drank when he drank, spoke only when he seemed to approve of it, and clearly their life revolved around him. I thought I was in a weird alternate *Sopranos* universe—that's what these guys seemed to mimic in their odd social fealty.

The other clique was made up of the three guys who didn't give a whit what Paul said or did. They had some kind of independent life outside of the hunting club—one was a cop, the others local laborers—but all absent allegiance to the loudmouth who ran the show. It turned out that Paul had married the governor's daughter or his niece and had sort of ingratiated himself into the semi-upper crust of Samoan society, and everything began to make sense. Paul, by the way, was shit-faced by the time he got to the island and kept drinking beer after beer after beer while we were mapping out what our evening hunt would look like, barking at his peeps and offering unsolicited advice at every turn. You can't really start hunting bats until the sun starts setting, so we had quite an amount of time on our hands while we were waiting for Afele to return to camp. We enjoyed talking to some of these guys, so we began to shoot b-roll and do some of the little nuts-and-bolts TV business that we needed to capture before the big scene, getting a safety lesson on the weapons, doing the meet and greet, and so on. Paul's crew were all perfectly nice, and they were extremely uncomfortable as Paul became drunker and drunker. At one point, he became so verbally obnoxious that one member of the hunt club who wasn't in Paul's little cadre of sycophantic toadies, a guy who was also a member of the Samoan Olympic team shooting squad, basically had to take his gun away from him. It was hysterically funny looking back, but at the time it was eerily surreal. Watching this drunk guy, clearly mad on the power of being the one big fish in a very small pond, having to be dressed down by the only teammate of his that he would listen to, reminded me of being in college, where one guy in the group always seemed to be the one who needed babysitting. And off Paul went, skulking down by the boat as Afele strolled back into camp carrying a couple of grubs. Hailing the conquering hero, swept up in the excitement of our friend's return, it took us a while to hear the shouts and ruckus down on the beach, and frankly we ignored him for a couple of minutes because he was the drunk guy. But then we hear the boat driver screaming over the sound of the breakers and the wind, and we think something has happened between Paul and the pontoon shuttle crews. We run down to the beach, and at this point the sun is setting and darkness is settling in, and the boat has come loose from its moorings as the tide has come up, and the wind is whipping up again, and the three of them, Paul and the two drivers, are in the water trying to hold on to the loosed boat. It takes a while, but once we have six or seven of us down in the water holding the boat, we can get another rope on it and tie it up. I should have thought—bad things come in threes, and this is only number two—but I wasn't really thinking straight. We almost lose our lives in the water getting turned sideways going out to Nu'utele, and now the boat breaks free of its moorings and we almost get stranded out there. Sometimes I think to myself that what we are doing is just a little too goofy and dangerous, and at that point in the evolution of the show we had no satellite phone with us and no way to get off the island if something really bad happened. The idea of being marooned was not appealing.

Eventually, we got the boat squared away, the dust began to settle and the magic begins to happen. The weather has cleared up, the humidity has dropped, the ruckus is settling down over this abandoned island, you see the shadows come out on this mountaintop, and we stand vigil underneath the ripe bread fruit trees and wait for the bats. Well, the bats on Nu'utele are not very far-ranging, and when I say bats, you're probably thinking of something flit-ting around the backyard in Connecticut on warm summer nights, a pest that weighs a couple of ounces and occasionally flies by accident into your living room, and you fetch a tennis racket and shoo it out the kitchen door. Guess again. These are fruit bats topping the scales at five kilos, giant tropical fruit bats, also known as flying foxes because they are so ferocious-looking, supersized and furry. This bat has as much relation to a bat in your backyard as my sitting in your garage makes me your car. It is an awesome sight to see hundreds of these things pinwheeling in the sky, circling down, down, down from the mountaintop caves they live in toward the bread fruit trees dotting the shoreline. All these bats do is sleep, poop, and eat ripe bread fruit. These animals are a rarity in the animal kingdom in that once you do kill them and begin preparing them for eating, you don't even have to clean them in the traditional butchery sense of the word. Even the stuff in the intestinal tract is good to eat, and the natives eat all of it. These animals are not purged or bled after harvesting; these things are simply held by two men over an open fire (with a six-foot wing span, it takes two to tango) to be scraped of their fur and roasted whole, simply scored with a little X mark in the chest so they cook evenly. These animals are supremely clean. All they eat and digest is bread fruit, and since that's all that's in their system their gastrointestinal acids and enzymes are relatively mild, so you can eat the whole animal with impunity. That's quite an unusual thing to partake of in the food world, an animal so clean and limited in range that you can eat every edible portion without cleaning it.

So we position ourselves in the jungle, spread out in a line in the little clearing between a couple of bread fruit trees heavy with ripe fruit, and we begin shooting bat after bat after bat as they soar into the trees, dropping four or five fairly quickly. The cop who was a member of the shooting team made one of the most miraculously hunting shots I've ever seen in my life. Out of the corner of his eye—I don't know how he could see it given that it was pitch black at night—he sees something fluttering about eye height and he dropped it on the fly in the dark about forty feet out. Turned out it was a true wild chicken, taken on the wing.

We had the five or six coconut grubs that Afele had scrounged up, we had a half-dozen bats and a wild chicken. Things were looking up. We head back to our shelter, burn a couple coconut husks, and start a roaring fire. We clean the bats one by one, stretching the animals across the fire, scraping their fur off as they scorch, and score the bats across the chest. We toss the bats on the coals and squat on our haunches, turning them every few minutes, getting hungrier and hungrier, just like a Sunday-afternoon weenie roast back home. Almost. Holding a bat whose wing span is about five or six feet from tip to tip, stretching one of these critters over an open fire to singe the fur, scraping off the hairy soot, taking a sharp knife and putting an X mark in its chest, opening it up so it cooks evenly, watching as the the guts start to puff out as the meat cooks—well, this is really caveman-style eating, to say the least.

Dining on bats in the great outdoors is a very greasy, smelly affair. You chew and tear as you go, the meat and sinew are fairly tough, and the process is slow and sloppy. We rinse ourselves off with buckets of rainwater, and finally cut down the cameras and the lights and pack up all of our stuff, but by this time it's about 11 at night and we are exhausted. We head down to the boat and load all our gear. By this time, the shooting club guys have gone off as quickly and mysteriously as they arrived, piling into their boat and heading off to Upolu. We start to putt out of the protected harbor beach area on Nu'utele, only to find that with the tide up you can't see all the giant rocks that were so easy to cruise around and through on the way in. The "crew" of our little tin dinghy had no idea how to get us out of the little bay on Nu'utele, and we discover that in fact they have never left the island after dark. We also come to learn, as we are going back and forth performing K-turns in vain attempts to get out into deeper water, that the crew is not sure how to get us across the channel to where the water is hundreds of feet deep. The water we are heading into is so deep that the angry swift current creates those huge waves between the big island of Upolu and the little island of Nu'utele just off the coast. The speed of the current in this deep V-shaped trough is scary fast, but eventually we get turned toward it in our little vessel more suited for flat lazy lakes than the deep South Pacific. We get about a half mile off the island, and despite the whistling winds and boiling seas you can hear the sickening scrape of rock against metal. I will tell you there is no worse feeling in the world than standing in a tin can of a boat with no radios and no life preservers, with a bunch of crazed, unseaworthy crew members, half in the bag at worst, hungover from their daytime drinking at best. That scrape of rock against boat meant just one thing and we all knew it, and if we hadn't already gashed open one of the pontoons and the boat was going to sink, it was about to. I considered my options quickly and figured out that if the boat started to sink, we could all make the decision to try to swim to shore for ourselves. What was really scary was that the boat was stuck on top of one of these rocks, and because the rocks were close to the surface they allowed rollers out in the open ocean to become breaking waves. The waves threatened to swamp the boat after flipping it over, which would have been disastrous. That's the type of scenario where people really get hurt and was when, we all realized at the same time, panic begins to set in. Everyone is screaming at each other. The guides and the crew were all vainly grabbing at poles that were stowed on the boat to push us off the rock. Two, three, or four waves in a row almost loosed us from atop this rock, but in doing so also almost flipped us over each time they swirled and crashed around the rock and our craft. Out of nowhere, Afele tosses aside his T-shirt and dives into the water in the middle of the ocean, swims around to the edge of the boat where the rock has snagged us, waits for the next wave to come, puts his little flip-flop feet up on the rock, and pushes the boat off from where we had been wedged as the water crashes over him. He nonchalantly hops back onto the boat, grabs the handle of the little outboard engine for our incompetent captain, and motors us off into the deeper channel.

Out in the deep water the rollers were surprisingly big and soft and the wind was nil. We flitted and threaded between the waves all the way back to the safe harbor on the big island of Upolu that we had embarked from fourteen hours earlier, capping one of the most energizing and thrilling evenings of my life. On this night I had thought on several occasions that I might lose my life, and it turned out to be one of those great days, a day that you look back on and say, yeah, I did that, making my bat meal taste all the sweeter each time I thought about it.

Journey to the Source
Why the Shortest Distance from Sea to Plate Makes for Amazing Meals

I am a traveler. I am not a tourist. Occasionally, I do touristy things. But I have spent about ten weeks' total time in the People's Republic of China and never seen the Great Wall. Go figure. Long ago, I developed a way of exploring a country by diving into their culture mouth first, mostly because I'm obsessed with food in a way that makes most cuisine-conscious culinistas seem only casually interested by comparison. As a young boy, I traveled a lot with my family, and it was through them that I got turned on to a new way of interpreting how to spend time in a foreign country. My dad and I spent as much time cruising the aisles at Harrods, exploring Chinatown, or shopping for socks at Marks and Spencer as we did looking at the British Museum's Elgin Marbles. I learned early on in life that you could view as much of Roman culture ordering shirts at Brioni as you could sitting in a tour, perambulating the Coliseum.

We traveled to eat, and often that meant going great distances in the opposite direction of the herd. In the mid-seventies, we were skiing in Val d'Isère and on our second day it started to snow heavily. When it stopped six days later, food delivery to the little ski town had been halted for three days. We ate sardines and crackers in the lobby of the hotel, and as the snow stopped falling, we anxiously awaited the first new truck deliveries through the pass, as well as some superb skiing. We were wrong. The pistes needed to be blasted with dynamite to make the runs safe from avalanches, and while cars could go out the pass when it was plowed, the four-wheelers were still a day away. No food, no skiing. So Dad piled everyone in the van and drove all day across France to Lyon, where we ate a dinner for the ages at Paul Bocuse, in the era when his eponymous restaurant was universally regarded as the world's finest. We spent the night driving back, skied the next day, and enjoyed the rest of our vacation. I remember the ease of the decision to bolt for Lyon as well as I remember the thumbnail-size mousse de foie gras course or the truffle soup en croute.

We simply wouldn't ever have considered staying trapped in town for one more day as an option, and hitting the road, traveling as far as we could in one day just for a great meal, was how we rolled. Literally. Trekking to the absolute last physical place you can, with a goal to seek out a unique food experience, is the best travel advice that I ever learned, and I learned it from my father. In Spain, we drove out from Madrid to a 400-year-old restaurant underneath the Roman Aqueduct in Valle De Los Calledos just for a taste of roasted baby pig. I remember driving an hour outside of Milan in his buddy's flashy Italian sports car to the little town of Bergamo, simply because they served up the best gnocchi and quail in northern Italy. As we feasted in that ancient restaurant with the twinkling lights of Milan in the distance, I clearly remember deciding that if finding the perfect meal meant going to the last stop on earth, it was certainly worth the trip.

Time is the enemy of great-tasting food, and so I believe in pursuing food at its source. I want whatever is freshest on my plate. I want lobster that goes from the sea straight into a pot of boiling water. I want shrimp that's pulled directly from a fisherman's raft through a rope-and-pulley system out of the bay and right into a kitchen. Those ingredients can't compare to the "sit around the food locker" stuff from a nameless, faceless mainline supplier. God knows how long those edibles spend in the depths of some industrial freezer, how far they've traveled to get to your plate, and how they've been handled along the way. With the exception of a few ingredients—wine and cheese come to mind—the idea that freshness counts is as old as the hills. Traveling in its purest form allows you to gain unbridled access to foods at their source.

Growing up in New York City, we rarely ate food at its freshest. You don't find shrimp in the Hudson River. There was lobster once, but 125 years ago they were overfished out of the tidal estuaries in and around the island of Manhattan. Every summer, my dad would drive me out to Montauk, Long Island. We'd sit at the dock, watching fishing boats unload crates of fresh seafood right out of the Atlantic. Like the paparazzi hot on some young starlet's trail, we would hound these crates to the clam bars on Montauk's docks just to eat the freshest catch.

There was one big tourist restaurant on the docks of Montauk called Gossman's. They had pretty fresh stuff, but their lobster was kept alive by holding them in aerated, ocean-water tanks. Standard ops then and now for larger commercial seafood restaurants. Minute by minute, day by day, the meat would break down. The lobsters became less flavorful, less briny, less saline, less intense the longer they sat in tanks. Time is the enemy of food, even when the food is still alive.

We skipped places like Gossman's whenever we could, in favor of smaller local clam bars. In those days, Salavar's was the working-class seafood shack we ate in, a small joint open at 5 A.M. to serve doughnuts and egg sandwiches to the commercial fishing crowd and dock crews. It sat about 500 yards down the road, but it was a world away in terms of culture. Real people ate, argued, and hung out at joints like Salavar's, Lunch (the Lobster Roll), and the Quiet Clam. This was the sixties, before the jet-set crowd had yet to discover the Hamptons. And these were the unspoiled clam shacks we spent our time eating in.

Now in his eighties, my father is still as tenacious a traveler as anyone. About five years ago, he moved to Portland, Maine. If you hold the state of Maine under a magnifying glass, you'll see its coastline looks like a thousand little fingers pointing into the Atlantic Ocean. In some areas, these peninsulas are protected from the brunt of the Atlantic storms by islands, creating quiet waters perfect for fishing and lobstering. I don't care how many times you've dined at fancy seafood restaurants in Chicago or New York: Until you've had lobster fresh from the cold waters of Maine, you really haven't had live lobster.

The very first time I visited Dad in Portland, he insisted we drive up to the Five Islands Lobster Company for what he felt was the best lobster roll in the state. Five Islands is a third-generation, family-owned lobster company. Their food shack is like Red's in Wiscasset, or Day's in Portland, one of those under-the-radar joints whose address is passed among foodies like heroin junkies trade reliable connections. I am probably performing an act of culinary self-mutilation by revealing my most precious source, but here it goes.

Five Islands is one of those rare food finds, if you can find it at all. You drive about forty-five minutes north of Portland on I-295, make a right, and head east on US-1. You begin to head east down county road 127, onto the paved road, turn left onto a dirt road, and you'll drive right up to the eighty-year-old, barnlike wooden structures where you can park and get some fresh air. Just look for the signs saying Five Islands Lobster Company—you can't miss it. The family still goes out every day and lobsters. That's their main business. You can sit and watch their boats coming in with crates and crates of lobsters, some headed off to the world's finest restaurants and fish shops. However, the family keeps the best stuff for themselves. Steamer clams, haddock, hake, clams on the half shell, local shrimp, oysters, or their famous lobster: It's fresh, delicious, and they're cooking it on the spot.

Enter the wooden swinging door and you'll notice the requisite mugs, T-shirts, and bumper stickers for sale at the counter. Crayon and marker-drawn cardboard menus line the walls of this crazy little room that houses a cooler you fetch your root beer from and the counter where you order. Somehow, they've managed to squeeze a kitchen into the back of this teeny space. Everyone orders the same things: Maine lobster rolls or deep-fried clams, or in my case, both. These items pair perfectly with their made-from-scratch dill-and-lemon tartar sauce, homemade coleslaw, and hand-cut French fries.

The thing that sets Five Islands apart from the rest of the clam shacks I love is not just that the lobster marches straight from the traps to the kitchen. This family takes their product so seriously that they don't want a giant food-service truck unloading on their dock. They could doctor up a decent tartar sauce from a jar, but they don't: They make their own from scratch, and the quality of their lobster rolls and hand-dusted fried clams is well beyond that of their competitors. The Five Islands lobster roll is a singular experience. You don't even notice the mayonnaise coating the meat, even as you put the overstuffed toasted hot-dog bun into your gaping maw. If you can stop yourself at just eating one of them, you're not really a lobster roll aficionado. I am usually good for two, plus a little side order of clams.

Now, there are two schools of thought when it comes to lobster rolls in Maine. The first kind, which you'll find at Five Islands, is a lobster salad coated with a gossamer-thin gloss of mayonnaise, salt, and pepper. The other kind of lobster roll, which they do best at Red's in Wiscasset, is simply a warm lobster plucked from his shell and put into a toasted bun and drizzled with melted butter. Most Mainers will argue at length about which version is the authentic Maine lobster roll, but frankly the point is moot. They both rock.

Just like lobster rolls in Maine, every country, state, or city has its own hidden gems if you know where to look. It's the same in the Philippines. In a country with more than 100 million inhabitants, it's mind-boggling to realize that few locals have ever traveled to the southern island state of Palawan. With its sky blue water, fresh produce, and incredible seafood, Palawan seems like heaven on earth—yet this picturesque locale is without a doubt the island less traveled. Simply put, people don't know it exists. Sitting to the north and east of Puerto Princessa, Boracay is the siren of the Philippine islands, luring in tourists with its famous diving, snorkeling, and beautiful beaches. Puerto Princessa is just a quick stopover on the way to someplace better. And I get it. It's not the most charming town. But it's the gateway to the rest of the island, which, simply put, is absolutely perfect if you prefer real, working beach towns to the all-inclusive, resort-lined streets of what used to be a working village, but now relies 100 percent on a tourism-driven regional economy.

Boracay may have great underwater activities, but you're not going to find a lot in the way of honest and authentic culture there, especially when compared to Palawan. For me, going to the last stop on the subway means actually going where the locals go, eating what the locals eat, and doing it in a place that still maintains its sense of local relevance. In a world that is becoming flatter every day, where globalization has killed so much indigenous food culture, these end-of-the-line locales are the last unspoiled destinations for travelers craving a real experience.

Puerto Princessa houses a few decent restaurants, and I did eat some superb meals at Kinabuchs. But if you crave a one-of-a-kind experience, you have to head into the most remote section of the surrounding mangrove forests on the outskirts of the city and find the Badjao Seafront Restaurant. Mangroves are like nature's take on the medieval walled city. These weedlike trees grow very quickly and become almost impenetrable within a few years. They densely populate Southeast Asia's coastal wetlands, inhibiting businesses there from doing much besides aquaculture. The mangrove forests are a haven for many species of all types and provide unique coastal protection from environmental disasters of both the natural and man-made varieties.

Ask any local or tricycle driver (lingo for a bicycle or motorbike with a sidecar) and they'll happily point you in the right direction. You turn off Abueg Road and park in a rather large field, make your way from your car to the little sign that says *Restaurant This*

Way. The Badjao Seafront Restaurant owners cut a half-mile-long wooden walkway into the jungle from the mainland side, which leads to a long, narrow teak deck. You realize about halfway down that you are walking along a wooden pathway built on stilts, and beneath you is the swampy waters off the Sulu Sea. At the end of this walkway, sitting like a glowing fireplace on a cold winter's day, is a gorgeous teak-and-mahogany restaurant, built on top of a floating raft on stilts, poking out into the bay.

Our local tourism department contacts and I sit down at Badjao and soak up the 270-degree view of the bay, dotted with small sanpans, little fishing and shrimping boats, gliding along one of the pristine inner bays of the Sulu Sea, framed by a horizon of mountains. The menu reads like a greatest hits list of the best of Philippines seafood cuisine. I was as giddy as a schoolgirl as I navigated my way through the dishes, sniffing with joy and spying on what other diners had ordered. I was blown away when I saw fresh whelks sautéed in coconut milk with shredded banana flowers making its way to another table, and I almost fainted with happiness when I peeked at the menu and saw it priced at three dollars a pop.

I took on the mind-boggling task of paring lunch down to seven or eight dishes. Luckily, everyone was into sharing. Our server offered up a mango-and-banana shake to tide us over. This was no ordinary shake. The Badjao Seafront Restaurant plucks the juiciest mangoes straight off the trees, adds bananas from the huge four-and-a-half-foot-tall bunch leaning on the bar, purees them with a bit of ice and a splash of water, and sticks a straw in it. I should tell you that the number-one agricultural force in Palawan are the banana farms—bananas of such sweet and primal excellence that you won't tire of them showing up at every meal. Look for roadside stands selling banana-Q, a local treat made by rolling fresh, ripe bananas on sticks in a bowl of crushed brown sugar and deep-frying them. Like a candy apple mated with bananas foster, just absent the snooty waiter and the rolling tableside cart.

As we awaited the arrival of our food, I wandered around the side of the restaurant, hoping to catch a glimpse of the fishermen navigating their miniature flat-bottom canoes. I looked on as they fished about a mile out from the restaurant, collecting shrimp and snapper from their little clusters of nets. It was a physical endeavor—pushing and pulling themselves around the bay, tossing nets, reeling them in, then poling or paddling back over to the restaurant, where they would disappear from view. I walked to the edge of the deck, only to discover they were literally hoisting baskets of fresh fish, shrimp, and crabs directly from the bay to the kitchen window, where they would be dispatched and, within minutes, arrive at our table.

I'd pinned myself down to the grilled shrimp, the monstrously large sautéed crayfish, and snails with the coconut milk and banana flower—a dish that I had always wanted to try but hadn't had the opportunity. It is literally the sturdy purple cone-shaped flower that grows from the bottom of the master cluster of bananas. The banana flower is available anywhere bananas grow, and every time I have seen it since tasting it for the first time in Palawan, I have asked if it's used in the local food. From Puerto Rico to Nicaragua, Okinawa to Samoa: It's an emphatic *no*. Filipinos, on the other hand, are addicted to cooking with it. The flower is sliced paper thin on a mandolin (or, if the chef has excellent knife skills, by hand) into little shreds, then sautéed with coconut milk. The flowers pair perfectly with something saline and gamy, like snails.

We dined on teeny grilled fish, served with Philippine soy sauce and a squeeze of Kalamansi—a gumball-size citrus fruit that's a cross between a lime and a tangerine. Kalamansi is to Palawan what salt and pepper is to America—readily available and dispensed on everything. The grill was fired by fresh coconut husks, which impart a superb light smokiness to the food cooked on it. The grilled shrimp and mackerel actually melt in your mouth. Seafood lumpia were rolled and fried to order, the whelks with banana flower had a strong injection of lime before they left the kitchen, and no one at the table could prevent themselves from inhaling the groaning platters of the food as they came in waves from the kitchen. With all the commotion over the persistent flow of dish after amazing dish (not to mention the fact that I was overeating to begin with), I'd completely forgotten about the final item, which had yet to emerge from the kitchen. I'd seen tuna collar on the menu and I thought to myself, *Gee, what a nice little treat. I'll have some tuna collar.*

Even casual fans of Japanese food are used to the minuscule hamachi collars sold in just about every Japanese restaurant. Roughly the size of a small envelope and about an inch thick, those collars are lightly salted to dry out some of the moisture, then broiled and served with grated daikon radish, a squirt of lemon juice, and soy sauce. The collar bone is covered with fatty, rich scraps of meat that you have to fight to unearth, but worth every minute of the canoodling it takes to extract the tasty morsels of flesh. That's half the fun, like a treasure hunt, and it's addictive, so I was looking forward to trying Badjao's version despite my straining waistline.

We'd finished up most of lunch when I realized, "Hmm . . . no tuna collar." Assuming they simply forgot, I asked our server where my tuna collar was and I was calmly informed that it was still cooking. I mean, this is a tiny piece of fish. What the sweet Mary and Joseph is taking so long?

As I'm discussing the situation with our server, out comes the tuna collar, spilling over the edges of a twenty-four-inch-long platter. Here is Badjao's version of this culinary gem: A seven- or eight-pound Flintstone-size roast of bone and meat from a gigantic yellow- or bluefin tuna. This fish had to weigh several hundred pounds when it landed in the boat. Brushed with sweet rice wine and soy sauce, served with fresh chilies and those little Kalamansi, this collar was quite the indulgent dish.

Foodies obsess about illegal foods like ortolans of western Europe, devouring whole roasted teensy birdies drowned in

Armagnac while a napkin is placed over their head to assuage the guilt factor. People wax poetic about attending foie gras orgies in New York's underground restaurants. Sure, you can have all that stuff, but the rarest of the rare food experiences is the opportunity to eat something singular and unique, in the main because the ingredients aren't available in any other spot in the world. An open source of giant fish, where chefs have inexpensive access to pristine precious ingredients, exists in very few places of the world. Consider this: At Tokyo's Tsukiji Market, just the collar alone would cost thousands of dollars, and here I was, for the equivalent of a few dollars, chomping away at this giant, charred, fatty piece of tuna goodness. I didn't have to force myself to eat the whole thing; I had a little help from my traveling mates. Going to the last stop on the subway in the Philippines afforded me the opportunity to dine in an environment where I wasn't competing with too many people, finding ingredients in their own terroir, so to speak (with a neutral carbon footprint, no less!), and without paying through the nose. Eat the same dish halfway around the world and not only will it be expensive and somewhat ginned up, but the flavor will be compromised, diluting the experience to the point that it is almost not worth doing in the first place. If something is worth eating, it's worth eating well, and that's the advantage of going to the last stop on the subway.

Muddy Waters
Ugandan Lung-fishing Can Be Messy

Lungfish is the common name for a primitive, freshwater, air-breathing fish that resides exclusively in tropical areas of Australia, Africa, and South America. Only six species of lungfish survive today, but fossil records tell us that lungfish were much more widespread and in more plentifully differentiated species in the distance past. Scientists agree that lungfish are closely related to the ancestors of the earliest vertebrates that adapted to live on land, which is very important, because lungfish are extremely unusual animals.

The name itself refers to the specialized lung that serves as the creature's main organ for breathing. This lung allows the fish to gulp air as an adaptation to low-oxygen water environments, such as swamps or bodies of water that frequently dry up. Most fish use their gills to pull the oxygen out of the water. Lungfish also have gills, but theirs are relatively small compared to their fellow denizens of the deep. Young African lungfish have true external gills, which degenerate with age. The single lung on the lungfish is more like a modified swim bladder, the air-filled organ that almost all fish use to help them float at a particular depth, saving energy while swimming around the ocean, but in lungfish the modified swim bladder can also absorb oxygen. Freaky!

When kicking back and chilling out, lungfish excrete carbon dioxide through their gills or skin, just like most other fish, but most other fish get oxygen only through their gills. The special lung on the lungfish also removes carbon dioxide waste when the lungfish is very active, an anomaly in the underwater world. African lungfish actually rise to the surface to breathe and can "drown" without access to air.

Lungfish have elongated bodies with a double set of fleshy limbs that resemble cylindrical fins. Their oddly shaped fanlike teeth act like an under-counter garbage compactor, ideally suited to their diet of fish, insects, mollusks, worms, crustaceans, and plants. These animals are very territorial and extremely aggressive, building nests where the male protects the eggs that the female lays until they hatch.

African lungfish aestivate, meaning they can become dormant, literally hibernating during dry periods or droughts for a few months if need be. If necessary, they can hit the rack for years at a time—*that's years . . . plural!* These fish burrow into the mud and secrete a covering of mucus around themselves. This mucus hardens into a cocoon, but the lungfish leave a small, closable breathing hole in the mummylike covering. The fish reduce their metabolism to a bare whisper and simply shut down, becoming essentially inactive. The protective cocoon softens when it gets wet—say, at the end of the dry season—and the fish can reemerge and live in the water again.

The lungfish, like its cousin the coelacanth, are commonly thought of as living fossils, a reference to the fact that these animals have essentially remained physically unchanged for hundreds of millions of years.

Oh yeah, and one more thing: When lungfish are in that cocoon and they get hungry, they eat their own bodies, tail first . . . and they grow back.

All of which begs the real question: *What in the name of all that is holy was I doing fishing lungfish?*

Let's start from the beginning. The moment Travel Channel picked up *Bizarre Foods,* I wanted to live with an African tribe. It seemed to me to be the ultimate family of *Bizarre Foods* experiences: Getting in with real indigenous people, many who live the same way their ancestors did thousands of years ago, would allow me the best opportunities to experience food and share cultures, and that's exactly what we found in Uganda.

Uganda is located in East Africa, and is landlocked by Kenya, Tanzania, Rwanda, Zaire, and the Sudan. Much like its neighbors', Uganda's past has been turbulent at times. Despite the fact that Uganda achieved independence from Britain in 1962, the establishment of a working political community within such a diverse ethnic population has been a Herculean task. The dictatorial regime of Idi Amin (1971–79) was responsible for the deaths of some 300,000 Ugandans. Guerrilla wars and human rights abuses under Milton Obote (1980–85) claimed at least another 100,000 lives. Since 1986, the rule of Yoweri Museveni has brought relative stability and economic growth to Uganda. However, the country is still subjected to regionalized armed conflict, partially due to its large refugee population and the prevalence of the Lord's Resistance Group, a separatist terrorist organization concentrated in the northern part of the country, which, for many travelers, has been essentially a no-go zone.

You're probably wondering if this is a safe place to be traveling in the first place. Trust me, I had plenty of those thoughts myself, and it seemed anytime I researched this trip, I stumbled upon words like "insurgent activity," "armed banditry," and "roadside ambushes." We were staying in the city of Kampala, located on the northern edge of Africa's largest body of water, Lake Victoria, for the first few days and last night of our stay, but for the majority of our trip we lived in an isolated village well outside the city. I always felt very safe in Uganda, but that's a relative term. Flying in to Entebbe Airport, you can see the decades-old hull of the famous Lufthansa jet, hijacked in 1972 and left as a "training tool" on the runway where it finally came to rest. Not the most charming of welcome mats in the Kmart catalog. Armed guards watched over us in Lwanika, hired to keep us safe. Frankly, I wondered how one old guy with a rusty AK-47 would fare against a jeep- or truckload of rebels intending to do us harm or steal our equipment. I bet my producer a hundred bucks that it couldn't fire if he pulled the trigger a dozen times, which was a bet he wouldn't take. Thankfully, it didn't come to that.

Kampala isn't exactly a hotbed of international tourism, but three minutes after leaving the airport, I saw traffic lights, an ambulance driving on another road, and a speeding police car, sirens blaring. I breathed a huge sigh of relief. Infrastructure like that means someone, or something, is at least nominally in charge. Having just come from Ethiopia, where I never saw an ambulance or police car during our entire eight days in-country, I can safely say that I was relieved to be in Kampala and not Addis Ababa or Harrar. Walking down the streets of Anytown, Uganda, from the biggest to the smallest, has the same challenges as walking down Mainstreet, USA. Look like a fish out of water, get treated like one.

Arranging a stay with an isolated African tribe is no easy feat. You can't exactly call or e-mail in your reservations. Our "in" with the Embegge tribe was through our local fixer, Haruna, a member of the tribe and a legendary local Ugandan musician in his own right. We wound up visiting and staying with his tribe in the village of Lwanika, located about six hours east of Kampala. It just so happened that our arrival coincided with the anniversary of his grandfather's death. Haruna's family, and his late grandfather in particular, are highly regarded in the community. In honor of him, they had prepared a huge celebration for the second night of our proposed stay, complete with a big, festive meal for the entire extended village. It was exactly what we were looking for.

We headed out to Lwanika by Range Rover, where we would stay with the tribe for four days. The drive was pretty much what you'd expect in eastern Africa. We started off on a main, paved highway heading out from the city of Kampala, snagged up for a good half hour in the early-morning traffic of the congested city. Eventually, that road morphs into a simple, paved road, then to a dirt road, and finally you're actually going all-terrain, driving over rutted grass byways to get to the heart of the village. In and around the village itself, we encountered a system of primitive dirt roads that connect the isolated villages of the region to each other. Villagers from one cluster of simple mud and straw homes would walk or bike from one to another to visit family or friends, or to help with work. While it's extremely rare for most villagers to venture into the big city, modern civilization has touched their lives just enough that they have the occasional need to go into another village or a bigger town. The most traveled members of the tribes always seemed to be those involved with dance or music, and most of these villagers spent a lot of time traveling throughout eastern Africa performing in regional festivals and contests.

This explains why we were greeted in Lwanika with an impressive amount of fanfare. All the women turned out, dancing and singing us into the main town square—just a dirt area surrounded by a cluster of four or five homes. It seemed everyone was curious about the arrival of these "mazungos" and their cameras. *Mazungo* basically means "whitey" in Ugandan culture, which never felt derogatory—they use it more as a term of endearment mixed with a healthy dose of good humor. The Embegge have an incredible sense of humor, and laughter is a regular part of the daily village cacophony of sounds. And why ignore the obvious? Mazungos just don't show up in their village all the time, especially soft fluffy ones like me. The Embegge were very found of using that term around me, mostly because I totally embraced the culture, even if it meant I ended up making a complete ass of myself. Unlike me, most mazungos don't dance with them, eat their traditional food, work with them, and sleep in teeny pup tents alongside their huts. I even went as far as joining the village's all-female cooking co-op for an adventurous lesson in cooking matooke—a common dish made from boiled and mashed green bananas. To the Embegge, this was probably the most bizarre thing they'd ever seen from any man, as the responsibility of preparing food belongs solely to females. In fact, once a male hits age twelve, he isn't expected to even sit in the kitchen. Taking an active role in their everyday lives, instead of simply staring and gawking from the safety of my Land Rover as most visitors do, afforded me a singular experience that meant we bonded in a way that would have been impossible had I only hung out for a few hours a day, then bussed back to a cushy hotel room somewhere.

Life for the Embegge is very rustic compared to life in the city of Kampala. For the most part, they do not wear Western clothes in the American sense. Women wear a traditional native shift, the same sacklike dress they've been wearing for years. Men wear pants and T-shirts in the village, or just shorts and flip-flops. Young men here dress like beach bums in Hawaii. But because national charitable organizations here in the States organize fund-raising drives on a grassroots level, you will often see whole families or villages decked out in prom shirts from 1997 in Cleveland, or see three boys walking together across a jungle field all wearing "Kimmelman Bar Mitzvah 2006, WE LOVE YOU KENNY!" tees. The families live in small, circular mud and straw huts, which they share with their goats, cows, and other animals, depending on the predators who live in the jungles nearby. Some families are situated in homes made of brick with penned enclosures for their animals. With each passing year, this is becoming more and more the norm. They cook over small fires, farm and hunt off the surrounding land, sharing what they can with their community. It's the pinnacle of sustainable living, except that buzzword doesn't exist there. It's just the only way of life they know. In America, eating well, eating sustainably, and eating off the land are increasingly becoming metrics of social status. In East Africa, it's the norm. And no one here is hungry, despite the embarrassing cliché of starving children plastered all over the media. Food choice is limited, and other health issues are in desperate need of attention, but the soil is fertile and the animals are plentiful.

The Embegge people were gracious, kind, and generous hosts, more welcoming than I could have ever imagined. However, I'd be lying if I said these few days I spent with them weren't one of the most physically, mentally, and emotionally stressful experiences of my life. You're constantly fighting the oppressive dampness and moisture, the heat, hunger, hydration, the overwhelming stench of rotting plant matter, and the constant threat of disease. From dusk until dawn, all mazungos must cover themselves from head to toe in clothing that has been treated with permethrin, a powerful insecticide that you must soak your clothing in, and wear heavy-duty DEET repellant. Despite the fact that you've essentially bathed in these chemicals, the biting flies, some literally the size of cigar butts, continue to seek whatever purchase on you they can. At night, from the safety of our fire and wrapped tighter than Tutankhamen in fine cheesecloth, you could see the mosquitoes in cloudlike waves flying around our heads.

On the day we arrived in Lwanika, we drove through the village and spotted a man sitting on the steps of one of the common buildings with a giant swollen arm. When I say swollen, I mean grotesquely swollen to the point that it was bigger than his body. He had elephantitis. When you see that kind of disease symptomology caused by insects, it makes you think about seventeen times before you run out into the jungle to take a leak at 4 A.M. Later that evening, I remember looking at the flap on my pathetic pup tent, seeing thousands of biting flies hovering outside. And let's not forget about the elephants or lions that could stumble into camp at any given moment. I spent most of those nights lying sleepless in my tent, too terrified to venture outside to piss for fear of being devoured by *something*. Ziploc bags come in handy.

I was quickly forced to face my fears on day two as I accompanied some of the tribesmen on a lungfish hunt. To be perfectly honest, I was really nervous about going lung-fishing from the first days of preproduction because of the horrific swamps in which they live. I was petrified of disappearing in a mud suck-hole or being devoured by snakes. I'm so thankful I never bothered to look at pictures of lungfish prior to this excursion. I never would have participated with such gusto had I known what was living just underneath the muddy water's surface. Screw the bugs and mud, these lungfish are intimidating.

Early that morning, eight of us marched from our tents through the jungle to the swampy rice paddies where the tribe farmed their grain. There were dozens of paddies, each a couple acres in size, all bordered by mud berms made of swamp detritus. Reeds, branches, and grasses are cut by hand and piled like dikes between the ponds to regulate the flow. These organic items decompose very rapidly, creating a mud topped by spongy grasslike mossy compost, which acts as pathways between ponds after years of being cut and piled and shaped. The waters here are filled with poisonous snakes—several of the most deadly varieties in the world, in fact—as well as some of the most infamous disease-carrying insects. Fabulous. The mud berms were so brutish to walk on, they actually sucked my Keens right off my feet. I went barefoot for most of the day after that, encouraged by local pals who reminded me that the only thing in the water was mud and plant life. A lot could happen to me out there, but stubbed toes and cut feet were essentially physical impossibilities. I had envisioned my body helplessly succumbing to the mud after accidentally stepping in a sinkhole, however, so I insisted on tying a rope around my waist—just in case.

Catching a lungfish is nothing like any sort of fishing I've ever done. First, you take a giant stick outfitted with four or five metal barbs, which are typically just pieces of stiff wire lashed to the end of the poles. It resembles a supersize fondue fork, maybe six feet long. Next, you jab the pole into these grassy, muddy walls, trying to find hollow spots where the fish nest. Occasionally, you'll spot a fish as it surfaces, breaking the thick brown water for a breath of fresh air. The lungfish we found were about four feet long, weighed about twenty-five to forty pounds, and had ferociously large teeth sprouting from their powerful jaws. They are extremely ugly and angry animals, and, as it turns out, they don't like to have their nests poked by mazungos. They like it even less when, upon finding their nest, you start hacking away at the mud walls with a machete. Here's the best part: Once these crazed, prehistoric creatures start to slither in, around, or out of their nest, you must blindly reach down into the mud and muck and retrieve them by hand. And considering their giant, sharp teeth, you better hope you find them before they find you. As you're trying to get your hands on the fish, your fishing mates attempt to jab the fondue forks into the fish to immobilize them. Trust plays an important role in lungfishing.

All the lungfish that we caught were found by hand, then speared once they were found. Holding on to a wiggling, thirty-odd-pound, ferocious half-fish–half-lizard animal, all while standing chest deep in filthy stagnant water in the middle of the Ugandan jungle surrounded by biting flies, leeches, ticks, snakes, and God knows what else, was one of the more intimidating experiences of my life. I couldn't have been happier that catching them actually happened a lot faster than I'd anticipated. Within an hour, we had five or six lungfish sprinkled out throughout our eight-man fishing party. Surprisingly, I'd landed one on my second try. The guides were cheering and screaming "*Mazungo! Mazungo!*" the entire time. Apparently, they had never even seen a white person try to catch lungfish, let alone actually score one. I am proud of many achievements in my life, but having dubbed myself the first mazungo lungfisherman in Lwanika is one of my all-time faves.

By this time in the morning, it had to be 95 degrees with 80 percent humidity. No joke. We were all such a dirty, muddy, sweaty mess, and I was just so thankful that the ordeal of collecting food was over. We carried the fish, impaled on our spears, over our shoulders and back to camp. Interestingly, lungfish is one of the only foods the women will not prepare. The lungfish is considered a "cosmic soul sister" to the female tribe members, and therefore the men take a turn in the kitchen. Unlike fish preparation in larger African cities, where a salt and sun-dried method is commonly used, the tribe usually hot-smokes them. This fancy-food term brings to mind images of these wonderful, touristy salmon shops in the Pacific Northwest, which couldn't be further from reality. The Embegge build a huge fire of brushwood, then place the fish fillets on a cooking grate, drying and charring them in the fire's smoke. Once the process is completed, you end up with an overcooked, rock-hard, blackened and brown slab of fish. In that state, it continues to dry out and can later be rehydrated in boiling water and braised in a stew with g-nuts, which is what we would call peanuts here at home. Peanuts are incorporated into a lot of Ugandan and East African cuisine, commonly mixed into a paste with sesame seeds and used as a condiment for meat, crushed and served sautéed with greens, steamed with beans and rice, or boiled in a soup that's used to rehydrate the lungfish, which is exactly what we did.

This was one-pot cooking in its purest form. The fish reminded me of carp, an oversize whitefish I've eaten plenty of in my time: kind of fatty, a bit fibrous, but definitely mild. This ferocious, prehistoric animal was more benign on the plate than I ever imagined. In fact, I've discovered that most of the time, the more ferocious and horrific-looking something is in real life, the more mild the flavor and timid the eating experience.

As we prepared our meal, I couldn't help but think about how many times this scene is repeated over and over again in every African village. Whether they are lungfishing or collecting wild vegetables, seeking out ingredients is such hard work that they collect the bare minimum of food, gathering only what is needed that day. They really don't have a place to effectively store food before it starts to go bad, bananas and grains being the two large exceptions. We caught five or six lungfish, well over the normal daily prescription, because the entire village was turning out that night for the big dinner celebration.

In addition to the lungfish, the Embegge killed a goat for stewing, something typically reserved for special occasions. We ate the fish, the goat, roasted squirrel, flying ants, crickets, millet porridge, matooke, yucca, cassava, sweet potatoes, rice and beans, g-nuts, and other root vegetables that night, all of which are commonly served in tribal Uganda. You see more unseasoned, nasty root vegetables in tribal East Africa than anywhere else in the world. I'd be just fine if I never saw another steamed banana or potato again after my three-week visit there.

Not a day goes by that I don't think of Haruna and his extended family. The journey was difficult, the stress was insane, and the unknown was all around you every second of every day, but the simple fact of the matter was that for four days I never once thought of a bill I had to pay or a call I had to make. My entire focus was on giving full love and attention to everything I was doing, whatever was right in front of me. It was life lived at its purest state in a country that Winston Churchill called the Pearl of Africa because of its magnificent scenery, robust wildlife, and the friendly native culture. I can't disagree at all.

THE LAST BOTTLE
OF COKE IN THE
DESERT

[Dying Breeds]

*A small octopus clings to Andrew's hand
in the waters off Huatulco, Mexico.*

The Last Bottle of Coke in the Desert

A Day in the Life of Tobago Cox

Everyone readily acknowledges that the world is changing, and our country has become obsessed with the *next new thing*, whatever it might be. I'm not above wanting the next best thing; in fact, I find I am just as interested in finding the latest Singaporean fish head curry spot as I am in downloading the latest application for my iPhone. On our planet you will come across people, places, things, ways of life, pastimes, cultural celebrations that are, in essence, the last bottle of Coca-Cola in their given stretch of desert. I don't necessarily mean to say that I am a passionate advocate for bringing back the days of the horse and buggy, although with our obsession with fossil-based fuels and the implications of what the car has done to the modern world, perhaps that's not a bad idea, but the notion that we can observe and participate in unique aspects of living history, meet people who are the last of their kind, take part in celebrations that are disappearing as the world becomes flatter and smaller, is one of the more thrilling benefits of traveling. It's not often that you get a chance to dive into those kinds of headlines the way you do when you travel to other countries.

With all the cultural clutter in the United States, it's hard to clear away the wheat from the chaff and find these dying-breed stories. But trust me, they exist here. There's the guy in Tarpon Springs, Florida, who makes the last brass, leather, and canvas diving helmets in the world. There's the eighty-year-old man in Staten Island who gets up every morning, opens up his little pizza shop, makes fifty pizzas, and drinks a bottle of Barolo at the end of his shift. He won't hire any employees, and when he can't work any longer he is simply shutting his doors. That's a dying breed. The guy who fixes Betamax tape players, he's a dying breed. There is something about finding these people in their own terroir, characters and places that represent traditions and pathways that have long since disappeared in our country, that makes for memorable experiences and even better storytelling, and the person who pops into my mind most often when I think of these experiences is Tobago Cox.

Tobago Cox was a national-champion weight lifter and body-builder, which is how he made his bones fame-wise in the islands of Trinidad and Tobago. In his sixties, he's got the body of a man at least thirty years his junior, with giant muscles and a puffy chest, chiseled and lean. Despite his intimidating physique, he's one of the most friendly, humble, and fascinating guys you'll ever meet. This attraction is only intensified by the fact that he has an incredible day job. He's the last "professional" conch diver in his country.

The coast off Tobago is home to some of the best conching in the world. Conch are giant, pink-lipped mollusks, and are a highly coveted creature, both for their gorgeous shells and the highly prized meat that can be gleaned from the saltwater snail that lives inside them. They traditionally live in shallow waters, sometimes only ten feet deep, which makes them fairly easy to harvest. As a young boy, I remember heading down to the Caribbean with my mother, who was writing a shell book back in the late 1960s. Despite the boat traffic, which often made inland sea life scarce, you could still walk out into the water back then, put on a snorkeling mask and dive ten feet down, and pull up a big conch. The beach bums would help clean your conch in exchange for the meat, and the tourists would take the shells home as souvenirs. Sadly, you can't do that anymore. Caribbean tourism has just exploded. That industry now drives the economic engine of the Caribbean, much of Central America, and the Yucatán Peninsula. Dishes like conch ceviche, conch fritters, and conch chowder have become the quintessential beach bar foods. Tourists clamor for them, and every beach lover wants to take home a conch shell souvenir. Rather ironic, considering that so few will ever see a live conch in their life. The demand for the meat and the shells drives the price of conch up, traffic increases, and *voilà*, they're a hot commodity. Although efforts have been made in the Caribbean basin to shorten the conch season and set fishing limits, less scrupulous commercial fishermen will take harvests that are well over the legal amount for huge profits. Consequently, something that you used to find anywhere you submerged your masked face is now an extremely scarce commestible.

In a world where giant fishing trawlers drag the waters of the Caribbean Sea for conch, Tobago Cox still does it the old-fashioned way. He's earned a living diving for conch since he was a teenager, and he's the textbook practitioner of the ancient art of open-water diving. We spent a day on the water with him, followed by a beach barbecue on a deserted island named No Man's Land, which lies just a half-mile off the coast of Tobago. The experience of being out in the water with Tobago Cox allowed us the rare opportunity to spend a day with someone who truly is the last bottle of Coke in the desert.

We started off our conch-diving excursion at Tobago's house, located on the east side of the island, where he keeps his small, rickety, wooden boat. Tobago's vessel is essentially an oversize wooden dinghy with a small, hand-built, plywood console in the middle that serves as his wheelhouse and protects him from the elements. The wheelhouse looks cobbled together with penny nails, sealing wax, fiberglass, and twine. There is nothing seaworthy about this teeny ship at all, except for its reputation: Tobago has been diving off this boat for more than forty years. I had no qualms about my safety, despite the fact that once again I find myself in a tiny vessel with no radios, no lights, no life preservers, no radar equipment or navigation equipment, no depth finder—nothing. I guess I just trusted that Tobago's life experience was all the equipment we needed.

On our way out to sea, putting out of the channel, Tobago explained that he had lived in the same house since he was a child. Growing up, he could literally walk right off his dock into the water, crawl around on the bottom of the inlet floor, and harvest as many conch as he could fit in his bag. He'd then sell them to local restaurants and markets, and that's how his career started. But over the course of time, he needed to go farther and farther out into the massive channel that separates the island of Trinidad from the island of Tobago. After a two-hour boat ride, which brought us seven or eight miles out from shore, we were finally in a place fit for conching.

In order to find the best spot, Tobago examines the water. I'm accustomed to seeing a lot of equipment on commercial fishing trips, from navigational gear that seems more at home on a NASA space shot, to depth and fish finders designed to pinpoint a single sardine, but Tobago just starts sniffing the air. It's absolutely astonishing. He checks the current with his hands and eyes, the direction of the wind with his nose, the weather and the navigational position by staring at the sky and the thin line of land on the horizon. He stares down into the water, dons an old Lloyd Bridges–style snorkeling mask, and looks to see if the ocean is too deep, which means no conch. If the current is too swift, that means no dive. He floats a diver's buoy today, for two reasons: to help us find him better with our cameras as he swims around, and to keep ocean liners, commercial fishing boats, and freighters from running him over. Good reasons.

Once we find some promising areas that are about thirty-five to fifty feet deep, over the side goes Tobago. His diving methods adapt to the change in water depths. If the water is only twenty-five or thirty feet deep, he'll free-dive with nothing but a bag of empty conch shells to help pull him down deep enough, the way a diver uses small lead weights. Down on the bottom he swaps each live conch for an old shell, balancing the "weights" to help him stay down. When he's in fifty feet of water, in a ferocious six- or seven-knot current, he uses a lead belt and oxygen tank. Once he sinks to the bottom, he'll pull himself along the ocean floor, an old spiky shell in each hand, his fingers curled inside and using the rough exteriors of the shell to grip the muddy, sandy bottom. The current is strong while he's literally pulling himself hand over hand, searching for conch. It takes him three or four dives and a couple of hours to find about ten conch and four spiny lobster. He always carries a spear gun—not for safety's sake, but just in case he happens upon something a little more interesting to wrangle into his net. This guy is one tough dude.

His son, Elvis, served as first mate today, helping circle the buoy as Tobago dove to the ocean floor, but typically Tobago takes to the sea alone. Like The King (early movie-star Elvis, not the 1970s drug- and booze-addled bloated version), this Elvis was a handsome, strapping man. Over six feet tall with movie-star, Michael Jordanesque good looks, he's the type of hunk you'd expect to see in fashion magazines, not helping his dad pilot his little old rust-bucket. Turns out this wasn't Elvis's bread-and-butter gig (which I will get to later), he was just there to steer the boat as a favor to his old man and help us with our gear. In fact, he had almost no water skills to speak of. Between dives, Tobago would snap, barking orders at his clueless son. Elvis was like a fish out of water, unable to tell his port from his starboard.

After a few hours, the clouds started rolling in and the wind began to whip up. Tobago surfaced and told us the conditions were too rough and dangerous for him to continue diving. Storm clouds were gathering, and he really wanted to get back to No Man's Land and fire up the grill. On our way over to the island, I asked Tobago if his son ever wanted to keep the family conch business running. Tobago explained that there was no money in it. Most of the conch sold to big hotels and restaurants is now imported, or farmed in

Asia and cheaply sold in cans or in frozen bags. The market for the fresh stuff, as delicious, fantastically sweet, and succulent as it is, hardly exists anymore. There's too much labor involved in shucking these massive beasts. Additionally, the youth of the Caribbean are more interested in becoming music producers, soccer stars, or workers at the local hotels. I guess the life of a humble fisherman isn't as sexy as it used to be. The humorous experience of watching this father and son argue all day turned poignantly bittersweet once I realized that when Tobago goes, the local conchdiving industry goes with him. I asked Tobago if he knew of anyone else who still dove anymore for these mollusks. He smiled at me and said, "No one, mon. I'm da last one."

I'm not sure what it is with the *Bizarre Foods* crew and boats, but it seems whenever we get on one, the shit hits the fan. What had been just a bit of bad weather morphed into a white squall within fifteen minutes. The wind and the rain became so fierce you couldn't even see the tip of the boat. My internal compass was off. I was soaked with spray and rain, nervous we were heading in the wrong direction. We were in the middle of the Caribbean Sea sans navigation equipment and unable to see our landmarks, but Tobago just smiled and told us not to worry, he knew exactly where we were going.

And he was right. He could have threaded that boat through the eye of a needle, despite the fact that the seas were pounding away at the boat, my cameraman got seasick, and the entire support crew in the chase boat was throwing up every ten minutes. It was a horrific afternoon at sea, and getting back to land took much longer than we had anticipated as our little outboard bucked against everything the sea could throw at us. Finally, after a very rough crossing, we pulled into the calmer waters a mile or so off No Man's Land, putted into shore, parked the boats about twenty feet off the beach, and waded toward the palm-lined pink sands, holding our gear high over our heads and thanking God we had made it.

Tobago's buddies had arrived about a half hour earlier and were waiting for us with a woman. The lady turned out to be a lonely, forty-something British divorcée who was staying at the hotel where Elvis worked. Apparently, Elvis made a living on the side as an opportunistic, resort-roaming gigolo and spent the rest of the afternoon lying next to her on the beach, helping her get her groove back. As the crew and I set up gear and blocked out the rest of our day, we couldn't help but be impressed with young Elvis, and we constantly peeked over our shoulders to see what he was up to and how he was working his mojo. He lovingly caressed his gal pal's stomach, played with her hair, nuzzled her neck and nibbled her ear, occasionally whispering sweet nothings into it. She loved it! Just try to make a TV program while the art of seduction, one that we later discovered was bought and paid for, is going on. I kept craning my neck, half expecting Benny Hill to pop up out of the sand dune. Sometimes you forget that the world still works in some pretty strange ways.

Back on the G-rated section of the beach, Tobago introduces me to his friends. First, there was Captain Frothy. To most of his buddies, he's just Frothy, but if you're on his boat, you refer to him as Captain Frothy. Next, we had Captain Frothy's nine-year-old son, Adrian, a very able-bodied young lad. And there was Skinny. Skinny was Captain Frothy's sidekick. Skinny ran just over six feet tall and had to weigh at least three bills. Frothy, Skinny, and Adrian had phenomenal cooking skills, and better yet—they all loved to eat. They were seafearing adventurers of the highest order. Captain Frothy's day job was running a waterborne adventuring company that took tourists on all sorts of different aquatic activities around the islands, but his real passion was food. Tobago asked him to join us to facilitate the chow side of things, and I was grateful to have some help. I certainly wasn't going to get any from Elvis.

We set up some worktables, unpacked the coolers, and got to work. We chopped vegetables, blanched and shocked the live lobsters, and extracted the giant conch meats out of their shells, which is no easy task. I had never seen a traditional conch harvester pull conch from its home, and let me tell you, it's truly one of the world's hardest bits of food prep. The shell is designed by nature to be impervious to intrusion and defy any attempt to crack it. The innards are coiled up inside the spiral caverns of the shell's interior, with the animal's long "tail" wrapping around the central column that the rest of the shell builds out from. Freeing the animal simply by pulling it out is a nonstarter—it's coiled too tightly, with an enormous amount of suction holding the conch firmly in place. I don't care if you're built like a brick shithouse— you're just not strong enough to pull it out. Sure, you can boil or brine the animal, pulling the meat out of the shell once it's died and shrunken away. However, both of those methods would mean ruining the meat for the type of cooking that we wanted to do, or that anyone with any desire to taste really good food would want to attempt. Extracting the conch alive and whole is not only ideal but, quite frankly, mandatory. To do that, you must take a hammer or a small crowbar or pipe and knock away at the crown of the shell where the biggest spike protrudes out. You goal is to open up an airhole there and release the pressure inside the shell. Once you've done that, you look for the whitish muscle and push it forward with a screwdriver or other narrow implement.

We did this to eight, nine, ten of these animals and trimmed away some of the intestinal products and the protective pincer that the conch uses to eat, move, burrow, and protect itself. It turns out that you can eat every bit of the mollusk if you need to, but some of the conch parts are tastier and more appetizing than others. Of course, the connective muscles and gastrointestinal tract can be eaten or discarded, and the animal has a large, crystal-clear penis relative to its body size, very long and thin with a small bulb at the end. Tobago told me that he has actually witnessed conchs mating on the ocean floor. The male extends this long, thin, transparent member, which looks like a tentacle from a 1950s sci-fi movie creature, and inserts it into the female from as far away as several feet. It's an odd coupling, but everybody in the conch biz swears it happens that way. Tobago and I ate a few conch penises together and had a few laughs as he tried to explain the whole conch mating ritual. I'm not proud of it, but if an animal has a penis, at some point I have put it in my mouth. It's just the nature of my job.

My favorite part of the conch is the giant, hockey puck–like disc of sweet, white conch meat that comprises the major muscle of the animal. Its texture is like a cross between abalone and raw steak, firm and yielding. The flavor rivals that of the sweetest hand-collected diver scallops you've ever tasted: saline, bright, and sugary sweet. In fact, most parts of the muscle you can just bite through without much work; it yields to the teeth and is insanely palatable.

I've eaten conch many times, sometimes frozen or canned, many times fresh, but never still wiggling and winking as it came out of the shell. That day on No Man's Land we feasted on the best-tasting conch I have ever had, and not just because it had been hand collected in cold, deep water, but also because it was so insanely fresh. That made our meal sweeter and more vibrant than anything that I could have hoped for. It was a truly sublime eating experience.

As the sun was setting, we pigged out on the kind of meal that you try to re-create for the rest of your life. A meal that makes all the other beachfront cookouts pale in comparison; a meal you would prefer to forget because it makes all the subsequent meals an emptier experience. Frothy, Skinny, and Adrian made a curry stew of fresh lobster and local vegetables collected at the market that morning, including cocoa, dasheen root, peppers, onions, sweet potatoes, and tomatoes. We made an incredible salad from some wild sea grapes I found. These are a member of the seaweed family whose little bulbous clusters coming off a central stem have inspired the locals to refer to them as sea grapes. We took wild limes, lemon, and fresh grated coconut and made a lobster ceviche, complete with the tomatoes and onions that we'd brought along. We ate it all with our conch, sitting in the sand on this uninhabited island with the sun setting in the background, the wind long since died down, and the seas as smooth as glass.

That part of the world has a confluence of so many cultures. You have the Creole, the African cultures mixed with Spanish, Dutch, and Indian influence, which makes Trinidad and Tobago's food scene a vibrant hodgepodge of international flavors on a par with countries like Singapore—a place everyone thinks of when the subject of a cultural culinary melting pot comes up. The meal had a little bit of all of those worlds thrown into the pot, and none of us wanted the day to end.

The poignancy of the evening was hammered home when it came time to say good-bye. Elvis was nuzzling the British lady in the back of the boat, and Frothy and Adrian and Skinny were stuffed to the gills, slapping one another on the back. Tobago was walking along the beach, not overly sad, mostly wistful. The afternoon had focused me around the fact that he was the last of his kind, but I didn't want to fetishize him. I felt bad that I had asked him so pointedly about it earlier on his boat; it seemed to be one of those issues he'd pushed to the back of his mind, and I had brought it front and center—perhaps insensitively? Tobago came walking back down the shore and seemed to read my mind. I began to apologize, stumbling over my words, and he stopped me, smiled his big toothy grin, and began barking orders at Elvis. We were all good.

The world is changing, and often I wish we could bring back the slower ways of doing things. There was a simpler time once, when diving for plentiful conch was a safe and economically viable occupation. It's not so easy to turn back the clock, and I am not sure we would want to. The world advances, and there is an ebb and flow of civilization that plays an important role in our historical and cultural development. Without internal-combustion engines there would be no rocket ships to the moon. However—and I don't think that you can lambaste and vilify someone for saying this—in an era when we are praising and even lionizing the slow-food movement, the concept of sustainability, and the notion of locavorism, we need to at the very least preserve the legacy of these people in a meaningful way so that future generations can get an accurate sense of what the world used to be like. The United States' high-end food culture is obsessed with sustainability, farm-to-table eating, snout-to-tail eating, and eating as close to nature as you can. I hope that some of that trickles down from the awareness of the privileged few to all Americans. Currently, you see a lot more of that kind of talk in the Wednesday Food Section of the *New York Times* than in the local mechanic's shop, with guys standing around the soda machine, wiping oil from their hands, and swapping stories about the best farmer's market to get heirloom dried beans from.

It's hard not to get emotional about spending the day on the water with the very last person in the world who harvests conch the old-fashioned way, one at a time with his own two hands. And the lessons to be taught about hard work and our rapidly diminishing capacity to save our planet from environmental disaster are best learned not from the nightly news but from men like Tobago Cox.

Saving Huatulco
Free Diving for Octopus

It might not seem like it at first glance, but Mexico is one of the most diverse countries in the world, ethnically, geographically, politically, and culturally. Every time I visit, I marvel at the abundance of things to do and how amazingly different one day can be from another. Americans love heading to Cabo, Mazatlán, or Cozumel, but my favorite destination has to be the country's southernmost state, Oaxaca. I'm sure you've heard of Acapulco, the region's most bustling beach town, overdeveloped in the extreme and filled with more ethnocentrist globe-trotting tourists than just about any location on the planet. But beyond that, Oaxaca offers the best of everything: gorgeous sand beaches, a phenomenally complex and varied food scene, and that easygoing vibe (in most towns) that nobody I know can ever seem to get enough of.

But the area has so much more to offer than sunbathing, Jimmy Buffet sing-alongs by the pool, and umbrella drinks filled with cheap tequila. The fish and sea life are plentiful, especially when it comes to deep-sea, sport, and hand-line or net fishing. With this readily accessible, renewable food source, it's not surprising that the locals made the most of it. The Pacific coastline of the state of Oaxaca is lined from top to bottom with fishing villages, both large and small, some thriving, some dying, and some struggling to survive the onslaught of the developers' bulldozers.

Take the city of Huatulco, which seemed to spring up almost overnight, but really has grown over the past three or four decades

from a lonely little beach, with some fun rock outcroppings surrounding a nice deep-water harbor, into a numbingly throbbing
hotel zone. Back in the day, this little beach town was wallowing
in huge puddles of financial success because of the fishing. The
sheer abundance of seafood that is available here is staggering:
mollusks, abalone, conch and clams, urchins, squid, fin fish, lobsters and all other manner of crustaceans—you can find it all in
the cool, deep waters off Huatulco. These days, tourism drives the
economy. Projections are that the once-tiny fishing town will support some 20,000 hotel rooms by 2020. In 2008, nearly 300,000
visitors traveled to Huatulco. Within twenty years, they expect
two million.

I spent some time in Huatulco a few years back, staying overnight in one of those horrific all-inclusive resorts on the beachfront, a place seemingly carved right out of a Hieronymus Bosch
painting of Dante's Inferno. The place was filled with lobster-
colored, margarita-scented tourists, most of whom never left the
hotel compound. Why should you? You'd miss all the free booze,
the pool volleyball with the bosomy bikini-ed staff, the free chips
and salsa—and God forbid you weren't first in line for the massive
buffet-style meals that made airplane food seem inspired.

Most vacationers talk a big game, boasting that they want to
dive into another culture face-first, but they never will. My fellow
guests were shocked as they watched me journey out in the morning to discover the real Huatulco. These are the folks who fear getting robbed or acquiring a serious case of Montezuma's revenge at
every turn; these are the people who think that everyone in the
city they live in leads a monastic existence predicated on a need to
walk the earth performing good deeds at every turn. They also
think that all indigenous peoples around the world are hustlers
and grifters, drug dealers and terrorists, every one of whom is
hell-bent on separating them from their wallets. I've said it before
and I'll say it again: The best experiences you will ever have as a
traveler require getting off your ass and spending quality time

with real people in real towns, cities, and villages. I prefer to do it by experiencing food and sharing culture.

Anyway, I'll get off my soapbox, but frankly people become so afraid of venturing into the unknown that they often miss what is right in front of their faces. One of the best meals I ate in Mexico on that trip came from the water right outside the hotel. I'd been up in my room, taking in the sunset from my balcony, trying to figure out what to do for dinner and where I could go to eat that wasn't in or near my hotel, when I noticed four or five kids diving off the rocks into the water. Each time they came out of the ocean, they dumped handfuls of shellfish into pails, which I assumed they would later hawk to local restaurants. I ran right down to the beach as fast as I could, asking if they had a knife or some sort of tool to open the shells. They did, and it turned out that not only were they trying to collect some seafood to haul to the back doors of a few local kitchens, but they would also hawk their wares on the beach to anyone willing to buy a plate. I ate a platter of fresh shellfish, one at a time, shucked by a nine-year-old kid right there on the beach. There was an assortment of eight or nine different pieces machine-gunned at me like a little mini raw bar selection on automatic fire. I've seen the same plate for hundreds of dollars in swanky Tokyo restaurants—orange and red Pacific clams, abalone, small whelks, oysters, scallops, all fresh from the sea. The big difference with this meal was that it cost about four bucks and I shopped for it from my balcony window.

While I love the Pacific shellfish, Huatulco is actually best known for a different sort of sea creature. The area surrounding the town's hotel zone, technically called Los Bahias de Huatulco, is made up of about nine bays that stretch for twenty miles along southern Mexico's Pacific shore. Much of the coastline is extremely rocky, with good currents and clean waters, making it the perfect breeding grounds for octopus. I love hunting and gathering food, so naturally I wanted to fish for octopus the old-fashioned way. Enter Francisco Rios Ramirez, an octopus diver with thirty years' experience under his belt. I'm beginning to think the fountain of youth is located in the long-lost city of Atlantis—either that or diving is great for your skin, since Tobago Cox and Francisco are two of the most fit and youthful-looking guys I've met in a long time. Francisco has a trim waistline, maybe thirty-four inches, but the guy weighs more than I do. He's solid muscle, with a huge chest and the widest shoulders I have seen on anyone his size. If I hadn't known better, I would have pegged him as an NFL linebacker, albeit a very short one. We met up with him at the docks in the sleepy port of Santa Cruz. We shared a coffee and a roll, got our gear together, and, under a cloudless sky, boarded his little boat, a small skiff with an ancient outboard motor, and headed out toward our first stop, Tagolunda Bay, which incidentally means "beautiful woman" in Zapotec, one of the area's indigenous languages.

Francisco dives into those bays nearly every day of the week, bringing in anywhere from twenty to forty octopuses per trip, each of which weighs roughly two kilos. His method is ancient and bare-boned, to say the least. Armed with only a thin, metal, yard-long stick with a hook attached to the end of it, and wearing only a tight faded Speedo, some fraying, cracked flippers, and an ancient diving mask, he flips over the gunwale and out of the boat. I follow him. He starts out by diving twenty feet under the water and hovering there for a minute or two. At this point, he's not even looking for octopus, just checking out the visibility and current, all the while he's expanding his lungs' capacity to hold oxygen. By the time he finds a good spot to look for octopus, he's able to hold his breath for four or five minutes, which seems like an eternity when you're sitting in the boat or floating nearby hoping your diving buddy—and only means of transport back to shore—isn't dead.

Francisco started me out on a few of the tamer dives, but after a few short lessons, we were off in search of our catch together. I should remind you at this point that I am five feet ten inches tall, weigh 240 pounds, and exercise as often as I can, which is about once a month. My idea of fun water sports is not heading ten miles from the nearest dock and free-diving in deep water with a swift current in the middle of the Pacific Ocean. But sitting with Francisco, prodded by his immensely toothy grin and halting guarantees of my safety, using my kitchen Spanish as our only means of communication, gave me all the confidence I needed. Besides, if we catch octopus, we eat octopus, right? The water in Tagolunda Bay, especially at the two outermost points of the bay, was some of the cleanest, most pristine ocean that I've ever spent time in. The seabed here is composed entirely of rocks and boulders, which means that no sand exists to be stirred up and cloud the water. These conditions are what Francisco looks for in a good octopus bed. You could see hundreds of feet in either direction. The water was teeming with bait and sport fish. The morning sun, facing away from the shoreline, afforded us some incredible light as it entered the water. It was just absolutely breathtaking.

I wish I could have enjoyed the setting as much as I would have liked while I was in the water itself. Even though I was with a pro, my nerves wouldn't subside. I was in water up to forty feet deep and fighting a ferocious current. In this part of the Pacific, you need to be careful not to get too close to shore or the rolling surf will smash you against the rocks. The entire time I was diving, I struggled to stay at least twenty-five feet off the shore, simply holding my position so I wouldn't get distracted by the job at hand and wind up tossed against the rocks.

I wasn't able to follow Francisco into the deepest areas (does that make me an octo-pussy?), but he pointed out clusters of dozens of octopuses a few yards below us. They are just so plentiful that you could actually just nab them out of the open space where they are eating or playing, doing whatever it is that octopuses do in the late morning. Francisco could pick up three or four at a time, swiftly swim back to the boat, and toss them in a live well. Of course, octopuses aren't always this easy picking. When they aren't feeding, they tend to squeeze their invertebrate bodies into the rocky nooks and crannies. Francisco poked around the large, round boulders that made up the underwater terrain, trying to coax the little cephalopods into the open. If he can't grab them in his hand, he'll hook them and place them in his free hand. Oddly enough, the octopus inadvertently aids this part of the process by clinging to your hand with its suction-cup-covered tentacles. Once back floating alongside the boat, Francisco demonstrated how to hold the octopus by putting your finger in and around the area of its mouth that sits on the underside of the head—right next to its gaping maw—and sort of squeezing and holding him there. Don't put your fingers in their mouths; they have sturdy beaks, and trust me, you don't want to get nipped by an octopus beak.

Within a few hours, we'd filled our boat with all the octopus we had come for, but Francisco wanted to make a few more stops on the way back to Santa Cruz and the dock. On our return trip, we went through the majestic Chahue Bay. The views here were nothing short of stunning: limestone cliffs dramatically plunging into the water, giant boulders with waves slapping over them. We dropped anchor and dove back into the water to scare up a few more octopuses and take advantage of a little more underwater sightseeing before we headed back to a small town called La Crucecita. This is where all the locals live, a cute hamlet with some of the best seafood restaurants in southern Mexico. It is also where I would finally meet up with Francisco's wife of twenty-six years and get to check out their other business.

Together, the couple runs a local eatery called El Grillo Marinero, which roughly translates to "the seafood grill," located at Carrizal 908 La Crucecita. It's a cozy, palapa-style shack with eight or so tables that features a seafood-intense menu: ceviche, seafood salads, traditional seafood appetizers, local shrimp, and about a thousand preparations of *huachinango*, the local red snapper, typically fried. Of course, the *especialidad de la casa* is *pulpo*, octopus. After we dropped our catch in the kitchen, Francisco went to get cleaned up. I stayed behind in the kitchen with Pola, who is known as one of the best seafood cooks in the area. While untrained, and humble beyond words, her skill set would be the envy of any of the world's great seafood chefs. She works efficiently and quickly, meticulously cleaning each octopus, discarding the heads and viscera, preserving the ink sac for later use. Next, she butchers them and tenderizes the octopus's tentacles by pounding them by hand against a large stone perched next to the sink.

If you're ever looking to cook octopus, be prepared for one of two things: (a) No work, or (b) A lot of it. When it comes to the giant ones, I really love to eat them raw, sashimi-style, which is delicious. If we're talking smaller octopuses, like the ones from Tagolunda Bay, their size makes for good cooking. Big octopus, especially if you want to cook it, means spending at least an hour beating the invertebrate against a rock to tenderize the meat. Then you must cook it for a long time, often a few hours. One of my favorite little seafood shacks is on the isle of Sifnos in the Cyclades, about half a day out of Piraeus in the Aegean Sea. There you place your order for braised octopus in wine and ink, and watch as the chef's grandma beats it on a rock for an hour in the water near your table. A few hours later your meal arrives, your patience aided by ample bottles of ouzo and retsina.

But lucky for me, all the octopuses here are small, and Pola made short work of kicking out several different versions, each one tasting more delicious and complex than the last. Francisco returned to the dining room and we sat down to eat. Pola started us off with octopus and shrimp cocktail, made up of steamed diced octopus and poached shrimp, cooled and sauced with onions, garlic, lime juice, cilantro, and fresh tomatoes, served in a tall sundae glass with spoons and fresh tortilla chips. Think cold poached seafood that melts in your mouth bathed in the best gazpacho you can imagine. As we inhaled that dish, the octopus platters came rolling out of the kitchen one at a time. Next was Creole-style Mexican octopus, sautéed with some garlic and onions, fresh tomatoes and peppers, and finished with a little bit of wine, braised all together for fifteen or twenty minutes and served in its own reduced pan sauce with some rice and soft corn tortillas. The second dish was fresh octopus cooked in wine with garlic and a healthy dose of the octopus ink. I adored this octopus version of a squid dish I first ate with my dad forty years ago when we traveled to Venice. The rich, thick black sauce that coats the octopus is slightly citrusy, and redolent in the most profound way of the dark, briny ocean. There is an earthy and deeply nutty taste that squid and octopus have, and the idea of cooking the animal in its own ink is the perfect combination, allowing not only the whole animal to be used at once but also providing a beautiful flavor contrast thanks more to the slightly lemony edge this particular ink offers.

The dish that absolutely blew my mind was the garlic-and-salt-glazed *pulpo de ajillo*, which is a very traditional Oaxacan treatment and a centerpiece of southern Mexico's grandmother cuisine. It's a dish rarely found in restaurants. Pola takes ten cloves of garlic and about a teaspoon of sea salt and pounds it into a fine paste in her mortar, rolling the pestle around the interior of the vessel with quick, precise strokes. There is not a grain of garlic that's larger than a piece of sand or talcum powder left in her mortar. Pola turns a burner on the stove to a very low setting and gets the pan hot. Keeping the burner on low, she puts a little bit of olive oil in the pan and begins to cook the garlic and salt paste until it's cooked through, custardy yellow, and sweet to the taste without that scorching acrid quality to it. She then adds the octopus, cut into pieces, and cooks it for a few moments, then adds a splash of wine, covers the pan, cooking it for about twenty minutes or until the octopus is tender. Then she takes the lid off and she lets that sauce and liquid cook down until it has evaporated entirely around the octopus, leaving all the flavor of that winey sauce concentrated inside this dish. All that was left other than the octopus was the garlic and olive oil; the liquids had done their job. She cranks up the heat for the last fifty seconds, basically caramelizing this garlic in the oil-coated seafood, where it clings to the octopus like a super-sweet garlic candy coating. Now the octopus itself melts in your mouth with a sweet earthy flavor that drove me nuts. Some people are crazy about garlic; I'm not one of them. But this garlicky paste of goodness is one of the singular great dishes that I have ever eaten in my entire life, a simple technique-driven dish that I have used over and over again back home with everything from shrimp to chicken. It's easy.

Hand fishing for octopus on a sunny day in the Pacific is deceptively intoxicating, but I was stuck thinking about the future of fishermen like Francisco. His tiny town of La Crucecita and the once-sleepy port of Santa Cruz, where there was a vibrant fishing industry just a generation ago, is now home to parasailing, scuba-diving, and sea-kayaking companies. The town's native culture is in desperate trouble due to tourism companies that can drop serious cash for the dockside real estate. They're squeezing out people like Francisco, whose family is one of the original five that founded the towns back in the day when there was only fishing—before electricity . . . before the monstrous all-inclusive hotels that now line the beaches.

What was being destroyed stretches far beyond the bulldozed landscape. From our boat bobbing offshore, I could see the giant fishing trawlers plying the waters on the horizon, scooping up every single fish they could like a vacuum. The effect of these massive trawlers on the majority of the world's conventional fishing fleets borders on the criminal. The equipment is nonselective, with bi-catch totals that are sky-high, about 60 percent of the total weight. Recent studies show that octopus trawlers are returning to ports with a greater percentage of juvenile octopuses, a telling sign that the species is overexploited. The long-term solution for this modern-day culinary Armageddon is to maintain catch levels that correspond to the potential of the stocks available. We have carbon-neutral living standards, so why not a species-neutral meal equation that would allow diners to sleep at night, knowing their dinner didn't negatively impact the life expectancy of the species? While the idea may strike some people as saccharine, I think it's a pretty important notion.

Promoting artisan fishing would certainly be a step in the right direction. Francisco's operation, old school as it may be, is a role model for how we can make it work. Take the animals by hand, catch only what you need, and let the fishery self-regulate. Once trawlers are sent packing, the octopus population will rebound quickly, due to their species' ability to reproduce in a short amount of time.

Of course, getting people to care about an alternative protein, like octopus, is a hurdle in and of itself. While octopus is wildly popular in most other parts of the world, Americans perceive shrimp, black cod, tuna, and salmon as the sea fare with the most sex appeal and most table-friendly attributes. However, octopus (and the small whole fish that the rest of the world eats regularly) should be on everyone's radar and dining room table. These are some of the best-flavored sea fare, high in protein, low in calories, usually inexpensive, and fairly easy to prepare. Eating alternative proteins is the only way to ease the pressure on center-of-the-plate commodity foods like chicken, pork, and beef.

Octopus is not a novelty item. It represents our salvation, which was one of the reasons I wanted to go diving with Francisco in the first place. We can control the degree to which we allow development to destroy the coastline of one of the most gorgeous physical landscapes in the entire world. We can control the degree to which we allow commercial fishing to destroy the sea life that has kept families employed for as long as there have been people there. As it stands, we're teetering on the verge of cultural homicide, watching something die and not doing anything about it. I'm not in the business of guaranteeing Francisco has a job and I'm not in the business of keeping the El Grillo Marinero afloat. I am in the business of advocating the preservation of a culture that will allow those elements of our human development to flourish so that one day my son can meet Francisco's son and they can go fishing.

Death Match 2009

Can a Matador Save Madrid's Historic Tabernas?

A restaurant's life span is much like a dog's. If it lasts seven or eight years, it's lived a healthy and decent life. If it makes it ten or twelve, and can put a little money back into the investors' pockets after paying off its opening and carrying costs, it's had a really good life. But if a restaurant is a couple hundred years old, passed down from generation to generation, and manages to continue serving up one of the best versions of its country's national dish, which once fueled the most machismo elements of the local culture—well, a restaurant of that caliber is more than just a precious family heirloom, it's a national treasure, the Lassie of the restaurant world. It seems that if a restaurant of that caliber is rotting at the core and fading away, it's worth fighting the upstream battle against the bulldozer of globalization. I'm not exactly sure how to go about it, but I do know that when you find an iconic restaurant withering on the vine, a place that is in and of itself a business, and represents one of the last bottles of Coca-Cola in the desert, it's definitely something worth hanging on to.

But that task is harder in a city like Madrid than in a city like Milwaukee. Milwaukee is home to several hundred-plus-year-old restaurants. If Karl Ratzch's restaurant were ever in danger of selling its last schnitzel, the city would pass an ordinance requiring everyone to eat there once a week. There aren't that many great restaurants in the town, and I am not calling Ratzch's great, but its place in the city's iconography is crucial to the local culture. At this point there is no great tidal wave of a food zeitgeist threatening Ratzch's or any of the other half-dozen ancient restaurants that made the city famous. The Serbian, Czech, Polish, and Ukrainian dining halls that make Milwaukee a great culinary treat for committed food freaks will still be there to visit.

Madrid is a different animal. It's truly earned its chops as one of the world's great eating cities, and simply walking down its winding, cobblestone streets really got my taste buds going. Madrid's food scene is made up of two very distinct culinary styles: traditional Spanish cuisine and extremely modern. I wanted to get started with a bang and raced over to have lunch at an eatery that defines cutting-edge cuisine. My first stop was La Broche, one of the country's legendary restaurants, which is saying a lot considering that some of the most exciting, innovative cooking on the planet takes place in Spain. Chef Sergei Arola, La Broche's chef and owner, got his chops working under culinary master Ferran Adria for many years, and his food philosophy and technical execution show it. His cooking style embodies that adventurous, bold, in-your-face cooking that Adria is known for, with an inventive, whimsical touch of what is most often called molecular gastronomy by those who need to put everything in a box with a name and a bow on it. However, Arola is supremely grounded in the strong elements of classic cooking.

Arola made four dishes for me in his kitchen, starting off with seared red prawns on olive gnocchi with an almond milk sauce. He spun fresh tagliolini pasta with seared morels, tiny smoky salty sea larvae, and Parmesan cream. Earthy and bold in the extreme. He topped the dish with an egg yolk cooked "sous-vide," or immersed in a hot-water bath, which gave it a raw look as it sat on top of the pasta. The first bite disappeared into my mouth with an explosive essence of poached egg, a perfect complement to the pasta and cream sauce, a mad scientist's nod to pasta carbonara.

He followed up the pasta course with a small plate of roasted sardines with black trumpet mushrooms. Simple and elegant, and the culinary harbinger of spring. The last dish went by the simple moniker of *roast beef*, which was truly the understatement of the day and demonstrates Arola's whimsical nature. He presented me with a few paper-thin circular slices of blood sausage, or *morcilla*, served on a disc of olive-oil-fried brioche crouton cut to fit perfectly beneath it. He topped the dish with see-through ribbons of warm, seared rare beef, crowned with an aromatic baby-herbed salad with little bits of microfennel playing the role of agent provocateur. A scoop of foie gras ice cream rounded the whole plate off. It was breathtaking to gaze at, and I could have stopped right there. But prudence ruled the day and I began to eat the stack of the beef "sandwich," scooping small espresso spoons of the foie gras ice cream onto each bite. Insanely good, and one of my all-time top twenty favorite dishes. I finished with some cheese and fruit and strolled out of the restaurant on a cloud.

How I had an appetite after I left is beyond me. However, all afternoon and evening long I managed to partake in a semi-traditional tapas crawl, stopping in every appealing tapas bar I could find, sampling small plates of *angulas* (baby eels), *pescaderos* (tiny sardines), salchichon sausage, Iberico dried cured ham, bouqerones, griddled razor clams, and dozens of other edible delights. It is often joked that Madrid's restaurants outnumber the local populace by about three to one, and Spaniards take advantage of that fact every few hours. They not only eat—they enjoy food. And there is a big difference. Business or social conversation is an excuse for snacking, and Spaniards have no issue in partaking in a leisurely lunch or eating well into the night, often not even starting dinner until 10 P.M. Remember, Spain is the culture that gave us tapas in the first place. There are a few ideas as to how this small-plate style of eating came to be. Some people will tell you it comes from farmworkers needing small bits of food to hold them over until the day's main meal was served. Others claim a Spanish king came up with the concept. By law, every drink needed to be served with a bit of food to soak up the alcohol in order to sober up the wine-guzzling workforce. In any case, it's a brilliant idea that still shapes the local and global food scene. Frankly, I find tapas outside of Spain one of the most tiring of food trends. The whole small-plate phenomenon is an overused food cliché that has spread to nearly every corner of the world. It's like Top 40 radio; the song is catchy, the hook is good, but when you hear it every hour on the hour it makes your head spin and you quickly tire of the song you fell in love with, killed by overexposure. But in Spain, tapas just sprouted organically. It's a grazing culture: You eat a wonderful breakfast and spend an hour or two enjoying a leisurely lunch. Midafternoon, you might stop at a ham shop before heading home after a day of work. From 7 P.M. until 10, you eat tapas and drink with your friends, hopping from bar to bar, finally ending your evening in a restaurant. It almost seems like work and sleep are the two things that break up one big meal. Suffice to say, Spain is my kind of place.

My tapas crawl that evening ended at the Museo del Jamón, a small chain of ham restaurants that are really cathedrals of worship for eaters like myself. The name roughly translates in the most dorky of ways as "the museum of ham." But the idea that great cured meats are under glass and safely away from overeager mouths, accessed only by an audio tour headset, is far from the case. Stroll into the store and all around you are belly-button-high marble counters behind which are more types of cured sausages, cured meats, meat salads, and traditional salume-style fare than you've ever seen in your life, hundreds and hundreds of varieties. Of course, they offer the all-star Iberico dried and cured hams as well as Serrano hams, Spain's version of prosciutto. Their Bellota ham was arguably the finest cured ham I had ever eaten; you could taste the wild-pig goodness, the acorn and hazelnut diet, the delicate salting and air drying, and the thin yellow fat streaked through the meat and rimming the edges of each slice tasted almost as divinely musty as the season's first truffle. And at over $100 a pound, it better be good! I have often wondered why a Museo del Jamón doesn't exist in New York. No one can resist the siren song of salchichon and cured ham of such high quality. Back home, the best Iberico, black-footed pig legs sell in some stores for hundreds of dollars a pound. And you have to buy a considerable amount in a store, or pay the markup to eat it in a restaurant, but at the Museo, if you're a pork junkie like I am, you create your own tasting experience. Point at five or six items in the deli case and ask for two slices of each. You can pay by the gram if you like. They'll gladly place your selections on a piece of a brown butcher paper and plunk it down in front of you at the counter. There are no chairs, just a bar with a foot railing you can lean up against. You eat some smoked and cured pork, some cheese, some olives, and some insanely fresh crusty bread and drink some inexpensive wine, beer, or orange juice. I know OJ isn't the beverage that first comes to mind when you think of ham, but the sweet, slightly sour, seasonal Spanish orange juice freshly squeezed one glass at a time is my beverage of choice here. It cuts through that fatty, porky goodness like a bunker-buster missile. That salty, smoky pork flavor paired with oranges just drives me crazy. It's like chocolate-chip cookies and milk. I'm not too proud to admit that I fed my pork jones at Museo del Jamón almost every single day I was in the city. Don't judge me! You would do the same thing.

So after stuffing my face for a couple of days, including a *percebes* (goose-neck barnacles) pig-out of Roman proportions at La Trainera, the best traditional seafood restaurant in Madrid, I'd sufficiently worked up the stamina to eat at Casa Botin. According to the *Guinness Book of World Records*, Casa Botin is the oldest restaurant in the world. The restaurant is scenically located on a narrow, cobblestone street about a block off the Plaza Mayor, which was the site of the heretical trials and subsequent witch burnings during the Spanish Inquisition. Botin cooks everything over wood in the same stoves and oven that have been pumping out suckling pigs and lambs every day since 1725. The ancient structure houses many small dining rooms, and shows its age with its tilted stairs, antique window casements, servers who look pulled right out of central casting, and ecstatic customers slurping down bowls of the classics: squid braised in its own ink and stewed partridge with polenta.

I spent most of my morning in the granite-floored kitchen, piling logs into the stove and cooking with the Botin staff, none of whom is younger than sixty. Hanging out in the kitchen has its perks. I scarfed down as much pig as I could handle, as well as plenty of *angulas*, freshly plucked at night as they make their way up from the Sargasso Sea. The kitchen prepares the delicacy using a simple glazed clay pot about five inches wide, heated to 600 degrees Fahrenheit. Once it's hot enough, they add olive oil, garlic, and a single dried hot chili. Next, they dump four or five tablespoons of these baby eels, which look a lot like vermicelli noodle pieces with eyes, into the pot and swirl it around with a wooden fork. By the time it comes to your table, they are cooked. An order costs up to $150, but it's a unique dish you're not going to find anywhere else. It's quite a treat.

After spending some quality time in the kitchen, I headed to a table to enjoy my whole suckling pig. More baby pigs, which are usually under a month old or weigh less than seven pounds, are consumed in Spain than in any other place in the world. The staff there was quite proud of me, looking on as I pried open the skull and made quick work of the ears, snout, cheeks, and brains, saving the tongue for last. Everybody in Spain eats this way, so I wasn't the only one in the dining room getting up to my elbows in pig head. And this wasn't my first trip to Botin, either. In the mid-1970s I went to Spain with my dad and our friends the Vales, with whom we traveled around the world on a regular basis. This meal at Botin was exactly the same as the one I ate there nearly forty years ago, except a little more expensive. Growing up in a family that placed a premium on collecting the most honest and authentic food experiences we could muster certainly made me the globe-trotting immersionist that I am. Eat first, ask questions later.

I was in town only a few days, so in true Spanish fashion, I headed to La Bola for a second lunch. La Bola isn't as old as Botin, but it's been open since the early nineteenth century. As I walked through its door, admiring the gorgeous woodwork and old-world leaded windows, I imagined what Madrid must have looked like 200 years ago. The city used to be filled with taverns, somewhere in the range of eight or nine hundred. Today, they're a culturally endangered species. Only sixty or seventy taverns remain, which is very sad. La Bola boasts an all-female kitchen, with a median age of seventy years. Everybody, and I mean everybody, heads there for one reason only: the legendary *cocido madrileño*.

Cocido madrileño is a very rich dish, and it makes for a one-pot progressive meal that every braised-food junkie needs to check out. The women start with a large decorative but highly functional clay pot, which resembles a flower pitcher, and fill it with lamb, pork, poultry, sausage, vegetables, and chickpeas, topping it off with a homemade broth that in and of itself makes a stunning restorative. They stack these pitchers upright, allowing them to essentially percolate on a wood-burning stove for hours. Once you order your cocido, a server takes the pitcher directly from the kitchen to your table, pouring the broth into a bowl filled with cooked fideos, thin Spanish egg noodles a little bit thicker than angel-hair pasta. It makes a lovely soup, and you eat that part of the dish first. When you've finished your soup, they dump the smoked meats and chickpeas onto the plate, serving it with small pots of sea salt, pickled hot peppers, and a puree of smoked and fresh peppers as condiments. Add the baskets of crusty bread to the table and you have a meal of legendary proportions.

After a midafternoon siesta (thank God for that traditional resting period), I went back to the streets for another tapas crawl with some friends.

. . .

We ended up spending the better part of the night at a restaurant that moved me like no other I've visited before or since. It was a crumbling establishment named Taberna Antonio Sánchez, after the son of the bullfighter who started the restaurant in 1830. Since opening nearly two centuries ago, the place has been owned by a succession of bullfighters, passed down from one to the other like a family heirloom. Today, the tavern lies in the hands of a seventy-year-old former bullfighter named Paco. Located near the Plaza de las Cortes & Huertas, at number 13 Mesón de Parades, this classic *taberna* is chock-full of bullfighting memorabilia, including the stuffed head of the animal that gored the young Sánchez.

Paco toured me around the tavern, pointing out the tables where famous writers like Ernest Hemingway came to eat, drink, and write late into the evening. The decor in this place is all original—tables, chairs, and even the wineglasses. They still use the ancient dumbwaiters, and house the kegs where they still store and serve the famous Valdepenas wine the taberna was renowned for. Paco led me by hand to the dark paneled walls where three unique works by the famed Spanish artist Zuloaga still hang. Zuloaga had his last public exhibition in this restaurant.

Nothing has really changed over the years in this historical Madrilenian tavern; the zinc countertops on the bars are still in use, photographs of old-time bullfighters like the legendary Frascuelo or Lagartijo still hang on the walls. The marble pedestal tables still are in use, the same tables where the authors of the Generation of '98—the group of creative writers born in the 1870s, known best for their criticism of the Spanish literary and educational establishments and whose major works fall in the two decades after 1898—argued late into the night. There are still the crumbling old posters advertising "torrijas" for 15 cents or warning customers that spitting on the floor is forbidden. The restaurant was most famously used as the setting for a scene in Pedro Almodóvar's film *The Flower of My Secret*.

After the tour, we pulled up a stiff, rickety seat at a small table in the corner to enjoy a house specialty. Bulls are revered not just in the taberna's decor and history, but on the menu as well. *Callos*, a casserole made with blood sausage and tripe, is a traditional comfort food of Spain. This version was unlike any I've experienced—so rich and sticky and filled with so much collagen that if you kept your mouth closed too long, your lips would literally stick together. Just like the history and decor, the dish was absolutely incredible. We ate *chipirones*, tiny squid, and other classic dishes that the restaurant has been serving almost without exception since the day it opened for business: stewed snails, San Isidro omelette, bacalao with onions, fried eggs on a bed of crisped potatoes, and the famous oxtail stew.

Sounds awesome, doesn't it? Now, if only the Taberna Antonio Sánchez could attract customers. I visited the restaurant on a Thursday night. Not a soul was in the joint when we arrived, not a body through the door the entire two hours we were there. It was downright depressing. Paco was so proud to show me his business, and how he ran this operation with just one cook and Paco working the front of the house. He'd stand by the door, just waiting for customers who were never coming. The roads around the tavern are silent, the streets too narrow for cars. It's an ancient working-class neighborhood, and years ago, this was where the bullfighters would come to see and be seen. These days, bullfighters are rock stars. They're not kicking back, eating callos, and bullshitting over a few beers; they're dropping Ecstasy and partying with supermodels in Ibiza. The neighborhood is changing. Wave after wave of immigrants settle into these affordable flats, and because the streets can't support traffic, the neighborhood is cut off like an island from the rest of Madrid, creating a pocket of decay. Developers take over the more charming buildings on the edges of this neighborhood, but the interior has yet to gentrify.

Additionally, the food that Paco is serving is simply not as popular as it once was. The restaurant seems doomed.

But Paco soldiers on, showing up every day to make the best callos in Madrid, giving anyone who will listen a history lesson from a guy who lived and loved in a way that doesn't exist in today's pop-culture, disposable world. Trying to leave on a high note, I asked Paco which bullfighter will turn bar owner when he's gone. He very haltingly told me there is no one—when he goes, the tavern goes. And then he said, "I am the tavern Antonio Sánchez." His stories, his stew, his stewardship will be gone and the tavern will go with it, making Paco without a doubt the last bottle of Coca-Cola in the desert.

Forgotten Foods
Juicy Cheese Worms Are Making a Comeback!

Running all over the world, hunting bats in Samoa, fishing with a Sicilian family, cooking donkey in a restaurant in Beijing, trying to experience food and share culture can lead you into some lonely territory. I often find myself spending time with folks living on the verge of cultural extinction, which can get downright depressing. However, the great thing about traveling is that for every sad story I unveil and undoubtedly sit with for a while, I find another person, ingredient, or culinary tradition that is all about revival and redemption. My recent trip to Nicaragua was all about this positive spirit, reminding me of the National Geographic documentaries I used to watch as a kid. I'd be mesmerized by the schools of salmon swimming upstream to spawn at the top of our Northwestern river systems. Without fail, there is always that last fish you're not sure will make it, and the cameras always made a point of telling his story. If you're anything like me, you're always rooting for that fish. Nicaragua, despite a century of constant struggles and hardships, is finally reaching the top of that proverbial stream.

Nicaragua is an overlooked destination for travelers, to say the least. Roughly the size of New York State, the country boasts two huge freshwater lakes, Managua and Nicaragua, as well as ocean borders to the east and west. In fact, it's believed Nicaragua means "surrounded by water," and originally stems from one of the many indigenous languages spoken by natives. The country is visually stunning and scenic, with tropical lowlands, sandy beaches, and narrow coastal plains interrupted by volcanoes. Hundreds of small islands and cays lie on the eastern shores, providing some of the best "let's get lost" islands in Central America. On paper, you'd think Nicaragua would be much like its Central American neighbors, infested with sunburned tourists escaping frigid northern winters, the kind you see teeming into airports with their cheap sunglasses and Abercrombie & Fitch pajamas, carrying their favorite pillows and checking that their Nascar carry-on didn't get scratched in transit.

However, until recently, that wasn't even a possibility. Nicaragua is like the kid on the playground who was bullied every day, teased by the girls, and just couldn't catch a break. In 1972, a devastating earthquake destroyed the downtown in the nation's capital, Managua. The entire area needed to be reconstructed in a completely new location on the far side of Lake Managua. The old downtown is nearly deserted. The businesses all moved, so the residential area around the old city center is nearly abandoned. The old presidential palace, Hall of the People, and the national museum are overrun by squatters. Nobody thinks it's safe. So with the new city that was erected five miles on the other side of the lake, it's sort of an odd town, missing a vibrant cultural center. Additionally, the area has been plagued by hurricanes, most recently 1998's Hurricane Mitch, which devastated the country.

The people experienced a huge political transformation as well. Although Nicaragua declared independence from Spain in 1821, it wasn't able to stand on its own two feet until recently. The country was mostly ruled by the Spanish elite until the Sandinista Revolution in 1979, which resulted in a short-lived civil war that brought a committed band of Marxist Sandinista guerrillas to power. Although the country's free elections in 1990, 1996, and 2001 all defeated the Sandinistas, it wasn't until Daniel Ortega's reelection in 2006 that the country could seriously start rebuilding. But Ortega is Ortega, and I am not sure this committed ideologue knows how to change with the times. Like that nerdy kid from grade school who had a growth spurt the summer after high school, ended up going to MIT, and married the hot girl, Nicaragua seems well on its way to greatness. I'm just keeping my fingers crossed that there are no more natural disasters, no more revolutions for a while, and that Nicaragua will get a chance to bloom on its own.

What I love about this country is that despite the hardships, earthquakes, storms, and revolutions, Nicaraguans are some of the most resilient, kind, caring, and open people I've met. They are for the most part poor, and yet everyone shares everything with guests. On my first day there, I met up with Sergio Zepeda in his small town of Masaya. He's a guitar maker now, but he used to be a famous musician in a boy band, sort of like the Nicaraguan Menudo. Here's a tip for anyone looking to eat well on the road: Hang out with musicians. Every time I'm with that crowd, I end up eating amazing food. Rockers eat late and at odd hours, with eclectic tastes and lots of free time on their hands. They're a great food resource for me. We started off at his home, where I sampled fresh cacoa beans for the first time. We hung out, ate, and played guitar with some of his pals, like La Vaca Loca, a superbly talented female singer/songwriter. We ended up going to a restaurant in Tiangue, where he introduced me to some of his musician buddies. We ate some *maronga*, a rice stewed in cow's blood; *morcilla*, another type of blood sausage; and *chainfaina*, a stew made of chopped-up bits of viscera, brains, and pig parts with some herbs. This dish is cooked until the meat falls off the bones. Then it's chopped up again and cooked down until it turns into a paste consistency, which is spread on tortillas. Don't get me wrong—I had a wonderful evening. Good food, great company. And the scene was amazing. A town square right out of the movies, with a narrow covered hut about forty feet long, under which there were dozens of old ladies cooking and hawking their wares. You order by pointing with your finger and young girls bring you your selections. There is an acoustic band playing classic Nica music, and the moon is full, rising over the ancient cathedral above us. However, the food lacked that one crazy item I'm always looking for.

Sergio asks if I had a chance to eat the iguana eggs. I hadn't, so he leads me over to a table manned by an old crone with three bowls in front of her, each filled with a light tomato porridge. Floating in the bowl are a dozen small golf-ball-size eggs. The embryo is encased in a soft, fibrous shell that you bite into and suck out the eggs. A horrific methodology, but pretty darn tasty. Very much like a chicken egg, but smaller and with a thinner and metallic flavor.

I spent the next day on a bus from Managua to Estele, a town high up in the mountains. You catch the bus at Mayoreo Market, roughly ten minutes from the airport. Selecting a bus is quite an ordeal, like selecting a gal to party with at the Bunny Ranch in Carson City. There are hundreds of idling buses, and since there are more seats than butts to put in them, each one is pimped out in order to attract riders, with young salesmen imploring you to take their bus, not the other guy's, to your destination. The buses are big American-style school buses, circa 1968, and I finally selected mine, a shimmering red and silver beast named *Tranquilo #7*. Every bus has a slick name. Before we hopped on our selected bus, we picked up some nut brittle from one of the hawkers, then set out on the Gringo Trail and headed north on the Pan America Highway.

I quickly discovered that a lengthy Nicaraguan bus ride is like a mobile progressive meal, with about as many stops as the local Lexington Avenue line on the New York subway. Every time we stopped, kids and older men rushed onto the bus carrying pieces of fruit, chopped watermelon, fried donuts, whatever it may be. By the time you reach your destination, you're stuffed. We ate *casillo,* a white cheese served in a plastic bag with vinegar chilies and tortilla, as well as *cuajada,* a curdled cheese made at a farm on a hill high above the highway. My favorite dish was *vigoron*. It was shredded cabbage topped with pork cracklings and dressed with lime and orange juice and bits of sliced tomatoes. It was fresh, crunchy, and totally hit the spot after I had spent the day in a hot bus. After disembarking, I wandered around Estele, checking out the amazing produce market there. Later, I hooked up with a pal who lives in the area. We hung out in Estele for a while, eventually making our way north into the foothills of the Cloud Forest. We stopped at a truck-stop place called Don Juan Papaya's for a little bowl of soup, and a short while later at Antojito's, where I met some of my friend's Peace Corps buddies. We ate some grilled armadillo and grilled boa constrictor in a restaurant that specializes in this local fare; it was superb, and I was stuffed.

We spent that evening at a place called Selva Negre, an old coffee plantation turned eco-hotel. The howler monkeys kept me up most of the night, but it was worth waking up in absolutely stunning surroundings, with a dense tropical rain forest high above the hot plains below. We finished the drive to Matagalpa that morning to hit the Sol Café. If you're a coffee connoisseur, add a visit to Sol Café in Matagalpa to your bucket list. The coffee business in Nicaragua is fascinating. Here is a food item representative of the campesinos' years of struggle against oppressors who've exploited their livelihood. However, like the rest of the country, this industry is bouncing back. The Thanksgiving Coffee Company, which operates out of the Sol Café, is a conglomeration of hundreds of local farmers, some of whom have only a few acres of trees to pick beans from. As a co-op, they sell to coffee companies all over the world. Starbucks, Newman's Own—you name it, they're buying coffee from Thanksgiving Coffee. The coffee association hired tasters and blenders to help craft a signature coffee style from beans that hail from different farms. When you see how slick and innovative this system works, you become a believer. This is going to work. They are a fair-trade coffee company and they receive a fair market price for their goods. A certain percentage from each sale goes to civic works projects such as local clinics or helping rebuild schools. We toured the facility at Sol Café, where local farmers bring their beans to be dried in the sun, graded again, and bagged for selling. Hundreds of laborers work in superb conditions, with benefits, and earn about 20 percent more in their pocket than at other agrarian enterprises in Matagalpa.

It's a really positive story, and just more proof that Nicaragua is a turnaround country. When I'm in Spain or Trinidad and Tobago, I'm often overwhelmed by how much of the indigenous culture is on the verge of extinction. But if I want to feel good about the direction of global food culture, I think of developing countries like Nicaragua, where cultural foods and traditions are on the rebound. These are the places where I get to experience the sheer joy of culture preservation. And what excites me more is that this notion of preservation has increasingly become important to Nicaraguans.

One of the great experiences along those lines came the next day when we flew to Blue Fields, located on the Atlantic coast of Nicaragua. Blue Fields is a Creole community, where everyone speaks English with a heavy Creole lilt. And given the fact that there are no roads to the area, Blue Fields is cut off from the rest of the country. You can get there only by boat from another port or by taking the one plane a day that stops in the teeny town on its way to Corn Island, a tropical paradise popular with the beach freaks. We spent the night in a hotel above a casino and journeyed the next day to the home of Edna Cayasso, a local grandma who specializes in the traditional Atlantic coast cuisine developed by the first Africans in Blue Fields. Edna, her three sons, and their wives and kids all live in one building, with Edna still ruling the kitchen. During our visit, she made *rondon*, a traditional Creole dish called "rundown" in creole communities outside of Sapanish-speaking countries. Rondon is a melding of flavors and cultures—born in Africa, filtered through flavors of the Caribbean, and now treasured by small communities who have eaten it for generations. It's a thick stew of meat, vegetables, and coconut milk, sturdy with sweet potatoes, plantains, yucca, and starchy tubers called cocos, which remind me of a cross between a cassava and a potato. The ingredients are thrown into a bowl filled with water. As far as protein goes, Edna opted for a chopped, browned *wari*, which is essentially a wild jungle rat that resembles a peccary. The starches and meat absorb the liquid as it cooks, resulting in a dish as delicious as it is diverse. Rondon is the quintessential Nicaraguan Creole food, and it is something that people like Edna Cayasso revere as more of a tradition than a simple dish. It's apparent that passing her passion for Creole cuisine on to the next generation is a high priority, as she insists her whole family make the dish together.

She served the rondon with coconut rice and beans, coconut bread, and two homemade beverages made from cassava and seaweed. These drinks are called seaweed pop and cassava pop. The seaweed pop was crafted from a puree of local seaweed, rehydrated with water, and seasoned with nutmeg. It's more of a sludge than anything else. I politely accepted the nearly inedible beverage, but in my head I wanted to run screaming from the table.

Finally, on our last day, I had the ultimate uplifting food experience I was hoping for in this country of redemptive experiences. We traveled south to Granada, a city where everything comes together—the Pacific, North, Central, and Atlantic regions—both in their food and heritage. Granada is a colonial Spanish town that has remained unchanged for hundreds of years. You can climb to the top of the public church's bell tower and look out over the rooftops. It's a sea of gorgeous curved clay-tiled roofs, not an antenna or satellite in sight. The smell of cooking fires wafts through the streets. It's an absolutely charming place, with artisanal chocolate shops, cozy city parks teeming with people and performance artists everywhere you look. The narrow cobblestone streets are a challenge to navigate, only because you spend the whole time craning your neck gazing at all the stunning Spanish Colonial architecture.

We were there the night of a big annual poetry and arts festival, where I had the pleasure of meeting the Nicaraguan vice president as well as a bunch of local dignitaries. I took a short break from the action to check out some Nicaraguan baseball T-shirts. As I sifted through the shirts, I noticed this Chinese guy running toward me. He immediately began screaming at me in Chinese. His interpreter eventually caught up, as did his security detail. Turns out this was the ambassador from Taiwan, berating me for not liking the stinky tofu I had eaten in his country. I'm just sort of holding my own, smiling and apologizing—I don't want to get involved in some international kerfuffle in Nicaragua. All of a sudden, his wife appears and starts chewing him out because, as the translator told me later, he was tearing me a new one over a food he himself did not even care for! Imagine, an American in Nicaragua getting a tongue-lashing in Chinese, translated into English, over a meal I didn't like from two years ago. It was pretty funny, and ended up morphing from an awkward altercation into a big lovefest. But I had to go, because dinner was at eight o'clock sharp and I couldn't be late.

I ended my night at a sleepy little restaurant and hotel where, I admit, my expectations were low. At first glance, Casa San Francisco, a quaint, family-run hotel about three blocks off the main square, was nothing special. However, once I entered the ancient courtyard, I changed my tune. Quiet and beautiful with a plunge pool surrounded by bougainvillea, the place just had that old Spanish western feel. I half expected to bump into Butch Cassidy and the Sundance Kid. And the surroundings were nothing compared to the food. Upon learning of my arrival, Chefs Octavio Gomez and Vernon Hodgeson went out of their way to up the ante a little in the kitchen. Vernon decided to reinvent a few rural dishes and raise them up on the altar, so to speak, exhibiting the kind of gastronomic and aesthetic flair that you expect from a New York City chef.

They kicked off dinner with historical local fruit flavors, serving a platter of *nispero, pera de agua*, green mangoes, and star fruit.

We washed that down with a *batido*, a sapote fruit milk shake. The main dish was quintessentially Nicaraguan with a modern twist—wild iguana, marinated sour orange, cumin, achiote, and garlic. They roasted the lizard whole, crisping the skin just like duck à l'orange—it was outstanding.

Aged Chontales cheese was the real star of the meal. It's a small wheel of soft, Muenster-like cheese, served in the ancient style of the Caribbean coast. You allow the cheese to age in the heat of the day, just long enough to produce large maggots. When you open the cheese, these juicy cheese worms, as they call them, are then eaten right along with the cheese, just hundreds of these suckers wriggling on the end of your knife. It's one of the most horrific and wonderful things I have ever seen on a plate.

The worm origin somehow remains a mystery, scientifically speaking. But I did manage to get the cultural story. One of the chefs explained that the cheese process originates from the time of the very first Sandinista Front. During that period, people near the front wouldn't throw away old cheese because it was so difficult to obtain any food at all in that time of war. Instead, they let the cheese ferment, hanging it in a sack to eliminate the *suero*, or liquid, from the fresh cheese. Once the cheese lost its liquid, it began the process of decomposition. It's at that time that the cheese develops and produces the worms, which continue to grow as long as you let the cheese ferment. Some people remove the worms and eat them fried; others eat them in their natural state. The whole idea of eating maggot-laden cheese is enough to boggle most anyone's mind, but what I couldn't shake is the idea that a traditional food like worm-filled Chontales cheese has been eradicated from this part of Nicaragua. Octavio admitted he's been clueless on how to make it, consulting aged family members to resurrect the delicacy. The cheese wasn't a dying breed—it was already dead and in the ground. When the chef learned I was coming to town, he saw the perfect opportunity to re-create this cheese for an audience that might actually enjoy eating it.

He started out with fresh country cheese, *caso cassero* or *caso creolo*. It's important you use raw-milk products from rural areas, because dairy products in the city use too much homogenization and scientific methodology to kill the bacteria and avoid decomposition. He crafted a basket of plantain leaves, hanging the fresh cheese from it to remove the *suero* for three days. Next, he rolled the cheese in fresh plantain leaves to hold its shape. On the seventh day the cheese started to decompose and produce eggs, which resemble fine grains of rice. It takes an additional twenty-four hours to hatch the worms. Luis served it to me four days later, which allowed the worms to grow to quite a decent size. Although nature does much of the work for you, it takes a lot of patience to stick out the two-week-long decomposition period. That, in addition to the fact that the cheese tastes like a rotten foot bomb went off in your mouth, has a lot to do with its phasing out. The cheese flavor is strong and pungent, which I adore. It reminded me of the washed rind cheese, The Stinking Bishop, that I eat whenever I can find some, but this one has the bonus of the wriggling worms busting out of it. Suffice to say, there's not a big market for Chontales cheese riddled with maggots. Despite the desirable protein in those worms, this process can goof up on you if the cheese doesn't lose its liquid. If that happens, the flavor will be kept even more rotten and putrefied and you can't eat it. So there is a very fine balance here. This isn't *Fear Factor* food, this is good cooking.

I lit up when I heard this story. For Luis to spend fourteen days creating this dish made me want to cry. Who goes to that kind of trouble for a stranger? People who are proud of their culture and want to share it with you, that's who. Octavio Gomez of Granada, Nicaragua, resurrected a regional, traditional dish that had died and gone to food heaven because no one was up to making it anymore. He breathed life back into a lost art form, and believe it or not, we devoured this cheese. It was fantastic; even the crew, who often forgo the bizarre fare for those faux-chocolate protein bars, liked it. The most disgusting-looking food is often the best-tasting.

As foul an idea as it is to shove a runny, smelly fromage, riddled with something you'd rather bait a fishing hook with, into your mouth, it was pretty darn tasty. Eating outside your comfort zone allows you to acknowledge the baggage that you carry into each meal, that evil corruptive contempt prior to investigation, which thankfully can disappear pretty quickly.

That's why I love doing what I'm doing. When I have those moments and I realize there are people like Octavio Gomez who share the same food mission as me, it makes me glow. My hat is off to him for putting his money where his mouth is, so to speak, by not only acknowledging a culinary dead end but doing something about it. And the best news of all came several months later when we heard that now the chefs at the Casa San Francisco are making this wormy Chontales regularly. Like the phoenix, it is reborn, one mouth at a time.

RANKED
AND FILED
[A Few Good Meals]

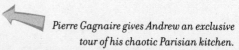 *Pierre Gagnaire gives Andrew an exclusive
tour of his chaotic Parisian kitchen.*

Paris

Best Food Day in My Life?

In the world of professional travel, as in life, some days are better than others. There are a lot of days that just don't measure up, and I've discovered that timing oftentimes makes the difference between a movingly memorable and an infamous experience. Nothing is more disappointing than flying into a Canadian lodge and being met by your fishing guide, who gushes about how many fish they caught yesterday. "You're going to be pulling them into the boat two at a time," he tells you. Up in the morning, big breakfast, down to the dock, and out in the boat.

All day under a hot sun with nothing but warm, soggy sandwiches for fuel and you haven't even had a nibble. "Ya should a been here yesterday," his mate calls to you from the gunwale as you putt back to the lodge, and you are reminded that this syndrome has reached epidemic proportions in the life of people who travel like you do. You finally score a table at some white-hot restaurant in another city, only to discover upon arrival that the chef whose food you are dying to eat is doing a charity dinner halfway across the country. It's hard to manage expectations when you've had your heart set on something for months, years, decades. You finally get to some remote corner of the world, only to find that whatever it is you're looking for just wasn't what it was cracked up to be. And there are many restaurants and food stalls, eateries, even types of dishes that have lived off of twenty-year-old reputations and are, as my friends in Texas like to say, "all hat and no cowboy."

Of course, when an experience lives up to the hype, it is truly a wonderful thing. Prowling through the dumpling shops of Taipei, deep-sea fishing expeditions off the coast of South America, strolling through Tsukiji Market in Tokyo, touring the caviar vault at the Grand Hotel Europe in St. Petersburg, Russia (where I was able to take a horn spoon and literally feast out of one-kilo tins of the best beluga caviar in the world), were some of the most notable eating experiences of my life. However, if you held a gun to my head and made me pick one food day as my all-time best, I'd without a doubt say it happened on my second-to-last trip to Paris. Imagine a one-day period spent hustling around the City of Light, stuffing my face all over town in some of the most famous eateries in the world. From a quality, variety, and sheer level of brilliance standpoint, the food purveyors and chefs that I encountered that day were simply mind-blowing.

Paris seemed the perfect place to create a phenomenal *Bizarre Foods* show. Many people thought it would be a tough sell. Unlike Asia and Africa, where a lot of the food is exceptionally strange to most Westerners in terms of recognition and sex appeal, Paris seems so tangible for any traveler. But I thought it would be the perfect spot to showcase what this show is all about. It's not about shock value or eating *Fear Factor* style. It's about exploring a city or region by experiencing the culturally significant foods that you find real people eating when you get there. I knew in my heart of hearts that so many things in Paris were bizarre (and I use that word on purpose, because I like to broaden its definition at every turn) because of the level of excellence and the brash boldness of chefs who create dishes that, from an intellectual standpoint, are incredibly challenging for people to wrap their heads around. And let's not discount the classics. *Tête de veau*, a potted calf's head in its own gelatin, is a staple of the Parisian *traiteur* and is certainly as crazy as any of the bits of rotted flesh, bugs, or entrails I've eaten on the show. Paris, with its culinary greatness as the main character, made a fantastic story.

We started out the day at six in the morning, heading around the corner from our hotel to the basement baking and proofing rooms of Poilâne Bakery, buried deep under the ancient streets of the city. Poilâne has been a Paris staple since it opened its doors in 1932. The French can argue forever about who has the best bread, the best croissant, the best pastry for hours on end. There are so many good ones, I'm not sure how you could begin to conclude which one is the best. But Poilâne's history gives their bakery more clout. So do the awards. And the claim by so many others about its greatness. Frank Sinatra and Lauren Bacall were members of the Poilâne fan club, and Robert De Niro loves to pick up a loaf at any opportunity. In 1969, owner and baker Lionel Poilâne was summoned by Salvador *freaking* Dalí to create sculptures made of bread. However, their biggest bread devotee is an anonymous New Yorker who coughed up a whopping $100,000 to Poilâne, requesting that his children and grandchildren receive a loaf a week for the rest of their lives. Seriously. It's one thing to be great for a couple years or a decade; it's another thing to achieve greatness for the better part of a century, to the point where hungry carbohydrate addicts regularly make a pilgrimage from all over the world to worship at the culinary altar of what they are baking at Poilâne. Now, that's something to brag about.

I may have had a better almond tart, pain chocolat, or baguette in my life, but I couldn't tell you where. I think that says a lot about Poilâne's greatness. Poilâne has three bakeries scattered all over Paris, but the original is located on Rue du Cherche-midi in the artsy Saint-Germain district. We rolled up to the shop and went inside. It took some time for our crew to set up, during which I found it painfully difficult, coffee cup in hand, to resist the temptation of snacking on all of the warm breakfast pastries and breads coming up from the basement kitchen. By the time I finally got to go downstairs, I must have looked like an elephant that hadn't had a drink in a week, such was the madness in my eyes—like I was on the verge of diving into the ovens. They didn't speak English, and

I only speak kitchen French, but I'm certain that when my chin dropped to my lap with my tongue splayed on the floor it was the international sign for *feed me, s'il vous plaît*. The building had to be a thousand years old, with the giant granite stone floor even older. I couldn't help but think about all the bread that's been pulled out of those ovens and the folks who ate it, the famous and the ordinary. How many lives had this bread touched? Amazing.

I get swept away with stuff like that. We build memories around foods because of the romantic relationship that we have with them. I love the idea of going into an ancient building, staffed with sixty-five-year-old ladies who have worked there since their teens, and eating bread that comes from a bakery whose sour starter still has the essence of the bacteria from decades ago, or longer! The sum of the parts here is greater than the whole. If you don't think that is true, then bread is just bread. But for me, there was no better place to start the morning than merrily chomping away on a baguette at Poilâne Bakery, watching the ballet of bakers deep in the bowels of the building as the world of Paris began its day a hundred feet above us. Sweep to the proofing box, trays in the oven, rotate the bread, adjust the racks, pull bread, cool, lather, rinse, repeat.

Next, I moved on to what the French like to call *léche-vitrines*, which literally means "window licking." And there is no better place to window-lick than the Place de la Madeleine, home to some of the greatest food shops in the world: Caviar Kaspia, Maison de la Truffe, Fauchon, Maille Mustard. Quite frankly, I really didn't know where to start. Luckily, I had a bicycle. When in Paris, window licking by bike is the way to go.

I decided to start at Kaspia, a tiny café that offers up caviar to eat in the café or take to go. I opted to eat in the shop, standing like a dork with a horned spoon in hand. After my carbohydrate feast at Poilâne, I couldn't imagine eating more bread, but when a plate of delicate blinis, miniature toasted bread crackers, and brioche toast points arrived with assorted caviars of all sizes and salt ratios (along with some hand-cured smoked fish), I thought I had died and gone to heaven. It was my third visit to Kaspia, and for me, a trip to Paris is not complete without stopping there. These folks know how to do caviar right. And the customer who wants to suck the most out of the experience ought to go big or go home. The gorgeous silver service, as expensive as caviar is, is best served in a luxurious manner. The silver platters, the paper-thin vessels holding the caviar, the crushed ice to keep it cool, the funky little forks, spoons, and paddles to scoop and dress each and every bite—it's a beautiful way to eat. If you're not going to go all out, what's the point of pressing those delicate eggs up against the roof of your mouth to begin with? You can't imagine what a treat it is to start off the day dining on some of the world's best caviar, including the increasingly hard-to-find Iranian caviar. Shopping for anything Iranian in the States is a delicate political issue; however, the French have an ongoing relationship with the former Persian empire, and God bless them for it, because it allows me the opportunity to eat Iranian caviar. I had only a few minutes to spend at Kaspia, but I made short work of four ounces of quality salted and cured sturgeon eggs.

Luckily, I didn't have far to go when I left. I moved two doors down to Maison de la Truffe. This restaurant and fine-foods shop has amassed a global reputation for not only supplying its customers some of the greatest truffles from Italy and France, but for its truffle-infused goods. Truffle butter, truffle oil, truffle salt, truffle cheese, and if you take a seat at one of their little tables, you can feast on truffles with scrambled eggs, gravlax of salmon cured with truffles—really anything you can imagine. I tried a fabulous black-footed cured Spanish ham rubbed with truffle paste, the meat shaved paper thin by hand and placed on little toasts schmeared with triple-cream-truffled cheese. If there is a truffle that should be paired with a food item, the folks at Maison de la Truffe have done it.

A shaving of truffle is like the aroma of a musty basement stuffed with seven million pounds of the earthiest mushrooms.

Just one thin slice of these oversized mold spores packs that kind of punch. With good truffles, the aroma and the flavor are absolutely explosive and huge in scope. It feels as if the flavor literally grows funkier and deeper inside your brain. While many purists, myself often included, consider the only way to enjoy fresh white truffles is paired with one or two other ingredients at the most, some of the best truffle flavor comes from the great culinarians and their ability to coax more flavor out of the truffle by pairing it with certain items, then layering those truffle flavors. That bite of truffle paste rubbed on cured Spanish ham was one of the most intense flavor moments of my life. Tasting the complex variety of truffle flavor compares to looking at a great painting where an artist has painted a sunset, then sanded away a bit and painted over it, then sanded away some more and continued painting. It creates such a vibrancy of color, a depiction that so closely resembles a real sunset. Layered and nuanced. Not just reddish orange, but hundreds of versions of that color, many of which are almost close to being the same, but not. It was said that the impressionist painters painted only their vision of reality, not reality itself, with many of them adapting a style that was completely juxtaposed to how it actually existed in nature. I can't help but look at Seurat's *Island of La Grande Jatte* or Monet's *Impression, Rising Sun* and think they've completely captured the way it looks in real life, despite the artist's liberty with our reality. And that is how it was with those truffles. I know it wasn't simple, I know it was a lot of ingredients, but those levels of truffle flavor still haunt me today. I nursed my tiny container of truffle salt, truffle mustard, and all my little truffle goodies that I brought home from Maison de la Truffe for months after I got home.

Of course, you can't leave there without having some of their foie gras terrines. A nice fattened duck-and-goose-liver terrine complete with truffles infused every step of the way, the terrine studded with truffle lardons and a bit of vintage Sauternes mixed in for good measure, all cooked and chilled into a nice beautiful block, sliced paper thin on toast liberally smeared with truffle butter—that is about as good as food gets. Talk about the ultimate food pairing! Feeling about 300 pounds heavier, I went back out onto the street and set out toward Fauchon. Ouch.

Fauchon is an overwhelming food superstore. It's not quite as imposing as Harrods in terms of sheer grandness, but the food halls at Fauchon are remarkable. I'd already checked bread off my list at Poilâne, smoked fish and caviar at Kaspia, and truffles at Maison de la Truffe, so I headed straight for the pastries. I walked out with four tarts—almond, orange, wild strawberry, and custard—each about the size of a golf ball. The combination of egg, sugar, butter, and flour is nothing new, and yet when you taste Fauchon's version, you can't help but think someone in that kitchen sold their soul to the devil. The talent level of someone who can take the same simple ingredients the guy down the street uses and make something that is five times better is truly genius. It all starts with the quality of French ingredients. Butter and eggs— the French worship these things, and take great care to ensure a food's integrity.

It reminds me of the way the Japanese treat food. There is just a level of respect for it not found in other cultures. I adore the Italians simply because they understand how to make food work in its simplest form. They are unapologetic about throwing a single piece of roasted fennel on a plate with a little grilled paillarde of beef. They do it so well and with such purity and innocence. They do stripped-down food as well as any Western country. I think the Japanese are their Eastern counterparts, where a single pickled plum works as a dish or a single cube of perfect tofu can stand alone in a meal's progression of flavors. From a skill-set standpoint alone, I think the French are to Europe what the Chinese are to Asia. They have the chops to combine flavors in a way that is bigger, bolder, and stronger than anyone else in a single bite. As I write this, I can taste that custard tart. Eggy and sweet, but not overtly, combined with the custard texture effortlessly

disappeared into crumbly leaves of pastry. An ethereal experience, to be sure.

We licked our last window at Maille Mustard Shop. Maille has
been pumping mustard since 1747. I say "pumping mustard" because they dispense it from a beer keg–like barrel. They always
offer their classic Dijon and three or four *moutardes du jour* on tap.
You can fill a specialty pot of mustard from the kegs or opt for pre-
packaged mustards, which are just fantastic. When Americans
think mustard, they think yellow, and maybe a spicy horseradish
variety. But Maille is like the 31 Flavors of mustard, offering up
dozens of options, somehow coming up with more flavors to add to
their repertoire every year. A preserved lemon and harissa de-
buted around the time I last visited, which might just be my new
favorite. The essence of North Africa in a jar, you can just taste the
saltiness and sweetness of the preserved lemon with that little
hint of citrus and the zing coming from the harissa chili paste.
The lemon-chili-mustard trifecta just smashed it out of the park.
Like a madman, I tasted every single mustard I could, and bought
a bunch of pots of Dijon for friends at home, as well as their tarragon mustard, which must be the best tarragon mustard there is.
A great marc du Bougogne mustard was so complex that you could
taste the fermented grapes through the mustard; it was just extraordinary. I carefully nursed those jars, using them with dis-
cretion to the very last drop. Before the mustard jars get rinsed out
and put in the recycling bin, I make a salad dressing, actually
shaking the oil and vinegar with the mustard. I want to use it all,
including the dry little crusty bits on the inside of the rim. That's
how much I love Maille Mustard.

Once I finished shopping, I headed over to Pierre Gagnaire
for lunch. Now, Pierre Gagnaire's signature restaurant at Hotel
Balzac is a big deal. He's consistently ranked in the top five restaurants worldwide, with his Parisian restaurant boasting three Michelin stars. He's a genius. He's a visionary. He's a classicist. He's
one of the most innovative chefs of his time, juxtaposing cutting-

edge technology with traditional cuisine. Gagnaire runs an operation that truly embraces the future while honoring the past at every turn.

We hung around a private room in the back, snacking on teeny hors d'oeuvres as we waited for him to return from a photo shoot. When I say teeny, I'm talking the size of your pinky nail. A tiny piece of crisped flatbread, inside of which was a little piece of smoked duck, topped with preserved Champagne grape with a dot of a mustardy sauce and leaf of microherb on top. I wondered if he had a team of little elves working in the kitchen creating these amazing, tantalizing treats. I could hardly control myself, pacing up and down, dying to get out into the dining room.

When Gagnaire arrived, he apologized and said he didn't have very much time, but invited us to spend some time with him in the kitchen. I nearly fainted. I'd anticipated stealing five minutes to fire off a few questions before one of his sycophantic toadies escorted me to the worst table in the restaurant. But to spend an hour standing next to Gagnaire in his kitchen watching him command his brigade and put out the lunch service was more than I ever hoped for. Gagnaire has an expeditor on the server's side of the line managing the tickets that the servers write up, making sure the food gets out of the kitchen and into the hands of the right customers at every turn. Hard job. The kitchen, in Gagnaire's signature restaurant, is a rabbit warren of little cubbies and cubicles. I have never been in a kitchen with so many corners, nooks, and alcoves! Finished plates are stacked up on one stainless-steel service pass, where waiters pick them up as they are worked over by the cooks and set them on trays. They then implore line cooks on the hot side, who carve roasts, plate chops, and put a piece of fish on a plate to do its thing. However, instead of everyone working in an elongated line with cooks working side by side, the kitchen is shaped like a starfish, with the points all turning in different directions. Pastries are down one little turn of the arm. Appetizers, cold and hot, off another. People operate in a vacuum, meaning you can't see where your other teammates are until you walk five feet to your left or right. Finding a final garnish or saucing takes some legwork. It was the most unusual high-end kitchen setup I've ever seen, and I've had the privilege of being invited into some of the greatest kitchens in the world. It was like a madhouse in there. This is an industry where most chefs strive to impose some kind of order on the frenzied chaos of a dozen or two dozen people cooking together. Gagnaire seemed more than willing to let this madness reign supreme.

Everyone treats Gagnaire like a combination of the Pope, the President, and Willy Wonka. He was the ringmaster. He walked in, and some of his more secure cooks were extremely happy to have him there for lunch service. When he's in town, Gagnaire works in the kitchen. However, his notoriety often takes him on the road. He might be in Dubai opening a restaurant, accepting some award in Asia, doing charitable work, or attending social functions as both a guest and a chef. I noticed a few young cooks who looked completely terrified, as though they'd never put out a lunch with the Master on hand (I'm sure shoving our TV cameras in everyone's face didn't help calm their nerves). Gagnaire was milking it, marching up to these fresh-faced cooks, screaming, *"What is this? What is this!"* and poking at whatever it was that they were attempting to cook. It was just hysterical. He was kidding, and the cooks were nearly in tears.

Gagnaire, for all of his greatness, reminded me again and again that he was just a humble cook. And he didn't just tell me so. He showed me, by making my first bite of his food a simple one. He could have begun with an incredibly complex dish that defied description, but opted instead for a piece of roasted leg of lamb. I wouldn't say lamb is necessarily easy or hard to cook. Certain preparations are more complex than others, but because of lamb's high fat content, its preparation is a little more forgiving than that of leaner meats. It can be served roasted to an almost well-done point and still retain a good level of moisture. He served nine- or ten-ounce (butchered and trimmed) whole legs of lamb from Bordeaux, where the skins had been rubbed with the pasty sediment residuals from the wine-making process as a way to show provenance to the area. We visited in springtime, when the lamb is just perfect. The animals had been in the market for only a short amount of time before Gagnaire made use of them. Without my realizing it, Gagnaire had placed one of the lamb legs into the oven twenty minutes earlier. When it was done, he took it out, grabbed a knife from one of his cooks, and sliced off a wedge. He poked the knife into the meat, handed it to me, and said, "Eer, tazte eet."

I'm rarely awe-inspired by movie stars, rock stars, or pro athletes (okay, I know I sometimes act like a child around pro athletes), but sitting in Gagnaire's kitchen, a guy I have worshiped for twenty-five years, floored me. The man was putting a piece of roasted lamb into my mouth while making a point about how flavor, not technique, is what lies at the heart of every dish. At that moment he's a simple cook slinging out simple roasted food. While I appreciated his point, you couldn't help but be impressed by the fact that he was anything but that. However, his genius hinges on his ability to stay connected to that simplicity, which is quite a feat considering customers wait months, if not years, for a seat at one of Gagnaire's tables. The confidence to put out a simple piece of roasted lamb with a couple of turned vegetables, knowing your patrons expect the best meal they've ever had, is just incredible. There is no doubt in his mind that his lamb will be perfect.

Before we left I tasted paper-thin, pounded pheasant breast rolled in a puree of spring vegetables and peas, cooked sous-vide and sliced into gorgeous little spirals. I tasted sauces. I tasted vegetables. I tasted roasted wild mushrooms, flown in during the middle of the night just so they could be paired with a sea bass dish. I tasted all the parts as plates were assembled, then later the complete dishes. I tasted soups. He shoved spoons into my mouth with the fervor of a mad scientist. I felt like I was one of those kids redeeming my golden ticket at Wonka's chocolate factory.

Gagnaire is a master of simple dishes; he's also at the cutting edge of modern cuisine. This has a lot to do with his close relationship with Herve This. This, pronounced "Tees," along with the late Oxford physicist Nicholas Kurti, is the man behind one of the biggest food movements in recent decades: molecular gastronomy. Amazing, considering that This is not a cook or a chef at all. He's a physical chemist at the French Institute for Agricultural Research. This field focuses on taking a scientific approach to cuisine. This and Gagnaire are great friends, frequently brainstorming complex culinary ideas. I was scheduled to meet up with This the following day, so I asked Gagnaire a little about their relationship.

"We discuss food," Gagnaire said. "We discuss ingredients, and Herve clues me in to possibility, and I clue Herve in to possibilities, because we both do things that the other one can't."

I asked if This had collaborated on any of the dishes they were serving that day. He immediately prompted his pastry chef to whip up a dessert called Spring Strawberries. A delicate demitasse cup housed thin, quarter-inch layers of strawberry foam, held between layers of homemade wild-strawberry gelatin, topped with wild-strawberry mousse foam, then even more layers of gelée, mousse, custard, and shaved fruit. A final inch-thick layer of strawberry foam was added, then finished with a thin meringue cracker made with egg whites and sugar.

I went to lift the cookie off the dish, but Gagnaire insisted I break it with a spoon. There was to be no gingerly removal of the cracker. He wanted me to be more violent with it, to not treat it as something so precious. He and This agreed that breaking the top would add an element of surprise and sense of humor to a deeply complex dish. With so much complicated work put into creating such a dessert, it's difficult to treat this cup like an ordinary dessert. But if you do treat it like that, you miss the point. According to Gagnaire, it is just food, after all. I find this an intriguing idea, especially from a man whose restaurant was a jewel box of an environment. Lunch for two can easily cost more than $1,000. I tried to put that out of my mind, and attack that gorgeous dessert with a spoon I did. The moment I dipped the spoon down into all that foam, it just kind of evaporated, much like watching locusts devour a field of wildflowers. It disappeared swiftly, yet slowly enough that you could observe it as it happened. Stirring the dish, you uncover layers upon layers of flavors. That last bit of foam, trapped between other layers, lingered with essence of strawberry in every single bite and let me know that Gagnaire's genius was one that could operate on so many levels, be it the complexity of the dessert or the simplicity of a lamb leg.

Badly in need of a nap, I left the restaurant and journeyed across town to Restaurant Michel Rostang. Rostang is a heck of a restaurant. He is a fifth-generation Parisian chef and hails from one of France's great cooking families. His grandfather's restaurant earned two Michelin stars; his father had a restaurant in the French Alps, near Grenoble. Joining them in the kitchen seemed only natural, and with that, Rostang attended culinary school in Nice, followed by a stint as a commis chef in Paris. He did return to the family restaurant in the Alps for a few years, but the siren call of Paris was just too tempting. He and his wife, Marie Claude, opened Restaurant Michel Rostang in 1978. Within a year, he had one Michelin star. A year later, two.

Since its inception, the restaurant has moved to a larger location, near the Arch de Triumph in Parc Monceau. It's a very upscale sort of place and always listed as one of the top restaurants in the world. With Michel Rostang, I wasn't looking for inventive modern French food, but instead one of the most classic dishes in the French repertoire: Canard à la presse, or pressed duck. Few restaurants serve that dish these days. In fact, there aren't many chefs who even know how to do it. And even if you can afford the multiple thousands of dollars price tag, getting your hands on a traditional duck press is nearly impossible.

An hour before dinner service, Rostang took me into his kitchen. Gagnaire's system was all about chaos. In Rostang's, you could hear a pin drop. Everybody worked with exquisite precision. I watched them prepping, making sauces, cooking broths, stocks, and reductions, watching the pastry chefs get their tarts and plates ready for that evening. The master led me around the kitchen, letting me taste all these little goodies. Eventually, most of the staff left to fuel up on the staff meal, a hearty chicken stew, leaving Rostang, his sous chef, and me alone in the kitchen. He shoved spoons into my mouth, allowing me to taste the sauces of the classic repertoire, all the while explaining how their kitchen worked—labor divided classically, as you would expect in any serious kitchen. Sauciers made sauces, gardes manger managed the cold side, and so on.

We got on to the topic of his classic style of cooking, and how he managed to survive doing these traditional dishes in an age where people worship whatever is new. He confessed to tweaking the same menu they've been serving for years by essentially lightening up dishes and modernizing the plating. They're doing phenomenally well. It made complete sense to me. Classics are classics for a reason. They taste good. The combinations work. The sauces are fantastic. These days, people want less butter and cream, more vegetables, and smaller portions, and creating the same dishes through a modernist's lens, he accomplished the mission of bringing the restaurant into the twenty-first century.

He made me a dish that was most emblematic of fusing the old with the new. His father was well-known for a sweetbread and crayfish dish, which is very popular when it pops up on their seasonal spring menu. Traditionally, it's composed of spring vegetables, crispy sautéed sweetbreads, and French crayfish sautéed in butter. The crayfish are then taken out of the shell and topped with a decadently rich crayfish sauce. With these beautiful little spring vegetables, baby turnips, bits of squash, peas, and chanterelle mushrooms, it's simply gorgeous. But where his father's dish was an assemblage in the middle of the plate, bathed in three or four ounces of this rich butter sauce whipped with crème fraiche and served in a pastry cup as a vol au vent, Michel modernized it. He created a pedestal, placing pieces of the poached crayfish, tiny squares of the sautéed sweetbreads, and individual vegetables all around the plate. He drizzled spare spoonfuls of the sauce all around, leaving the diner to pick at the little jewels of the ingredients separately. The essence of the dish was unchanged. The sauce had been lightened, the portion was smaller, but the inventiveness and wittiness were there. Even the puff pastry vol au vents were transformed into small puffs the size of gumballs and employed as a garnish. While not on the level of Gagnaire's kitchen in terms of its modernism, it certainly was a memorable changing of the guard at Rostang's. And the flavors and compositions were stunning. With that, we proceeded to the dining room.

After that dish, I was ready for the main event. Pressed duck is an entire roasted duck, cooked at a very high temperature for only twenty-five or thirty minutes, which essentially crisps the skin and ensures that the rest of the duck is warm but very rare. At that point, the muscle just begins to tighten with the heat, allowing you to cut away the legs and carcass, as well as bone out the breasts with ease, slicing the meat paper thin. The bones, skin, and all the rest of the body-cavity viscera are placed in a cup that resides in a large, silver contraption resembling a giant French coffee press. The cup has many holes and works as a colander as you wind a handle, which smashes the contents, releasing the blood and liquids from the duck into a beautiful silver bowl. Next, it is skimmed and strained. The juices are reduced tableside with wine and stock. This deep, rich, earthy wine sauce—basically thickened with the animal's own blood and juices—is poured over the thinly sliced duck. And that's all it is; that's what the dish is about. For anyone who appreciates food, it's a must-see, must-eat. Words cannot describe the simplicity of this dish and the complexity of its flavor. It's deep and minerally in a good way, but the tannic wine notes pull back the sanguine quality of the rest of the sauce. The duck itself dissolves in the mouth.

After tasting Rostang's pressed duck, I'd come full circle, tasting my way across all of Paris. I thanked him profusely, then excused myself from the table (surprise, I had no room for dessert), flopped into the car, and crawled up to my hotel room. I took a long shower and crashed into bed to try and digest. I reflected on this incredible food day, trying to wrap my head around all the amazing things I'd eaten and just how lucky I was.

I spotted my knapsack in the corner of the room and noticed a small bag poking out of it. I crept over and pulled out a bag of cookies and mini tarts that I still hadn't finished from my morning trip to Poilâne Bakery. I ended my day as I had started it, with a little sweet from Poilâne Bakery, and if you have a food day that can beat that one, I'd love to hear about it.

Welcome to a Wazwan
The Meal That Nearly Killed Me

One of the best meals of my life also happened to take the longest to physically consume. It also was the meal that began the latest in the evening and finished the earliest in the morning. To get the full picture of it, we sort of have to backtrack.

India, much like its food, is complex and teeming with contrasts. Its capital city of Delhi perfectly exemplifies the zeitgeist: gritty and ugly, yet simultaneously elegant. It's modern and ancient, affluent and poor. It's a city of Sikh temples and red clay mosques. There is poverty and sickness. There are beggars in the streets, as well as serene parks and gorgeous architecture. It's an international megacity, with more than 13 million people, making it the second largest in India. There are dozens of indigenous ethnic groups and religious cultures. Throw in the expats and the thriving tourist business and you can see why Delhi is a pretty potent cultural masala. From some of the best restaurants in the world to humble everyday cafés, you can find every one of the many Indian cuisines represented in Delhi. Fortunately, I had the opportunity to dive mouth first into several.

Delhi is the oldest continuously inhabited city in the world, going back at least 2,500 years. The ruins of seven other cities have been discovered there, and it is said that Delhi's food descended from the medieval lashkars who were garrisoned around the forts of the old capitol. Today Shahjahanabad, or Old Delhi, is home to an army of office-goers and shopkeepers who trade in everything from spices to tapestries, bridal trusseaux to electrical fittings. If you venture through the tangle of streets and dark alleys into busy boulevards, you are likely to find surprises lurking around the corner, especially when it comes to street food.

Traditional street foods are continuously bulldozed under in a busy, hectic city like Delhi; the creep and crawl of expansionism forces them out physically, and the legal process forces them out before they ever go into business. But you can find cold, spiced milk froth, tiny stands that serve *nahari*, and vendors selling fruit puree sandwiches. I explored Charri Road and sampled all these goodies there. Food and eating are such a strong element of each and every Indian culture. And interestingly, the one thing that brings most people together in most parts of the world is often what keeps people apart in India. Culture and religion in India segregate people, especially when it comes to food. Some eat meat. Some won't even allow meat inside their homes. Some fast in order to be closer to God; some others say fasting is the path to weakness and is therefore evil.

I visited one place, however, where all cultures, all religions, all walks of life can sit down side by side and share a meal: the Langar of the Gurdwara Bangla Sahib, also known as the Kitchens of the Sikh Temples. Sikh culture promotes nonviolence and vegetarianism. Sikhs are strong believers in Karma and attribute karmic values to everything they do, including the air they breathe, the water they use, the light of the sun and moon, as well as the food they eat. Sikhs are considered the most egalitarian society in the world. This ideology is embodied in the two daily meals served at Gurdwara Bangla Sahib, where anyone can volunteer to cook in the *langar*, or kitchen, and thousands of people from every race and religion are welcome to eat free of charge. They serve between eight and nine thousand visitors daily, with no division between a lunch and dinner hour. It's always mealtime at the langar, and everyone who enters understands that the food is an offering from

God. It's more a place of community and spiritual experience than simply a setting for a meal.

The food served at the temple is by no means fancy, consisting of basic staples: dahl, a spicy dish made from lentils, tomatoes, and onions; roti, an unleavened griddle-baked flatbread; and curried vegetables. I helped roll out roti, then stew the dahl and vegetables, which went on to feed thousands of my newest friends. As we all ate together on the cold, marble floor of the temple, I couldn't help but think that this meal was what humanity is all about. Literally sharing food and culture. It was quite fantastic, although I must admit, I was glad to be excluded from dishwashing duty.

Interestingly, a simple ingredient also has the ability to bridge the gap between religious and cultural sects. Where religions demand adherence to exclusive diets, milk is one of the only items common in India in homes across the nation. To the Hindus, who make up more than 80 percent of the Indian population, the cow is revered as sacred. Thus, milk is a sacred ingredient, often used not only in food, but for spiritual cleansing purposes as well. Believe it or not, India is the largest producer of milk in the world (eat your heart out, Wisconsin). Drinking milk isn't all that weird to Americans, although I find it incredibly interesting that human beings thrive on this white secretion from the mammary glands of cows.

From main dishes to specialty drinks, milk plays a huge role in Indian cooking. Not all Delhites are comfortable with the suspect processed version that you and I buy at the supermarket. Instead, they rely on fresh milk from the cows down the street, and, yes, in one of the largest cities in the world, the milkman keeps his own cows in his own house and delivers milk daily. He milks the cows into large cans, hangs them off the handlebars of his scooter, and off he goes. I tagged along with one of these guys and watched his delivery, which allowed me to visit the Indian sweetshops where they use milk to make some of the world's best desserts. *Kulfi,* a favorite dessert of mine, is essentially the Indian ice cream that comes in a variety of unlikely flavors, such as rosewater, pistachio, and saffron. The milk used in this treat is simmered down, not whipped, which results in a solid, dense frozen dessert similar to frozen custard. We always think of Paris and Italy as the global leaders in the sweet departments. Nobody ever thinks of countries like India and Japan, despite their great tradition with them.

I encountered many other unique dining traditions in the city. Old Delhi's jam-packed and bustling Nizamuddin neighborhood is the place to experience the red-meat-rich (they typically opt for buffalo) Muslim cuisine firsthand. Located just outside Jamaat Khana Masjid, Delhi's largest Muslim mosque, this area boasts many authentic Moghul cafés, where I indulged in *nayaab maghz masala,* or mutton brain, cooked with cheese curds and curry. They're also well-known for *kalije,* which is a savory liver-and-kidney stew, chopped kidneys and testicles, as well as *nalli nihari,* a spicy stew made with buffalo marrow, feet, and skin.

And then there is Bengali cuisine, which hails from India's eastern state of West Bengal. Bengal's culinary traditions are founded on the rich selection there of grains, sea foods, bananas, and spices, primarily their customized blend of *nygela,* made of black mustard, fenugreek, fennel, and cumin seeds. I visited one of Delhi's newer neighborhoods, Nehru Place, where I had the pleasure of cooking lunch with chef Joy Banerjee. Joy is an expert on Bengali food and specializes in re-creating family recipes of a bygone era. He mans the kitchen at Oh! Calcutta, named after the avant-garde Broadway musical from the 1960s.

Despite the fact that Oh! Calcutta may be one of the worst restaurant names of all time, cooking lunch with Joy was one of the best eating experiences of my Indian sojourn. The banana is extremely popular in Bengali cuisine, mostly because it's convenient and abundant. Additionally, every part of the plant—flower to trunk—is edible. After watching the complex preparation of each banana specialty, which included peeling the banana tree trunk itself and exposing the heart of a foot-long blossom and stuffing the leaves, I feasted on Bengali dishes like sautéed tree trunks, fish bathed in mustard oil and wrapped in banana leaves, and *moocher ghona,* a dish whose centerpiece are the foot-long banana flowers.

In addition to offering some amazing street food and wonderful cafés, Delhi also houses some of the best fine dining in the world. Bukhara, a tandoori eatery *Restaurant Magazine* has often touted as the best restaurant in Asia, is one such place. It's a see-and-be-seen favorite of rock stars, presidents, and royalty, and a must-go for any restaurant aficionado. The food is exquisite. Their tandoori is beyond compare, and I've eaten tandoori in the best street stalls and most elegant restaurants globally. Bukhara does simple tandoori cooking better than anybody—it's magical. What's more, the casual atmosphere in a place as renowned as Bukhara is rather bizarre in and of itself. The dishes are unpretentious, and patrons are urged to eat not with silverware but with their hands. In fact, the chef insists on it, claiming it brings the whole eating experience to a heightened level, giving diners a deeper connection to the food.

These snapshots of Delhi's dining scene depict a piece of a puzzle that, when put together, create the vibrant food culture that is Delhi. Each piece on its own would make for a great story; however, no single experience can compare to the deeply complex and lavish meal I had with a group of Kashmiri hipsters.

Food in the Indian state of Kashmir isn't just about eating, it's an all-sensory sacred tradition. Kashmir cuisine is as much about art and style and ritual as it is about the food. I've met Kashmirs while traveling through India, growing up in New York, as well as in Minnesota, where I've been living for nearly eighteen years. Without question, these folks are some of the most outgoing and outrageous personalities I've ever met. They are all about the party. That boisterous characteristic is not very surprising, considering that the state was a big hub for every spice and silk route that you have ever seen on an ancient map. Persian, Afghan, and Central Asian merchants passed through the area, and while for many it was just a stop along the way, their influence stuck with the Kashmir people.

Kashmir dining traditions are lavish and decadent, with an obvious passion for hospitality. Traditionally, Kashmir hosts lay out all the food that he has at home before his guests. Then the guests fulfill their role by doing full justice to the meal—and thus was the Wazwan feast born. A Wazwan meal can consist of as many as forty courses. Organizing this meal is not for the faint of heart (nor is eating it, as I soon found out). Not only must the host select the numerous courses, he or she must also be willing to perform certain traditional ceremonies that accompany each dish.

Leave it to renowned Kashmiri fashion designer Rohit Bal to take on the daunting task of creating one seriously over-the-top Wazwan feast. These meals often entail many days of preparation and hours of cooking. I received the invite the first night that I landed in Delhi. And while I was completely wiped from traveling, I could not resist the opportunity to hang with this guy. Torturously fun-loving Ronit enjoys a good party—I mean, he's the Isaac Mizrahi of India, after all. I couldn't think of a better host for this kind of spirited feast, which is typically for special occasions and weddings these days. The colorful meal is really a ritual in and of itself, the preparation of which is considered an art form. The chefs, who are called *wazas*, pass this trade on through the apprentice system, from chef to chef to chef. While the traditional number of courses is thirty-six, there are sometimes a few more or less, and the preparation is traditionally done by the *vasta vasa*, or head chef, with the assistance of wazas.

I arrived at Rohit's home, located in one of the glitzier sections of Delhi. His neighborhood is absolutely beautiful, complete with parks and oversized three- and four-story brownstone homes. Rohit lives on the top floor of one of these gorgeous buildings. Even though it was 10 P.M., I was one of the first guests to arrive. As we entered Bal's home, I could smell food coming from all over the place, but curiously, his kitchen was empty. Apparently, the wazas had spent the previous twenty-four hours cooking, chopping, dicing, pureeing, boiling, sautéing, and baking in the hallways of his building. The wazas arrive with pots and pan, burners and bowls, cutting boards and curios, and they take over. I may have been the first guest to arrive, but I was certainly not the first to start partying. The host and a couple of his inside coterie started partying much earlier. You know how some people have a cocktail or two before guests arrive, just to kind of quiet the nerves? That's Rohit Bal. They were nervous hosts, and if I'd been in his shoes, I may have been on edge as well. The parade of models, filmmakers, restaurateurs, designers, and TV anchors . . . it was as if a Who's Who of Delhi society paraded into his house that night, as well as several childhood friends from Kashmir. Drinks flowed heavily, and food was absent. There were no appetizers. I found that really curious until I realized that no person in their right mind would want an appetizer before downing a thirty-six course meal.

So there I am, the American sober guy, surrounded by beautiful Indian A-listers downing booze like frat boys on spring break. I was nervous. I mean, I didn't know anybody at the party, and everybody looked so fabulous. Within no time, the Kashmiri knack for hospitality kicked in, and I started getting into the groove. The evening ended up being a real learning experience in Indian high society. I didn't just learn about food, I learned how to pose for a picture. Rohit, who regards events as an art form, hired a photographer to document everything. Apparently, a great photo involves leaning out over your waist slightly and tilting your head down just enough to hide a double chin. And you must stare down the camera, looking very severe. It's quite something.

After about an hour and a half, we finally sat down for dinner. Rohit cleared out his entire living room, outfitted with bright lights and a Cashmerian silk carpet. Everyone was seated on the floor, in groups of three or four, on top of gorgeous pillows in a semicircle, where we began with the first ritual of the evening. A Tash-t-Nari, an ornate silver basin, is passed by the attendants for guests to wash their hands. This ritual is less about hygiene than it is about symbolizing the cleansing of the soul and ridding yourself of negative energies.

Next, large serving dishes are piled high with heaps of rice, then divided into four quadrants with seekh kebabs, which are made up of ground, tubular meat sausages that have been skewered and grilled. It's perfect for this kind of shared meal—four guests get to eat off the same plate, but everyone has their own personal zone. Four pieces of different types of purees and yogurt sauces and sides of barbecued lamb ribs sit in the platter as well. The meal is accompanied by yogurt that is garnished with Kashmiri saffron and different salads and pickles and dips, and you just kind of start eating the moment the food arrives.

One of the cornerstones of the wazwan is making a whole lamb part of the process, ensuring that every piece of the lamb is utilized. The most notable ingredients in Kashmiri cuisine are lamb and mutton. More than thirty varieties of lamb are raised in that part of the world, and this multicourse meal makes use of the animal in nearly every dish. It's even considered a sacrilege in some serious Kashmir homes to serve any dishes that are based around lentils or grains during the feast. We were offered handfuls of fried lamb ribs dusted in turmeric, chilies, and lime. It was deliciously fatty and rich, which from a flavor standpoint I absolutely love. However, and I kid you not, after two or three of these mini racks of ribs I was almost full. At that point, it was almost midnight; I'm ready to go to sleep. But the next thing you know, the food starts pouring in.

Every time you finished a course, more food would arrive. Fried lotus stems. Cottage cheese squares. Bowls of chilies and radishes and walnut chutneys. A parade of four or five different stewed lamb dishes, one after another after another. Lamb curry cooked in milk. Jellied bouillon made from the meat and bones. Eggplant and apple stew. Rogan josh, a very spicy lamb stew. Another lamb stew made with tree resin. Mustard oil–based roast lamb. Cockscombs. Saffron-infused lamb. But the highlight was *gushtab*. I know this doesn't sound very luxurious, but I think of this hallmark dish as lamb bologna balls. Food books describe them as balls of chopped lamb with spices, and cooked in oil, milk, and curds. That doesn't even begin to describe the process. The chefs take raw lamb, a bit of garlic, and some mild spices and begin to pound it with a mortar and pestle, adding handfuls of minced fat as they go. I spoke to one of the wazas, who explained how they literally pound this stuff for hours, basically fluffing it up, then demolishing it into a paste. They don't pass it through a sieve, but it literally takes on the texture of a hot dog. It sounds almost like I'm denigrating it to say it tastes like bologna, but it tastes like the best lamb bologna you ever ate. So light, with so much fat beaten into it. It holds a ball shape so you can cut it with a knife, and even though it has a hot dog–like chew to it, it also has this melting, unctuous quality—it disappears down your throat as quickly as you're chewing it. It's one of the most glorious dishes that I have ever tasted.

We had thirty-six courses, and finally, at 2:30 in the morning, I needed to be thrown in a wheelbarrow and rolled back to the hotel. I was the first to arrive and I was also the first to leave. Despite the warnings to slow down and not eat it all at once, I pushed the pedal to the metal. You have to pace yourself. But of course, how can you pace yourself when the first thing you taste is lamb braised in chutney, with fresh plums, lime juice, and spices. It tasted unlike anything I've had before, and I probably will never experience it again. Holding back is way too tall an order for someone like me.

I can also have a hard time when people are drinking all night long and I don't drink at all. I'm okay after the first round of stories, and I'm just fine when the voice volume increases. Usually, I'm good for the second go-round of the same stories, but when you've heard the story so many times you could tell it yourself, it's time to head home. And so I wandered out to the streets of Delhi looking for a cab, desperate for a few hours to lie down to try and digest this amazing meal. Nobody loves lamb more than I do, but the next day, sort of like a tequila hangover, I swore to myself, *I am never eating lamb again.* I had lamb fat coming out of my pores for days. Of course, with such an amazing array of lamb dishes available in that city, it was only a matter of time before I caved on that one.

Mary's Corner

The Quest for the Best Laksa in Singapore

New Yorkers, Chicagoans, let's face it, really most Americans, think that they know what characteristics make for the best hot dog. Some say it's all about the sauerkraut or relish. Others think it's Heinz ketchup and yellow mustard. And then there is that group of people who believe one drop of the fancy red or yellow stuff completely ruins a tube steak. But at least we can all agree that encased ground meat served on a bun is the foundation for a basic hot dog.

Well, Laksa is to parts of Southeast Asia what hot dogs are to America. This dish is one of the most popular soups served in that region, especially Singapore, Malaysia, and Indonesia. There are many different styles of preparation, and everyone has an opinion about what makes one bowl better than another. Laksa is a spicy noodle soup that originates from the Peranakan culture, a heritage often referred to as Baba or Nonya. As a group, the Peranakans formed when the Malay Indians merged with the Chinese in the eighteenth century. Many different dishes symbolize Peranakan culture, most notably *otak-otak*, a sausage made of ground and seasoned forcemeat and steamed in thin portions in bamboo, banana, or other edible leaves. It can also be grilled or baked. To some people this is the most popular and iconic of all the traditional Peranakan foods, but my favorite regional dish is Laksa.

To understand this dish is to understand two things: One, it's an easy, cheap meal in a bowl, with lots of noodles and shellfish in the broth. Malays, the Singaporeans, and Southeast Asian food freaks argue about what makes for authentic and honest Laksa. To me, that sort of culinary dialogue often misses the point. You can argue about whether or not crispy shallots belong on top, or whether little strings of cold omelet should be julienned and stirred in, or how thick the broth should be, whether it should be thin and sour (as it often is in Thailand), or thick, rich, and creamy with a sturdy foundation of coconut milk. And let's not even get started on noodle options. To me, these are all specious arguments. Who cares? All those soups belong in the Laksa family. It's like arguing over pizza. It doesn't really matter whether it's from a grocer's freezer or a neighborhood wood-fired-oven joint, it's all pizza as long as it tastes good to someone. I've often thought that what propelled Laksa to such incredible heights can largely be attributed to the jump in American tourism over the last forty or fifty years, where gobs of foreign visitors came back to their hometowns raving about the best meal-in-a-bowl. The obsession with this high-energy, big-flavor dish reached staggering proportions because the combination of flavors is just simply off the charts. When it intersected with a large enough group of new diners— well, let's just say that a tipping point was an understatement. Any traveler who goes to Singapore and doesn't have a bowl of Laksa might as well call the trip a waste of time. Once you have tried it, you become consumed with it, scouring foodie chat rooms and Web sites to discover who has the best Laksa in town, and not just the one where you live. We all have our opinions. I certainly have mine, but we'll get to that later.

I've been dying to get to Singapore for as long as I can remember, and finally had my chance in 2008. On most trips, the first glimpse of a country comes as your plane prepares for landing. Sometimes it's what you see through the window; other times it's what you hear over the intercom. This is especially pertinent when landing in Singapore. It's not your polite "Please fasten your seat belt. Thank you for flying Delta Airlines." Instead, it's a kindly auditory welcome mat stating, "It is 98 degrees Fahrenheit, 34 degrees Celsius this morning in Singapore. Please mind overhead compartments, as luggage items may have shifted during flight. And please remember that swearing, spitting on the ground, or the use or importation of illegal drugs, even for personal consumption, is punishable by death." It's the kind of thing that makes you gasp the first time you hear it.

The city-state of Singapore is certainly a unique place. It's a very small island, roughly four times the size of Washington, D.C., with about four million inhabitants. Singapore is one of few city-states in the world. There is Monaco and the Vatican City, which is certainly rarefied company. Singapore, which boasts a gorgeous natural harbor with very deep water, is strategically positioned in the Pacific Ocean among the low-hanging Southeast Asian countries. Take a look at a map and you can see why this was the perfect place for the British East India Company to send one of their most aggressive agents, a gentleman named Sir Thomas Stamford Raffles. He set foot on the island in 1819 to create a British trade port, intending to compete with the Dutch, who were Europe's big trading force in the region. It was founded as a British Colony in 1819, but joined what's called the Malaysian Federation of States in 1963. Currently, Singapore is predominantly populated by people of Chinese extraction, who make up 76 percent of the total population. About 15 percent are the indigenous Malay people, and about 8 percent are Indian. I was shocked to discover Indians made up such a small percentage of the Singaporean population, given that Indian culture is so vibrant in Singapore and quite predominant when it comes to the local zeitgeist. You can't turn around in the street without seeing the wide swath of Indian influence in Singapore. Considering the country's diverse cultural makeup, it's easy to see how—and I admit, I hate this term—one of the world's most famously original fusion cuisines was born here. English, Dutch, and European influence on a Chinese and Malay culture, with free-flowing Indian exposure, spices, food styles, curries—this is the stuff that creates the ultimate hybrid food palette.

Eating has become a national pastime in this modern, bustling country. People eat all day long, and so my first job was to find out where most people do their chowing down. My priority was to check out the hawker centers, and I do love me some street food. I think it's the best way to eat, because you have so many options. Some stalls are more like restaurants, offering five or six dishes, while others specialize in one dish, like barbecued ribs, stewed mutton, or otak-otak.

I was ecstatic to visit People's Park, which boasts hundreds of stalls. I also checked out the Zion River Food Side Center and Adam's Road Food Center, which is in a Muslim neighborhood, so all the food there is Halal. People's Park is the one that I returned to on several occasions, and it doesn't hurt that it's right in the center of town. Many Americans get flustered in hawker stall environments in foreign countries, freaking out about whether or not they'll be hovering over a toilet for hours after having a few bites of street food. I wouldn't stress too much about that in Singapore. These hawker centers are spotless. Singapore has a deservedly well-earned reputation for strict laws (I mean, they outlaw *gum*, for Pete's sake), so the extreme cleanliness of the country is not surprising. This is a country in pursuit of excellence. They want to be the best when it comes to a hybrid food culture. They want to be the most crime-free country on the planet. They want to be the cleanest city in the world. Given some of the places I visit and the things I eat on *Bizarre Foods*, it might surprise you that cleanliness around food is extremely important to me. Not just from a visual standpoint—I actually get concerned about my well-being when I see a lot of filth and degradation. That's no environment to be preparing food in. Sadly, that's how much of the world operates—including the United States, which is ironically one of the filthiest food countries with respect to kitchens. Everybody hems and haws about what to eat while traveling, but I'd be more concerned about picking up a bug from something at a giant American chain restaurant than at a Singaporean hawker stall.

Hawker Centers are government run in the sense that the government owns the space and leases the stalls. This allows them to keep the place clean and well-managed. Fortunately, the government understands that they have no business cooking food. Let the artists, the chefs, come in there and do their thing, and let them do it in an environment—the physical space—that the government maintains. The centers have tables as well as lovely little gardens where you can sit down and enjoy your food. But first you have to decide what to eat. You claim a numbered table, then walk around to the stalls that stretch for half a mile in a series of indoor and outdoor courtyards in People's Park. You order, and let the hawkers know your table number. Once your grub is ready, a runner will ferry the food to you. Pretty sweet, huh?

I was fortunate enough to dine at People's Park the first time with Violet Oon, the Julia Child of Singapore. She was an absolutely fabulous host, and she knew her way around the Singapore food scene and was game for trying everything. I immediately developed a serious food crush on her. We ate fantastic frog porridge and slurped pig soup filled with all the different parts of the pig: liver, heart, lungs, and so on. Grandma is in the back of the stall, stirring ten-gallon pots filled with a generations-old family recipe. I know it sounds overly romantic, but that's truly what it is. The pig soup broth base was top-heavy with sweet spices like cinnamon and star anise, ginger, lovely braised greens, and a hint of fresh lime juice to lighten it up. The soup also incorporated melting bits of braised pork rib, shoulder, and paper-thin slices of the pig heart, tongue, liver, and other effluvia. I know that might not be up everyone's alley, but don't knock it 'til you try it. We picked some dishes from a duck stall where you can get wings, tongues, split roasted heads, and sliced duck breast. We devoured the classic Hainan chicken, which is a steamed bird that tastes like no other chicken you've placed in your mouth. It's the way chicken used to taste everywhere, I imagine, and the better hawkers purge and then gorge their birds on a diet designed to increase the brittle nature of the skin and the meat's fat content. They drizzle the cooked poultry with an aged, thickened, sweet soy sauce and serve it with classic Singaporean-style fried rice. People's Park was just a phenomenal experience.

Violet turned us on to a place called Tian Jin Hai Seafood Restaurant. Tian Jin Hai is the brainchild of Francis Yeo, who ran a successful seafood hawker stall at the Jackson Center for ten years. When the center closed a few years ago, he went on a long holiday and decided to open in another hawker center when he came back. However, when he returned he discovered his space wouldn't be ready for a while. This is one of the drawbacks of the government owning all the hawker centers, and it's a fairly common story in Singapore. On one hand, they are clean and organized. On the other, bribes or cash don't speak as loudly as connections do. And sometimes vice versa. Yeo sought out another option, stumbling upon a place at the edge of town in Punggol's Marina Country Club. A Taiwanese chef had recently closed down his restaurant at the marina and the space was vacant. Yeo took it over and opened his restaurant a few months later. Unlike the cramped and hot Jackson Center, this dockside restaurant sprawls over a series of patios, some covered, some open-aired, with thirty or forty tables, a bar, a semi-open kitchen, and a beautiful view of the water. Instead of little stools and tables, there are lazy Susans and fancy chairs. Obviously, prices have gone up, but Yeo offers the best seafood I tried in Singapore.

Yeo earned the reputation for incredible chili crab at his former hawker stall. Chili crab, the Singaporean national dish, features giant mud crabs with thick shells and stout claws. He offers eight or nine different varieties on his menu: black pepper, rice wine, black bean, the traditional sweet chili, just to name a few. The crab is broken apart and lightly steamed so it just holds together. It's cooked again in Chef Yeo's killer sweet chili sauce. It's a great dish to pick through, spending some quality time cracking and working the meat out of the crab's nooks and crannies. You suck on the thick, sweet chili paste that gets all over your fingers and your face. It's probably the only time that making a huge mess is encouraged in Singapore. After I tried chili crab a couple different ways, I cleaned up with some hot towels and moved on to Yeo's newest creation: steamed shark's head.

This is a dish that Yeo claims he invented and, interestingly, it's a dish that has no meat on it at all. Singaporeans, like the rest of the world outside of our country, eat from snout to tail, using every part of the animal, because they have never lost connection with the idea that they should never waste a thing. Finances dictate it, as does culinary ideology. Yeo noticed this was not the case with shark—the heads always went to waste. He experimented with the shark's heads and ended up with a novel dish you're not going to find anywhere else. He starts by stripping down the skin, trimming the head, and cutting out the gills. You're left with a pointy, triangular piece of bone with thick slabs of what look like gelatinous, pale, white tendons hanging from it. These are the connective tissues that make the jaws of the animal move up and down with such mind-boggling strength. Yeo makes lateral incisions perpendicular to the bone so that all these big flaps of tendons protrude like little fingers. He steams the shark's head in light sweet soy sauce and rice wine, which removes the pungent (and often nasty) off flavors typically present in fish heads. After four hours of steaming, those gelatinous pieces of cartilage melt in your mouth. Next, he puts this head on a platter, drizzles it with a sturdier soy sauce, and finishes it with shaved ginger and scallion. You pull off these little bits of cartilage from the head and eat them. The texture reminds me of perfectly cooked sea cucumber, yielding a slight crunch as you sink your teeth in but melting away after just a hint of pressure. It reminds me of bone marrow's rich, buttery flavor. This is one of the most unusual dishes I've ever had, but trust me, it's absolutely addictive; it sounds straight out of a sci-fi movie, but the flavor, texture, and novelty simply blew me away. It's certainly not the type of thing anyone would ever order on their own, but it's worth a try if you get the opportunity.

Just across the city is a completely different food experience. I toured Little India with Anita Kapoor, a local Indian woman who works as food writer and a local TV host. She is superbly knowledgeable and understands the food scene in Singapore, especially in her neighborhood. The highlight for me was the Banana Leaf Apollo. This is an Indian restaurant that, though not responsible for inventing fish head curry, takes credit for making it globally famous. We sat down in this cafeteria-style eatery where you dine on banana leaves in the traditional style, ordering rice, some condiments, and bowls of curried fish heads. These aren't tiny fish heads, either, but taken from giant red snapper with enough of the neck in place to provide ample meaty benefits in addition to little tasty treasures like the cheeks, eyes, tongue, and bits of skin. When cooked correctly, a fish head offers so much tender and delicious meat. Frankly, I get bored with mildly flavored, everyday fillets, so every once in a while a more aggressive fish concoction just hits the spot. The spicy curried broth loaded with root vegetables, greens, onions, and tomatoes is the perfect partner to a fish head. You scoop up bits of the fish head and the broth onto your rice and eat everything by hand. Never use your left hand at the table! Indian culture reserves this hand for more personal bodily functions.

My food crush, Violet, and I met up for a second date later in the week. She introduced me to one of the most interesting approaches to cuisine I've ever experienced. The Imperial Herbal Sin Chi Café and Restaurant in Vivo City, located on the beautiful harborfront walk, specializes in TCM, or traditional Chinese medicine. The restaurant sets out to not only nourish, but cure whatever ails your body. The menu is chock-full of exotic ingredients: antelope horn, dried sea horse and cordyceps, deer penis—nothing illegal, mind you. Once we arrived, we sat down with Dr. Fu, a TCM physician.

He took my pulse, examined my tongue, and checked my body by prodding and poking me all over with his fingers. He did a lot of staring at me. The consultation ended with a prescription for particular foods to cool down my body parts that had gotten overheated, warm up my parts that had gotten too cold, tone down my yang, replenish my ying . . . You know the drill. You aren't required to undergo the medical examination in order to eat at this remarkable eatery, but I don't understand why you wouldn't. I suppose many customers, especially locals, already have an herbalist prescribing food for their health, so they just go in and eat the fabulous cuisine. If you're currently in between herbalists, check out Dr. Fu, who thought some scallops with egg white, deer penis soup, crocodile soup, and a bracing eucalyptus tonic was just the thing I needed. I'm not certain I felt much different afterward, but it was easily the best-tasting medicine I've ever had.

No trip to Singapore would be complete without eating at a Peranakan restaurant. This was the stuff I was most eager to try. Peranakans are also known as Straits Chinese, named after the Straits Settlement, a group of territories created by the British in Southeast Asia in 1826. Basically, the term refers to people in the region of Chinese descent. I learned there are all sorts of names for the different types of Chinese in the region. Once Violet and I were comfortable with each other, she gave me the rundown on the lingo. The whole concept was fascinating given the obsession with political correctness in our own country, but there are two terms I will never forget. The first came up in conversation as Violet and her best friend spoke over lunch one day about flying to Los Angeles, where her best friend's daughter was getting married. I said, "Congratulations." Both women gave me a happy but not completely thrilled look.

I said, "What's wrong?"

They replied, "Well, he's ABC." I had no idea what they were talking about. They explained, with a healthy dose of humor, that ABC is the acronym for "American-born Chinese," which I inferred to mean not completely ideal. They also refer to ABCs as bananas: yellow on the outside and white on the inside. It's pretty humorous. Friends of mine here at home have heard the term "Twinkie"—yellow outside, white inside—but mostly from the mouths of other Twinkies. Maybe I'm crazy, but I can't tell if it's offensive or not. I can tell you that during the conversation I was frozen in my chair, smiling, hoping not to laugh too hard, or even laugh at all.

Peranakan is old-school Singapore and refers to the earliest Chinese who immigrated there and intermarried with Malays, spawning a culture and cuisine unique in its own right. Singapore's Katong District is the place to see and experience this culture in action. The historic neighborhood houses a famous spice garden containing more than 100 different spices that grow abundantly in Singapore. It was there that I met up with a young chef named Ben Seck who comes from a family that specializes in Peranakan cooking. He introduced me to one of the strangest fruits I've ever encountered. The fruit, which grows on giant Buwakala trees, contains a black nut called a Bualkeluak. What's bizarre about this nut is not its flavor necessarily, but the fact that it is extremely poisonous. Detoxifying the nut is a tedious process (which I am baffled that someone ever managed to figure out in the first place), beginning with breaking the fruit open and picking out only the seeds. Next, the seeds get buried in volcanic ash for 100 days. After the nuts are dug out of the ground, they are soaked in water for three days to wash away the ashes. After all this, each nut must be smelled before it is chopped up to ensure it hasn't gone bad. Just one bad nut will spoil an entire dish, making it toxic to consume. Once you've culled the good nuts from the bad, you can begin to work with them.

The Seck family restaurant, True Blue, is an extremely popular restaurant in Singapore. Ben shares the cooking duties with his mother, Daisy Seah, who is arguably the most famous Peranakan chef in the country. The restaurant is located in a restored two-story town house, and walking through the front door is like stepping back 100 years. What's special about the food is that the recipes are not written down. Rather, they've been passed from generation to generation. Mother and son created some of the most interesting, authentic dishes using the Bualkeluak nuts, including a duck soup that was just absolutely glorious with the cooked fruit. The paste from the nut smells like coffee and dark chocolate, almost like a fermented mocha taste with elements of burnt caramel and bitters. The paste works on the plate much like a condiment, and once you crack open the cooked nuts, you can spread the paste on anything. It enhances everything it touches, sort of like a naturally occurring Pernakan version of Vegemite. I sampled a braised-chicken dish with fermented shrimp paste and rice. Somehow, when mixed with rice, the Bualkeluak lost some of that coffee and chocolate flavor and instead offered a light, citrusy finish. The nut can change flavors depending on what it's cooked with, making it the Zelig of the food world. This is a very complex and interesting ingredient, but it's not the quintessential Peranakan dish I'd been dying to try.

No one is exactly sure how Laksa earned its name. One group claims it stems from the Hindi Persian word *Lakhshah*, which refers to a type of noodle. Some say it's derived from the Chinese word *Lasha*, pronounced "lots-a," and means "spicy sand," due to the ground, dried shrimp that typically goes into the soup. Another theory is that it's a Hokien term, where it literally means "dirty" because of its messy appearance. But regardless of how it came to be, Laksa generally describes two different types of noodle soup dishes, Curried Laksa and Assam Laksa. Assam Laksa is something that I've seen more often in northern Southeast Asian countries, especially in the upper half of Thailand, where the base for the soup typically is a sweet-and-sour fish soup. In Singapore, Laksa is usually built around a curried coconut soup. Most of them are yellowish red in appearance, with dried prawns that give them a shrimpy flavor, complete with a curry gravy or soup. Thick rice noodles, called Laksa noodles, are typically used in this dish.

However, sometimes a thin rice vermicelli is used, and these are called *bee hoon* or *mee hoon*. Foodaholics will argue that one noodle or the other makes a Laksa more or less of an authentic experience, but I'm not sure it's as easy as that.

I was turned on to curried Laksa growing up in New York City, where we ate a lot of Thai and Indonesian food. The main ingredients of the Laksas that I knew as a kid were pieces of tofu and fish, shrimp, sometimes cockles or clams, and maybe bits of julienned chicken if you were at a fancier restaurant. Many places add a nice kick by cooking chilies in the broth or by putting a spoonful of nuclear hot sambal on top just before serving. Of course, the variety of the options—even in New York—is nothing compared to how divergently this dish is represented in Southeast Asia. Malaysians often use Vietnamese coriander and cilantro in theirs, and refer to it as *daunkesum*. In Panang, where I went four or five years ago, the dish is usually called curried Mee because of liberal use of mee hoon noodles. Curried Mee is a delicacy to the Malaysian Chinese community, especially when served with cubes of congealed pork blood. There so many versions of Laksa, it's hard to keep track. My personal favorite is Nonya Laksa, made with coconut milk. Katong Laksa, a variant of Nonya Laksa, comes specifically from the Katong area of Singapore, where they cut the noodles into smaller pieces so it can be easily eaten with a spoon. Some people say Katong Laksa is the true Singaporean national dish. I've only tried the variety with cut-up noodles two or three times, but to me, the curried Laksa with long, thick noodles is king. What can I say? I'm a slurper.

There was a place called Tongjimian in the Golden Mile Food Center that I just adored. Another spot, Sungei Road Laksa, served a very traditional Laksa with fresh coconut milk in it. On the East Coast Road there were a couple of places, including a joint called 3-28 Katong Laksa, that one of our drivers wanted to show us, mainly because they pound their own shrimp paste there. It rocked. All the good stuff starts with a combination of lemongrass, galangal, chili paste, candlenut, and blanchan, which is fermented shrimp paste, along with coriander seeds and turmeric. It's finished with shrimp, tofu, cockles, and sambal on the side. All of these soups were quite good, but I've got to tell you, the Laksa that I had at Mary's Corner still remains the best I've ever eaten.

I spent my entire trip to Singapore carrying around a notebook with "Mary's Corner" listed on the back. No address, just a name. Whenever we were out and about, I begged our driver to pull over if we ever glimpsed it. Near the end of the trip, we finally found this humble little restaurant. As is often the case with any good eater, sometimes you have to take hostages, and at times my crew suffers the slings and arrows of being pulled like little bits of flotsam and jetsam in a storm all over cities in search of certain types of food. This was no exception. I made everyone have some.

Mary's is situated in the Nan Sin Eating House on East Coast Road, with two or three outdoor tables. Orders are placed at a window on the street that fronts into the postage-stamp-size kitchen. You get your bowl, sit at one of the tables, slurp down your soup, and move along. At peak hours, the line stretches around the corner, with most people opting to have their Laksa to go. On our visit, I took a moment to peer into the kitchen, where I could see down a narrow space that reached about forty feet back into the rear storage rooms, all the way through to another business in the building next door. Hey, it's Sinagapore. This interior hall led to the prep area, where I spied Mary presiding over a giant vat, almost like a garbage can, of boiling soup. The noodles are cooked separately and the old crone puts them into a bowl and ladles the liquid gold over the noodles, scatters poached shrimp, bean sprouts, cilantro, sambal, and bits of tofu on top, and hands you a steaming hot bowl of goodness. While this might sound like a simple operation, the guys she's got making noodles to order would beg to differ. And when I say made to order, I mean made from scratch, hand-rolled in multiple portions, batches-to-order. That to me is one of the hallmarks of a great Laksa. Are you pounding your own paste for your soup? Are you making your own noodles? At Mary's, they cook thirty or forty portions of handmade noodles at a time. There's not a knife; there's not a cutter or machine. Instead, they use that old Chinese repetitive knead-and-fold methodology. After repeating this process for about eight minutes, the noodle maker basically raises the tube of dough up over his head and slams it on the table, where it explodes into a thousand strands of pasta. It's one of the most glorious techniques I've ever seen.

Mary's Laksa is impressive. Sure, it had the sandy, ground-up dried shrimp. It had the rich coconut milk I adore. It had the traditional, thick white Laksa noodles. And, yes, it had a curry flavor. But what really put this soup in a league of its own was the fact that it wasn't made with a fish soup base, but instead was created with a strong, rich, briny, and crustaceously awesome shrimp soup. When cooked with the coconut milk, you ended up with one of the best spicy Asian shellfish bisques that I've ever encountered. Sprinkle that soup with some ground nuts, the bean sprouts, the cilantro, a lime wedge, sambal, the blanchan, and you have a dangerous sweet, sour, salty seafood noodle explosion on your hands . . .

I realize I throw around superlatives a little too much, and I'm always warning myself not to say things like "it was the best bowl of soup I had ever had," but boy, I'm drooling just sitting here writing this. I can taste that shrimpy goodness and can almost feel the sweat popping between my eyebrows, which lets you know the soup is perfectly and intensely infused with chilies. You can't stop eating it. I admit, I might be romanticizing this soup a little because the nearest bowl is 3,000 miles away. Or maybe it's the fact that I may never have the opportunity to devour it again. But having said that, the simplicity of the dish, the freshness of the noodles, and the immediacy of the cooking preparation made this my ideal bowl of Laksa. It's hard to pinpoint the best bowl of chili I've ever eaten or the best fried chicken I've ever tasted, because so many places serve up stellar versions of those two dishes. That's why I don't want to be Jane or Michael Stern, but I've discovered that when you set up readers with high expectations, it's the readers who are usually disappointed. Sometimes I wonder if my faves will ever be your "best." After all, we each have our own favorites and our own set of rules that we measure excellence against. But Mary's qualifies using any set of standards, and frankly, I can talk about great places a million miles away and rarely receive letters saying I am wrong. But I encourage you to see for yourself.

So I sat at Mary's at four in the afternoon, eating my last lunch of the day. The streets bustled around me, with motorcycles and pedicabs darting here and there, cars honking, blaring tinny Southeast Asian music from their speakers. And as pedestrians bumped into my table in the endless stream of Singaporean street life, I sat there slurping Laksa, knowing there was no other place I wanted to be. And as for traditional Peranakan food—well, I think it is really special; a cuisine that people believed was nearly at the end of a culinary cul-de-sac. Luckily, folks like Ben Seck and Mary kept it alive long enough for it to enjoy a new wave of popularity. And thankfully, due to Singapore's strategic location (for travelers, especially business travelers), the local eateries will be open for a long time, doing very well.

Simple Foods
Noodle Houses of Guangzhou

My love of Chinese food borders on obsession. For the record, this Chinese food I speak of is not a plate of indistinguishable, fried hunks of meat, tossed in a wok and coated with a sticky corn starch–based sauce. That's not Chinese food. That's like calling Cracker Barrel authentic American cuisine. But for every fifty subpar Chinese restaurants serving buffet dinners yoked to the American way of eating, there are a surprising number of authentic restaurants doing that cuisine justice. You don't need to travel to the People's Republic to find authentic Chinese food. I've experienced some of the most authentic Sichuan food in St. Paul, Minnesota. All that is required is access to ingredients and a good skill set in the kitchen. Honesty and authenticity don't have a lot to do with location, although it often helps.

Few people in the world have a more passionate relationship with food than the Chinese. Due to large-scale immigration from the southern province of Guangdong to the rest of the world, Cantonese cuisine is by far China's best known. Cantonese cuisine originated in Canton, which is now called Guangzhou. With its fertile soil, perfect for growing all kinds of vegetables and raising healthy animals, as well as proximity to rivers, lakes, and oceans, every ingredient you could possibly want is within reach. And if these people can reach it, they'll eat it. An old Cantonese adage says, *If it walks, swims, crawls, or flies with its back to heaven, it must be edible.* Cantonese live by those words. They will eat anything and everything—not because they are obsessed with exotic foods; it's just that if it tastes good, they'll eat it.

The simply named Guangzhou Restaurant is the city's most popular. Founded in 1935, this restaurant is the oldest operating restaurant in Guangzhou. You would think that with a country as storied and steeped in history there would be some form of eatery still in operation predating 1935 in this eater's city, but there isn't. Its original name was Xi Nan Restaurant, but when the People's Republic was established, it changed its name to the nondescript, egalitarian name it has today. Despite the name change, the food remained the same. In fact, many dishes are just as famous today as they were at its inception, most notably their dim sum.

The restaurant is located on the busy merging of Wenchangnan Road and Shangxiajiu Street, one of the most famous intersections in the Li Wan District. Over the years, it's expanded from just a restaurant on the first floor to a catering and banquet service, housed on the second and third floors. They feed as many as 10,000 people a day at that original location, also running affiliated branches from Hong Kong to Los Angeles. I'm sure you can eat a fine meal at any of their outposts, but you can't beat a meal at the original.

The main dining room is all about classic Cantonese food served in a beautiful classic setting. An antique, stained-glass window from China's Chang Dynasty hangs in the main dining room, with a giant Rongshu tree sprawling overhead. The restaurant is composed of numerous courtyards and rooms connected by arcade corridors. The waitstaff, donning the Chang Dynasty's traditional servant uniforms, gives the dining experience the air of taking a step back in time. Add the fact that they've mastered Cantonese cuisine, and you have a hard time convincing me that if you could only eat one meal in Guangzhou, it shouldn't be here.

The Guangzhou Restaurant is known for its dim sum, which was decent but not half as good as that found at other places I'd visited in China or Taiwan. But if you're looking for traditional

Cantonese cuisine, look no further. Cantonese cuisine offers a rather mild flavor profile and consists of contrasting elements. When it comes to flavors and styles, you're not going to get a one-note Charlie, and when dinner is all said and done, often you've enjoyed a steamed dish, a cold dish, a boiled dish, a spicy dish, and a double-fried dish. I had duck soup with Chinese watermelon, and a bowl of creamy, northeast Chinese peanuts simmered with the black skins still intact. Interestingly, they use a lot of milk skin in dishes, which struck me as odd. Milk skin is made by boiling fresh milk until a fine layer of skin is formed. After the milk cools, the liquid separates from the skin, making a congealed, fatty, egg white–like substance that offers a textural counterpoint to most other dishes. Remember homemade chocolate pudding as a kid? Remember peeling back the skin that formed on top, and how dairy-ish it tasted? Like the sweetest milk imaginable? Well, that's what they serve here. While I didn't care for the milk skin in savory dishes, I really liked it served as a dessert. Their double-skin milk, braised with sugar forming yet another layer of skin, is even sweeter still. Caramel heaven.

The dish that sticks out most in my mind is their Wenchang chicken. Such special care goes into creating this impeccable dish that it's difficult not to swoon over it. These chickens are to China what wagyu beef is to Japan. The chickens are tenderly cared for, raised in coops high off the ground, and fed a specific diet of coconut, peanut cakes, and banyan seeds. As a result, the meat becomes fatty, with the skin turning yellow and very brittle when cooked. Guangzhou Restaurant's version is cooked twice, steamed at first, then deboned, plated, and steamed again to heat it back up. It's finished with a light, aromatic sauce of aged soy sauce and faintly salty and briny abalone. For those of you who stray away from the boring chicken options on a menu, one bite of this delicate, succulent Wenchang chicken will turn you into an evangelist. It's even said that a Cantonese meal without traditional Wenchang chicken is really no meal at all.

If you're looking for something on the lighter side, check out the restaurant's old-school tea service. Carts equipped with hot-coal-filled iron pots wheel adjacent to your table, keeping tea hot for the duration. Tea drinkers sit in their own corridor, sipping tea out of these tiny cups and eating elegant snacks. The teapots were just charming and looked to be hundreds of years old. The pots were chipped, cracked, and discolored, yet beautiful in their ancient state. Weaving my way through table after table, the sounds and scents of bubbling tea, echoing in the narrow rooms, the smell of jasmine and oolong and pu-er in the breeze—I couldn't help but be impressed.

But my meal at Guanzhou Restaurant that day was just the beginning; I needed to see for myself one of Cantonese food's crowning glories, the noodle house. Noodles are the primary component of many Chinese dishes. At one time, all noodles were made by hand in homes and restaurants. Modern machinery has since taken over that process, but fortunately for me, the art of hand-pulled noodles is still practiced at the Jiu Mao Jiu Noodle Restaurant. This place is all about the noodles, and they make dozens of varieties there from scratch.

Jiu Mao Jiu Restaurant is located on the other side of town in the Tainhe District, smack dab in the middle of an office park. When have you ever found a decent meal on the first floor of a nondescript office building? From the street it looks like nothing is there—no signs and no big car-size plastic noodle bowl hanging from the roof over the door—but the place is packed, with the smell of ginger, garlic, and that welcoming starchy humidity that I associate with great Chinese food hanging in the air. You hear the clitter-clatter of metal on metal—the sounds of chefs feverishly working dough on giant metal tables and wooden chopping boards.

Jiu Mao Jiu, also dubbed the Noodle King, takes its noodles seriously. Hand-pulled noodles are unique to China, and this is where it all started; the noodles are made by a trained cook who spends years perfecting the art form. The noodle paste or dough is handmade in massive work bowls, and through a series of stretching and pulling techniques the dough becomes pliable, then gets rolled back up into a ball. The ball is rolled out into a fat tube until it is about four feet long, then the ends are joined, the dough is twisted, and the process repeats a hundred times. Every time the ends are joined, the middle of the long tube of paste is swung so it twists around itself, then gets stretched again. Then, on a cutting board, the noodle maker begins pulling the paste with his arms outstretched, folding the thick strings of paste in two with fewer refolds in between stretches. He pulls again and again and again until the strings of pasta paste become longer and more numerous, thinner and thinner, finally turning the mass into very fine noodles. It's an art form requiring extreme dexterity.

Stir-fried dishes are cooked in a closed kitchen here, but all the noodle stuff is done in the open. It's a slightly less cheesy Benihana teppanyaki show that concludes with food that actually tastes really good. You can also watch as these pasta experts turn balls of noodle dough into delicate noodle chips right before your eyes. They take a sharp tool that looks like a four-inch spackling knife, then strike the ball of dough sitting in their opposite hand outward, away from their body, sending little chips of raw noodle dough into a giant wok of boiling water six feet away. These fat, thick doughy globs get cooked, then sauced. The process reminded me of flipping playing cards into a hat, except that these guys had great aim.

Jiu Mao Jiu also creates noodles literally as thin as silk thread, formed through a process where they keep folding and refolding the noodles, weaving and reweaving dough to a point where they dramatically smash them on a table, exploding the dough into hundreds of thin noodles. It's like Rubik's Cube—I have seen it done, but I can't explain it.

The Chinese equate long noodles with a long life, and thus have created a method that turns dough into spaghetti-sized strands of single noodles that stretch hundreds of feet long. In fact, the only restriction to a noodle's length is how much dough is available. These long, singular noodles are the crux of big noodle bowls here at Jiu Mao Jiu. In a quality restaurant like Jiu Mao Jiu, it's one noodle, just piled in there, coiled on top of itself. This is executed by weaving the noodles by hand, then spooling the dough from the noodle maker's hand into a giant bowl of water. The strand of dough is quickly pulled from the bowl and tossed into a cooking pot. The dough is cut only when they feel they've achieved the right noodle proportion. One giant long noodle will easily feed two or three people. Order up a bowl of minced pork with black bean sauce, and out comes a big soup bowl filled with enough noodle to feed two or three people, the whole dish swimming in porky, beany goodness.

Noodles, of course, need accompaniments, and the kitchen was just as skillful at dressing up a noodle as they were in constructing them. I fell in love with this dish called Cat's Ears Noodles. These tiny noodles started out life as flat dough triangles, no larger than a half-inch wide at the base, and were pinched together in such a way that when dropped in the water, they swelled dramatically, eradicating the harsh, angular edges. The end result: curled shapes that looked just like teeny cat's ears. When these noodles were fried in a wok with a light vinegar sauce, bits of minced meat, and scallion, the first bite exploded with flavor. The tart edge to the sauce just made the dish seem lighter, allowing you to eat a lot more than is probably advisable.

I was amazed by a dish called Kow-low-low, which literally translates to "standing shoulder to shoulder." This dish is made with sturdy, thick, macaroni-shaped hollow noodles lined up vertically, symbolizing strength and unity. The noodles are put into a dim sum steamer standing on end, packed tightly so they don't topple over on their sides (then they would be cheek to jowl, a slightly less Maoist food metaphor than shoulder to shoulder). A plate of these conjoined noodles arrives at the table with a rich, earthy, oyster sauce, sautéed minced pork, ginger, and aged fermented black beans spooned over the top. Using your chopsticks, you pull apart these starchy tubes that have been steamed together, dripping with the meaty, rich, salty, sweet sauce.

In addition to phenomenal noodles, I sampled stir-fry dishes that remain some of my all-time favorites. I'll never forget the twice-cooked pork with garlic sauce, which had the wok dragon's breath still on it. That's the kind of charry, smoky flavor and aroma you'll get only from food that's been properly scorched in the hottest of woks and then whisked to your table so fast that you can still taste the wok's heat with your first bite.

So with all apologies to those of Italian heritage reading this book, as amazing as many of the pasta dishes that I've eaten in Italy are, and many Italian restaurants around the world that I have visited and fallen in love with, I'd have to say without a doubt that the best noodle experience I've ever had has been at Jiu Mao Jiu in Guangzhou.

Eating My Words

When the Most Obvious Choice Is the Best

I didn't grow up in a "food is fuel" kind of home. As a child, food played a magical role in our daily lives, part of our Jewish heritage, part of our New York City lifestyle. Sharing food and eating meals together shaped our family life.

My first memory of eating Chinese food goes back to the mid-1960s. My dad and I left the Ziegfeld Theater at Fifty-fourth Street and Avenue of the Americas after taking in one of those epic David Lean films, hopped a cab to Chinatown, and headed for Bobo's. In the decades before it closed in the nineties, falling victim to increased competition and the ever-expanding New York food scene, Bobo's was *the* place in Chinatown. I vividly remember eating spareribs there for the first time, as well as Dragon and Phoenix, which sounds exactly like the kind of dish a five-year-old goes gaga over, but was in fact the gussied-up fancy name that Bobo's gave their traditional lettuce package offering. The Dragon in the dish was the shrimp, the Phoenix represented by squab. The shrimp and squab, ground fine, were served wok-tossed with micro-diced vegetables and bathed in sweet, spicy, and salty flavors in a hot, hot mixture that came to the table in a small oval platter with a lacquered enamel spoon. The textures were incredible. You scooped up gobs of this mixture and placed it in shallow, crisp, and cold iceberg lettuce cups. The leaves gave in just enough to the hot mixture that you could roll it up and put it into your mouth with great ease.

All great food is about contrast, if you think about it: the cool crunch of a pickle on a hamburger; the toasted bun served with a yielding hot dog; a crisp cone filled with cold, soft ice cream. Biting into that lettuce package was a revelatory moment for me. It was the first time I had eaten Chinese food in a Chinese restaurant, and it opened my eyes to a world of flavors and textures and ingredients that I didn't know existed before.

I'd eaten Chinese food once or twice, but mostly the cheap take-out versions or the nicely turned out homemade chow mein my mother served at home. My mother attended Mills College in San Francisco in the late 1940s, where she met Vic Bergeron's daughter, rooming with her for several years. Even if you aren't familiar with the name, you're certainly aware of his legacy. He spear-headed the creation of one of America's most famous fusion cuisines. Trader Vic's merged Chinese, Hawaiian, Polynesian, and Californian food all under one umbrella. After college, my mother and her roommate moved to Los Angeles, where one night they invited Vic over for dinner. Neither girl could boil a pot of water, and consequently the meal failed miserably. After calling the restaurant to send over a dessert that hadn't burned, he insisted the girls learn to cook in his kitchen. So my mother learned to cook at the original Trader Vic's. I remember her version of chicken chow mein topped with crispy egg noodles, which I nicknamed Chicken à la Goosh as a toddler. It was delicious, and we ate it at least once a week.

We loved Chinese food in our house, but the Bobo's meal was the first time I'd tried it at a restaurant. By the late 1960s, higher-quality Chinese restaurants had started to pop up outside China-town in greater numbers, offering adventurous diners more options. The Zimmern family took advantage. Regional Chinese cuisine was slowly becoming the rage in New York. Today, people like to think that midcentury New York was as diverse and accessible from a food standpoint as it is today. It wasn't. New York supermarkets were similar to Iowa's in the sixties, old-fashioned and devoid of international flavors of any kind. Nary a caper in sight. The late sixties and early seventies marked the beginning of the New York City food explosion for diners and, more important in a sense, for home cooks. Next thing you knew, customers were clamoring for different types of vinegars, exotic Asian ingredients, and tropical fruits in their local markets. Italian and Chinese immigrants propelled that movement upward, with their swelling population expanding businesses, especially restaurants, out of their traditional neighborhoods and into other parts of the city.

In 1970, Uncle Tai's Hunan Yuan opened on the Upper East Side. This Hunan- and Sichuan-style restaurant was the first to gain any traction with mainstream New Yorkers. The movement hit like a tidal wave. People were eating food they had never tried before. Chinese take-out shops opened, hawking pot stickers and steamed dumplings for the first time in great numbers. Dumplings are so much fun to eat, especially for kids. Traditional dumplings are soft and doughy on the outside and filled with ginger-spiked pork inside. Easy to eat, kid-size, and kid-friendly. My four-year-old son can't get enough of them, and I remember it being the same way for me. As a nine-year-old, I was a dumpling freak. There was so much excitement surrounding Chinese food at that time, and my father and I would scour the city looking for hidden gems.

This was an exciting time for New York's food scene. Craig Claiborne, Pierre Franey, and Mimi Sheridan dominated the food journalism scene. All of a sudden, people talked food in a much different way. Julia Child's and Graham Kerr's TV shows energized the city, and food slowly became the currency of the realm. After my parents divorced in the late sixties, my dad moved to Greenwich Village, where the action was really taking place. Balducci's, Jefferson Market, and other food shops started carrying exotic fare—things like extra-virgin olive oil paired with the fresh mozzarella—that you previously could find only in Little Italy. Those were the kinds of ingredients that people really got excited about having access to. It seems odd now, but back then, being able to buy fresh herbs or hoisin sauce in a specialty shop was a big deal.

Our family tradition became Chinese food on Sunday nights. We'd order takeout all the time from Richard Mei's King Dragon, on Seventy-fourth and Third, a restaurant right next door to where J. G. Melon is today. At least once a month we would eat in the restaurant, most of the time with my dad's mother in tow. King Dragon offered traditional Cantonese food, with a few choice steamed or fried dumplings on the menu. Sometimes, if I'd done well in school or had just gotten over a cold, my parents would treat me to something off their menu, and my passion for Chinese food really started there. It still remains my favorite comfort food.

These days, my family doesn't do too many Sunday-night Chinese dinners. However, we love the opportunity to eat dim sum on a Sunday morning. *Dim sum* literally translates to "touch heart" and consists of tender, endearing small-plate dishes. Some people refer to it as Chinese tapas—it's an entirely different tradition, but I guess the same sort of sentiment is at play. Sharing small plates over conversation and having casual snack foods that sum up to a meal is something that everybody enjoys. I almost regard dim sum as my stock-in-trade in terms of eating. I'd rather sit down at a Chinese restaurant and eat twenty different plates of small goodies than just about any other meal I can think of.

In high school, my friends and I would often head to Chinatown on weekends in pursuit of great dim sum. Clark, Toby, Eric, Aaron, and I hit the subway, most times venturing to Num Wah. For generations, this was the "under-the-radar" place for enjoying dim sum on weekend mornings. *Shao-mai* dumplings, *char siu bao* (barbecued pork buns), and crispy shrimp wrapped in rice noodles, then deep-fried so they looked like they were dunked in futuristic spiderwebs were always on the table. Paper-thin sheets of bean curd, wrapped around vegetables and braised pork, chicken feet simmered in black bean sauce, teeny sparerib nuggets just about a half-inch wide, with a bit of meat clinging to them, bathed in ginger and garlic. Sticky fried rice, loaded with Chinese sausage, roast pork, and beaten egg, stuffed inside a lotus leaf and then baked again. This was a hungry, teenage boy's heaven, and we regularly gorged ourselves. We'd follow it up with nickel pinball games at the Chinese arcade down the street. We always ended our sojourn with a stop at the Dancing Chicken. This oddity was a large chicken-wire-wrapped box sitting on a table. Insert a coin, and a small door opened in the back of the box and out would come a rooster. He danced around for a few seconds, then raced back into the door. It was hilarious. We'd bum around downtown, sometimes grabbing another meal, then climb back on the subway to make curfew. That was a great day for us, and not an unusual one. So if that's how I was as a child and a teenager, you can understand how my passion for dumplings grew with time.

It took a trip to Taiwan to find what may have been the ultimate dumpling experience. Interestingly, I tried with all my might to avoid this particular dumpling house. I'm the kind of guy who likes to go to the last stop on the subway. I don't want to go to the obvious place that every guidebook recommends. I like the challenge of discovering that obscure, hole-in-the-wall joint. It's usually these sorts of hidden gems where I find the best food, but often the most obvious answer is the right answer, and so it was when I finally got to Taiwan.

While we filmed in Taipei, a nice crew dinner was in the works. We had a local producer, Josh, who expertly guided us though the show. He's a wacky genius, very creative—a geeky filmmaker with a great eye for both story and shot detail. He led us to some great locations, already knowing the best shots and setups to take advantage of. He was just fantastic to work with, as was his crew, composed of three dynamite PAs. Apparently, these guys met while practicing kung fu in the local gym there. Some of these guys were national-caliber champions, with others still climbing the ranks— an authentic group of big, bad-ass motherfuckers. These guys are all big eaters, and on the night I suggested we have dinner together after work, they all wanted to head to Din Tai Fung.

Din Tai Fung? I couldn't have been more disappointed. The *New York Times* called it one of the ten best restaurants in the world twenty years ago. It's a dumpling house turned chain restaurant, with three or four now in Taipei, even locations as far away as Singapore, Hong Kong, and Los Angeles. The idea of the place struck me as a soulless choice, like a Ruth's Chris steakhouse—decent food, I suppose, but surely there had to be something better in town. I didn't want to eat there. I was convinced it was way too commercialized. I wanted to go to the sleepy, out-of-the-way place where all Taipei's foodies gathered in hushed tones to eat dumplings.

We piled out of a few taxis and walked toward the giant, glowing red sign outside Din Tai Fung. A steady stream of customers flowed in and out on this weekday night. Taipei is a city of restaurants, most of which do a nice trade, but find the one that's packed all the time and you'll know you've found a winner. Din Tai Fung was packed. I sat outside as we waited twenty minutes for a table. I had a very visceral reaction waiting for dinner, with my stomach in knots, my mouth salivating uncontrollably. I had started the evening not wanting to go to Din Tai Fung, and then standing outside in the drizzling rain waiting for a table, smelling the restaurant every time the door opened, seeing the faces of the guests as they left—well, my viewpoint did a slick 180. The anticipation just killed me, but I was trying to keep my expectations low. I repeated mantras in my head to stay calm, otherwise whatever I ate would inevitably fall short of living up to my expectations. My serenity level is directly tied to my level of expectations, and I didn't want to swing and sway too violently in the opposite direction of my earlier disdain for my companions' choice of eatery.

Our table was finally ready. I walked in the door and the humidity level was electrifying. The kitchen was a glassed-in gigantic space of a room divided in half. A glassed-in refrigerated room for dumpling making on one side, a glassed-in steaming room on the other. More than a dozen cooks, outfitted with aprons looped around their necks, neat hats on their heads, rolled dumplings like a synchronized swim team of the highest caliber. They stuffed these doughy little skins, packing them into well-seasoned racks, some lined with cabbage, some not, some lined with banana leaves, some not. They created different shapes of fish dumplings, *shao-mai*, which have a delicate little empire waist, pushed up and open-faced at the top. Closed soup dumplings, half-mooned fish dumplings, crab roe dumplings, chicken dumplings, green veg-etable dumplings, pickled vegetable dumplings . . . I'd really never seen anything like it. In the room with the built-in steamers, chefs rotated orders. Dumpling racks were stacked along the wall. A cook would assemble your entire order, rack of this dumpling, rack of that, and then stack them up and steam your order all by itself in its own glorious edible tower. Your entire dumpling and steamed-foods selection would arrive at once, which I happen to love.

When our waitress came to take our order, I simply said, "Bring us one of everything you have." I think they offered a dozen types of dumplings, plus appetizers, soups, and more, but the dumpling offerings totaled only about twelve different types. She looked at me like I was crazy. I realized that was a lot of food, but there were nine people in our group, with a few of us hungry souls who I knew could really pack it in. She called over her girlfriends, all speak-ing Chinese, pointing and giggling at me. I asked our Taiwanese crew to please explain to her that I was as serious as a heart attack. I'm on the other side of the world and I want to try everything on the menu. So, finally, after much negotiating, we placed our order.

We ended up putting a pretty good dent in the food, which ad-mittedly made me feel pretty smug. On the other hand, I've felt terrible about it ever since, because I must have come across as such a piggish snob. Through our interpreter, I made sure to let them know I had traveled a long distance to be there and I wanted to try one of everything. I promised that if we didn't eat everything we'd make sure the food didn't go to waste.

The meal began with small bowls of boiled peanuts, and shredded spicy cabbage pickled with hot toasted dried chilies. We made quick work of those. I love meals like this when you actually get the traditional nibbles germane to a food's region. These little treats get the taste buds going. Next came steamed chicken soup as well as some braised beef noodle soup. Then came the noodles, one mixed with pickled mustard greens in a very light sauce, and another in a thick sesame-and-peanut-paste sauce—extremely spicy and redolent of chilies and ginger and sesame oil. After we demolished those, out came the dumplings, stacked to the ceiling.

Now, the dumplings there are very, very unique. The most popular dumplings in the place are also the most widely imitated. They are called Xia Long Bao, which literally means "small basket buns." These are delicate little nuggets of minced pork encased in very thin dough that is a cross between a pasta sheet and a bread dough. If the dough is too thick, they become bready and awkward to eat; too thin and they fall apart. The Xia Long Bao is the quintessential Shanghai-style snack, supposedly invented in a little town called Nanxiang, which is now essentially a first-tier suburb of Shanghai. I have never had a better Xia Long Bao than the ones at Din Tai Fung.

Perfection requires a lot of attention to detail. The refrigerated room is necessary because there is so much liquid in Din Tai Fung's dumpling mixture. Their dumplings are often referred to as soup dumplings because of the explosive rush of liquid hidden inside. When making many of these types of dumplings, the stuffing mixture needs to be cold and gelatinous, almost solid really, to construct the perfect dumpling. If the filling is kept well chilled, it's easier for the chefs working with it. But when steamed, the Xia Long Bao literally burst with soupy goodness. You can get a horrible case of burnt pizza mouth on these things if you're not careful. The key is waiting just long enough for them to cool slightly, but not so long that you can't chew them well. Unlike certain types of pot stickers, which you can nick with your chopsticks so they can soak up some dipping sauce, soup dumplings need to be eaten whole. And speaking of sauce, DTF offered the typical ginger-infused black vinegar or ginger-and-chili-infused vinegar; sometimes I take a little bit of soy drizzled in—but the sauce at this joint was drinkable, it was so good. The broth used in the making of dumplings here is one of the best-kept secrets in the food biz, but a surprise visit to the kitchen gained me a peek into their soup pot loaded with pig's trotters and shrimp shells. The gelatin in the pork allows the stock to chill to a solid form, and the pork/shrimp combo is what makes the soup so addictive in its hot liquid form.

This was the ultimate dumpling feast. Steamed pork dumplings, traditional Xia Long Bao, and assorted round little soup dumplings twisted at the top. We had a steamed crabmeat-and-pork dumpling, which I just adored. Crustacean and pork dumplings are my faves. I love the texture of the lobster or shrimp or crab swimming in the porky soupiness as you chew. Half moons of steamed vegetable-and-fish dumplings, platters of steamed green-vegetable dumplings—usually a trio of mixed greens, some pickled, some just minced fresh, some mixed with pork. You can see the brilliant emerald green through the thin sheeting they come enrobed in. We devoured mushroom dumplings and indulged in the best shao-mai I've ever had. Shrimp and pork varieties, about an inch and a half high, pinched in the middle so they look like little nuclear power plants. The night's specials were over the top in flavor and presentation. They brought us these shrimp dumplings, decorated like a teeny shrimp replete with tails and eyes. I've never seen anything like it anywhere else in the world except in some of the dumpling palaces in Xian in the People's Republic.

The buns came next. We powered through their *char siu bao*, a light doughy bun filled with barbecued pork, steamed and baked buns filled with mixed vegetables. There were sweet red-bean-and-sesame buns dotted with a circle of filling on the top to distinguish them from the savory varieties. We had a black glutinous rice dish that absolutely blew my mind, it was so dense. It was pitch black and looked as if it had been steamed in banana leaf and unfolded onto the plate—like a power bar of rice. We had plates of sautéed water spinach called *on-choy*, mixed greens and gai lan bathed in oyster sauce, and sugar snap pea shoots wok-tossed with ginger and burnt chilies.

Somehow, we found room for the two entrées listed on the menu. One was a chicken steamed over rice and the other one a fried pork chop. They were both admirable dishes, but if you ask me, a waste of stomach space when there are such incredible dumplings to be had. Almost no one orders them. Din Tai Fung is all about the dumplings, created in the male-dominated kitchen, served by giggling girls in short skirts, thick stockings, and clunky high heels. A huge winner.

The only real downer of the evening was the red bean rice cake dessert. I often find Chinese desserts to be disappointing. Quick, name your favorite. See? We had mashed red bean and glutinous rice patties that our Taiwanese cohorts just wolfed down. Me, I just don't get the sweet bean paste mixed with rice. Not enough contrast in flavor or texture for my taste, but so be it.

Bingyi Yang, Din Tai Fung's founder, arrived in Taiwan in 1948. He began working in the cooking oil business. Ten years later, his oil store closed. However, Yang remained optimistic and managed to open his own oil shop in 1958, called Din Tai Fung Oil Store. Din Tai Fung turned into a successful oil shop, so much so that he opened another location in the bustling Xinyi Road area. In the 1970s, cheap tinned salad oil flooded the market, leaving Yang's business hanging by a thread. Taking the advice of a friend, Yang and his wife turned half of the shop into a steamed dumpling operation. They never advertised, but word of mouth brought people in. Eventually, business exploded and they soon stopped selling oil altogether. Locals and travelers alike flocked to their restaurant, where everything is made by hand and quality control is job one. These guys do it right, with a refrigerated room to roll dumplings and a hot room to steam them. Sitting at long banks of tables, cheek to jowl with diners not in your party, it's definitely intimate, but boy, you will not find better dumplings anywhere in the world. If you have never had a soup dumpling with paper-thin translucent skin, dipped into a little bowl of red or black vinegar infused with fresh ginger, and finished with a drizzle of aged soy sauce, you have not lived. When that mixture of soup, meat, and sauce explodes in your mouth, it all marries together harmoniously, which is why I think dumplings are the world's most perfect food.

Fish Heaven
Finding Perfection in a Ginza Basement

Although it has yet to achieve the everyday normalcy hot dogs and donuts have in this country, sushi is perhaps the most popular food in the United States, possibly in the world. Over the last five years, hundreds of millions of Russian and Chinese middle-class consumers came online, joining the legions of global sushi nuts. Demand increased so drastically that the prices high-quality fish were able to garner at wholesale fish markets around the world hiccupped forward almost overnight, responding to and then reigniting a giant sea change in demand.

Oligarchs, dictators, Mafiosi, supermodels, and food freaks—anyone with deep pocketbooks—scrounge for reservations not at French tables of gastronomy, but at the handful of high-end sushi restaurants around the world. A food that was originally thought to be peasant fare (pickled fish) ended up having rice and *nori* applied to it as a way to keep gamblers from marking their cards, dice, and gambling debts. Later it became the ultimate Japanese snack food, captivating the imagination of hundreds of millions of consumers around the world.

I remember going out to Montauk on Long Island to go bluefish fishing with my dad when I was six or seven years old. We were going out on one of the big party boats that left from in front of Salivar's Dock. Later that afternoon when we returned from our day on the ocean, we saw these giant 300- or 400-pound beasts being slung on derricks from the docks, then hoisted into open-air dump trucks wheeled up to the water's edge. I asked my dad where these big fish were going, lying in the bins on the backs of these trucks. We found out that these behemoth fish were being driven mid-island to a cat-food factory for processing. My, how the world has changed.

Those same fish now regularly garner $150,000 a pop at Toyko's Tsukiji Market, where they are flown fairly regularly. The boats that catch the primo tuna will actually have graders flown out to the vessels by helicopter. They'll inspect the fish, pull it into the helicopter's belly, and whisk it away to an international airport. Fifteen hours later, it's auctioned off at Tsukiji Market. Sadly, in the food world today, the currency of the realm is expensive fresh fish, the very thing customers in Japanese restaurants, and a host of other styles of eateries, crave the most.

I remember when Japanese food was essentially a handful of little yakitori-style restaurants in Manhattan. I was probably eleven or twelve when my friends, the Wakabayashi family, began taking me to Tenryu on a weekly basis. Invariably, one of our appetizers was a large platter of assorted sashimi and sushi. Around the same time, I began accompanying my dad to lunches and dinners at the old and long-since-closed Edo Restaurant in the West Forties. Like most sushi newcomers, Tekka-maki was the first thing I fell in love with, those small chunks of tuna rolled in rice and nori. I eventually graduated to eel, freshwater and saltwater; hamachi; then to geoduck, known in Japan as mirugai. This gigantic saltwater clam soon became my favorite.

The first time I tried uni, or raw sea urchin, was at Hatsuhana. The liver-y and softly textured creamy roe of the sea urchin isn't for everyone, but I adored its one-of-a-kind saline and minerally flavor profile. This was the place to eat sushi and sashimi in the late seventies. I would sit mesmerized for hours as I watched the brigade of sushi chefs with long, thin blades turning four-inch chunks of cucumber into paper-thin sheets. They would make their thin cucumber paper, rolling it around in thin warm slices of unagi, then slice it thin, creating little eel and cucumber pinwheels, one of their first signature dishes.

I love sushi and sashimi, and I've eaten some great fish in my day. Still, to my mind, one of the great experiences in my food life was getting up at oh-dark-thirty and heading over to Tsukiji Market to watch the fresh and frozen tuna auctions. Participants still dress up in the ancient uniforms, march into the auction room, and barter away for some of the most beautiful fish you've ever seen in your life. I've had the honor of escorting 300-pound fish from the market floor at four in the morning to a dealer's booth. This wholesaler cut up the fish, dispensing pieces to sushi restaurants around the greater Tokyo metro area who had placed orders with him that day. I watched the cutters take six-foot-long samurai swords and divide the fish into panels, separating the chutoro from the otoro and the toro from the guro. He weighed the different cuts of tuna, wrapped it up, and sent it on its way.

I've learned more about tuna from spending a few days at Tsukiji Market than I ever did eating and working in restaurants. I've prowled the market extensively, hopping booth to booth, tasting tuna brought in from different parts of the world. I've had wholesalers lead me by the hand to the carcass of mammoth bluefin and yellowfin tuna, where they'd run a spoon along certain bones or along the spinal cord, collecting scrapings of particularly fatty or noteworthy bites to educate me on what to look for in terms of fat content, flavor, and texture.

I've eaten some of the most world-renowned sushi. I've been lucky enough to dine at Nobu Matsuhisa's restaurants many times. I've probably visited eight or nine of them globally, often getting fed by the Master himself. I didn't think anything could top having Nobu Matsuhisa himself prepare uni, raw scallop, a selection of toro, and more for me, standing behind the sushi bar at his restaurant one night in Los Angeles. This was the thrill of a lifetime—until I got a chance to eat with him in the kitchen of his Tokyo restaurant a year later. If you've never eaten poached octopus eggs cooked in dashi and mirin, accompanied by some fresh fried frog, I implore you to get on a plane and head to Tokyo immediately.

And speaking of frog, not in my wildest dreams did I ever consider eating frog sashimi. They serve it in Japan at a little getemono bar called the Asadachi, which hysterically translates to "morning erection." Tokyo's getemono bars are notorious for serving food-forward, psyche-challenging dishes, so if you're jonesing for a grilled lizard, that's where you go. Businessmen flock to these little restaurants to eat for sport, usually as a way to celebrate the closing of an auspicious business deal. Eating frog sashimi involved more audience participation than I'd anticipated. I actually selected my live frog from a basket. The chef then took a penknife and ripped its skin off. He served me paper-thin slices of the frog's flesh with a bit of soy and lemon sauce for dipping, along with a separate bowl for the still-beating frog's heart.

On several occasions I've found myself at Jewel Bako's sushi bar in New York City. One of the greatest things about frequenting the same sushi bar is building a relationship with the chef. I often turn the ordering over to Yoshi, one of the great sushi chefs in the city, who hand-selects cuts of fish for me, like teeny filets of melting silver needlefish flown in from Tsukiji Market. He scores the skin with the sharpest of knives, finishing it with a blowtorch to char the skin. The flesh, still cold, is placed on some of the best vinegared rice I've ever tasted. If you're really up for a challenge, try Yoshi's live lobster sashimi washed down with a hot and comforting bowl of lobster miso soup.

I am not, by the way, in the business of animal cruelty, and the debate can rage on for decades about whether or not a lobster has "feelings," but there are many cases (oysters, clams, to name a few) where lively freshness is imperative when dining, and frankly, in most cases I am very content being ensconced firmly at the top of the food chain. I would also say that many of the more extreme examples of my dining on live animals falls into the experiential category and not into the everyday-habit category.

That's not supposed to make you feel better if you are against this sort of thing, but it makes me feel better.

I've dined several times at Nozawa in Los Angeles. At the turn of the millennium, when Nozawa was the king of raw fish in Los Angeles—a city unrivaled in its passion for sushi—he turned out some of the most incredible food that I've eaten in a sushi bar: freshly steamed Dungeness and king crab in two separate hand rolls, flesh still warm, plucked from the shell by his wife and his assistant, who help him run the tables. I remember those crab rolls like it was yesterday.

Nozawa's reputation for phenomenal food is almost eclipsed by his ironfisted approach to serving sushi. He's not far off from Seinfeld's infamous Soup Nazi when it comes to personality profiles. He plates the food, giving you the portions that he believes you should have. You do not ask for seconds. You do not over-order. If a dish is not accompanied by soy sauce, pickled ginger, or wasabi, it is not an oversight. He wants you to eat a certain piece of fish without it. This man isn't looking for you to have a pedestrian experience. If you challenge him, you run the risk of being kicked out.

I've actually seen him give customers the boot, something I never thought I would see in my lifetime. Before my Nozawa experience, I'd seen it only once before: at 150 Wooster, Manhattan's hottest celebrity-driven dining spot in the eighties. I was in there one night and looked over to see a regular, seated at one of the premier tables, sent out the door midmeal, dinner hastily packed up in hand, because they wanted to give Mick Jagger and his entourage that table. But that's nothing compared to Sushi Nozawa, where nearly every time I visited someone got kicked out for not playing by Nozawa's rules. He's got opinions, to say the least.

The sushi in New York, Los Angeles, and other major cities around the globe is superb, but if you want the best, go to Japan. In recent years, Tokyo has emerged as a big player in the global food scene, possibly even more so than Paris or New York, especially in the last few years. Consider the controversy that sparked after Michelin assembled their first-ever dining guide for Tokyo. Michelin, famous for their tires, is just as famous for their restaurant and hotel guides. More than a century ago, the Michelin Company created the guide to help traveling salesmen find restaurant and hotel recommendations on the road. Today, it's sort of the ultimate restaurant guide, dealing mostly with European offerings. Eventually, they started covering the United States, and a couple of years ago they announced a plan to put together a Tokyo book.

The total number of stars given to Tokyo restaurants eclipsed that of Parisian restaurants, sending off a firestorm of conversation in the blogosphere and in restaurant kitchens worldwide. Which one is the greatest eating city? I've spent a lot of time eating my way around the world's food meccas, including Paris and Tokyo. You can't convince me that Tokyo *isn't* the most exciting food city in the world—let's put it that way, and that says a lot. It's sort of like asking, who's the better basketball player: Magic, Bird, or Michael? Who's a better golfer: Jack Nicklaus or Tiger Woods? It's hard to say.

There certainly is a lot of culinary magic going on in Japan, and not just with their restaurants. Good Japanese cooks, and I've had the pleasure of working with many in my life, are brilliant replicators. So precise, with impeccable knife skills. Their diligence, discipline, and powers of concentration are far beyond the average Western cook's. Give them a classic French or Italian dish and within a day they can nail it every time. The great French and Italian restaurants in Tokyo are hindered only by availability of ingredients, which in the age of the airplane does not limit them much at all. But the last time I was in Tokyo, I had the opportunity to have a meal alone by myself in an empty restaurant in between lunch and dinner that stands to this day as the greatest single sushi experience I've ever had.

Sushi Mizutani is a teeny restaurant in the basement of the Ginza Seiwa Silver Building, right around the corner from the

Shimbashi Station. Open six days a week, serving lunch and dinner Monday through Friday, I'd have to say this gem is the best
sushi restaurant in the city.

Don't go with a crowd—you won't want to. Go with one good
friend—preferably someone you feel comfortable pawning the bill
off on. You'll easily spend $200 to $300 a person—and with Mizutani's amazing sake collection, probably a lot more. Depending on
how the space is configured, you might even want to go alone—the
place holds only between eight and ten counter seats. Behind the
counter is a space that is only big enough for one person to walk
through at a time, and there is only one chef here, so no need for
more room. A table for two, tucked away in the corner across from
the sushi bar, may be used at dinnertime, but only when the chef
Mizutani deems it fit to seat someone there. He loves to dole food
out himself, lavishing stories on his patrons, allowing them a
front and center seat to what may be the greatest set of sushi skills
operating in the world. Mizutani is the man. Every bite of food in
this restaurant passes through his hands at some point.

The real magic happens before the restaurant even opens, when
Mizutani himself, along with his assistant, prowls the markets,
collecting the best product available in the city—and with almost
fifty years of cooking under his belt, he knows what he's looking
for. He's a neat and tidy little man, very thin with a big, round face
and easy smile. His giant round glasses emphasize the sloping
features of his face. He's probably approaching seventy if he's not
already there, but he has the energy of a man half his age.

His restaurant is spare and without pretention. You actually go
down into the building's basement, where you'll find a nondescript
sliding screen door. You knock and enter. It's one of the more hid-
den-away restaurants that I've ever experienced, especially for one
of this caliber, but Mizutani doesn't want it any other way.

He's been there for years now, doing what he does like no other:
simply providing people with the best. The best-quality fish and
shellfish, the best aged soy sauce, the best shari (vinegared rice).

Every ingredient has a special provenance. His rice, for example, comes from a handful of growers at a very special farm a couple hundred miles away. The vinegar is made in a renowned prefecture in northern Japan. Dishes have few ingredients, but each one is of the highest quality available, bar none. This all sounds very serious, but the restaurant's vibe is anything but. It's hard to contain yourself when you're just blown away by this food.

Dinner reservations are scheduled months in advance, if you can get in at all. Lunch, of course, is less crowded and you might be able to weasel your way in, especially early or late. I couldn't get there during regular service hours, so Mizutani met with me in between meal periods. I watched as lunch emptied out before I sat down to eat alone with him, chatting with him about his craft.

I think the food world has sort of come full circle in many ways. It used to be that all food was served on platters. Think of Erroll Flynn's *Robin Hood*, in which the banquet scene reveals that in that day and age, and it is historically correct, all the food was on platters, with everyone sharing family-style. Over the course of the next couple hundred years, as the food idea slowly turned into less of a classist exercise, taverns came into vogue, and then restaurants. Real restaurant culture developed in Europe in the early nineteenth century, but tavern culture, places to have a meal, existed for centuries. Individual foods plated in single servings is a relatively modern convention.

For hundreds of years, it was restaurants themselves—not the food or chef—that were famous. Certainly, many chefs garnered fame for inventing certain dishes at certain restaurants, especially in America. Chefs of the Delmonico Restaurant in the nineteenth century were justifiably famous, not necessarily by name or face, but by reputation. And it didn't matter who was cooking—you always knew someone good was there, much like Commander's Palace in New Orleans today. This has been home to some of the greatest chefs working in the South. You knew every time you went there, year in and year out, that it was going to be good.

Over the course of time, the restaurateur, the owner, became famous, or the man running the room. Pavilion in New York was a famous restaurant, but when Andre Soule was in his heyday, in New York's Truman Capote era of the fifties and sixties, Pavilion reigned supreme. People flocked to Pavilion, and everyone remembers Soule and the restaurant but not the chef or the food. Which isn't to say it wasn't good or he wasn't a star; it's just that society in those days placed a larger premium on other facets of restaurant life than it does today.

For the past few decades, restaurants have been all about the chef. Thomas Keller, Wolfgang Puck, Charlie Trotter . . . These guys are regarded more like rock stars than chefs. And deservingly. I'd put myself in the long list of people who'd be willing to wait for weeks in a freezing cold rain for a meal at the French Laundry.

These days, the ingredients are as important as the person cooking it. You go to many restaurants not just to see what a certain chef can do with a given menu or oeuvre, but to eat ingredients available nowhere else. Sometimes the chef and his ingredients are synonymous. People flock to Blue Hill in New York not only to taste Dan Barber's food, knowing that means the most farm-fresh ingredients. In terms of menu, only the most discriminating of chefs can offer the kind of shopping Barber is capable of, mainly because he grows and raises much of his ingredients. Today, it's all about ingredient worship, and I think sushi bars are the most obvious places to witness that development.

When it comes to ingredients, Japan's respect for food matches Italy's passion and simplicity. Like Japanese cuisine, Italian food at its essence is extremely simple, extremely seasonal, and not overly complex or clichéd. But the Japanese are indeed special. I think it's the only culture in the world where a single pickled plum served on a giant plate gets the kind of oohs and aahs that are otherwise reserved for more ambitious culinary pyrotechnics. In Japan, "simple" really works in a way that it doesn't elsewhere. It's pretentious when I see that type of cooking in other restaurants;

they are just imitators and replicators, as opposed to true disciples. When you're in a Japanese restaurant where a chef is actually making complex philosophical decisions about what to put on a plate, it can get really impressive. Japanese chefs would never serve that plum at its peak of ripeness just sitting naked on a dish; they would feel rightfully obligated to cook or prepare it in some way, even subtly. I mean, that's why you go to a restaurant, right? If you want to eat the perfect raw plum, you go see a farmer; you wouldn't go see a chef. But—and it's a big but—if anyone cooks food in a more naked or exposed or simple oeuvre than the Japanese do, I haven't seen it.

Great Japanese chefs do just enough to those items to heighten the eating experience without killing the ingredient. An ingredient captured at its peak moment of texture and flavor may not need much tweaking, which is why Mizutani's "less is more" approach works.

Mizutani himself greeted me at the door while his wife and assistant tidied up the kitchen and helped with some mis-en-place work—it's still a restaurant, after all. He invited me to sit at the sushi bar and asked me for my order. Who would better know what to order than Mizutani himself? I opted for an omakase-style meal, where you let the chef take the reins and pray for the best.

Of course, I had nothing to worry about here. Mizutani serves only the best. Japan grows great rice, and Mizutani has been getting his from the same family for years. All their rice is hand planted, tended, and harvested in small batches. The care with which Mizutani prepares the rice is astounding. He washes and dries it, then gently cooks and seasons it with his specially formulated vinegars to give it a faint sweetness. This special care affects the way he cuts and stores his fish, and the way he handles individual pieces of fish, especially ones with a high fat content—like certain cuts of tuna—not allowing the warmth of his hand to change the texture of the fish. Rice. Fish. Plate. Simple, but not easy.

I watched as he handled the mackerel, or saba. He cups the fish in his hand, keeping his palm in contact with the rice for a different length of time, depending on the fish itself, transforming the flavor for the better, making it less fishy and less oily, as the warmth of the rice and his hand actually draws some of that oil from the fish into the rice itself. In a sense, he cooks with his hands.

What blew me away the most were the little things. I received the fish one piece at a time, and each one had a story. This mackerel was caught by his friend; that scallop, hand collected by divers he knew in the north—and he bought only four or five a day when they were available at the Tsukiji Market. I received a thin slice from the top of the scallop, still in its shell, and watched as he draped it on top of the shari, the vinegar rice with the barest brush of wasabi. He invited me to dip the piece of scallop sushi in soy sauce, which is so phenomenal that I contemplated drinking the stuff like a shot of espresso.

It's not that Mizutani serves the most unusual fish. My meal ran the full gamut of traditional fish, such as kagai, mirugai, and hokigai. However, superior freshness, presentation, and symphony of texture exalted this meal to a new level. I ate several different types of flounder, called hirame. The dorsal fin was one of the most fabulous textures of any sushi I've ever eaten: crisp and corrugated, sweet and briny. The monkfish liver was kissed with sake and mirin, warmed ever so slightly. He followed up with paper-thin slices of abalone draped over rice sushi style, chutoro (which is the meaty and fatty cut of bluefin tuna taken from the belly), incredibly fatty otoro as well, along with maguro.

The squid was so fresh and delicate, cut with a dazzling sort of diamond cutter's expertise. Millions of little knife marks ran across the flesh in a crosshatch pattern, allowing the fish to literally disappear on your tongue. I had two types of eel, freshwater and saltwater, braised in a soy, sugar, and mirin sauce, reduced down to a syrup. The fish is cooled and cut to order, sauced and thrown under a broiler to char the edges, then draped over small balls of rice.

Mizutani served the best uni that I've ever eaten in my life. He directed me to his uni guy at the market. A few days later, a friend and I bought a whole tray of uni, about 500 grams. We demolished the whole thing with two spoons, standing in the area between food stalls at 10 in the morning as cleanup crews hosed down the market's walkways.

The shad that I had, a small bony fish that is also called kohada, is usually a very pedestrian sort of fish in America, but in the hands of Mizutani, it was absolutely insane. His knife work is amazing, and he left little bits of skin on the shad but cut away other little pieces of the skin so it simply disappeared in the mouth. I had aji, a Spanish horse mackerel minced as a little sashimi course, that was ethereal. These offerings are normally fishy even in the best of eateries; here they aren't. And his cooking skill is amazing.

Everybody raves about his tamago. This egg dish is placed in a square or rectangular pan, cooked in thin sheets and folded on itself, then pressed into a block. It is typically sweetened, and it makes a great last bite in a sushi meal. Mizutani's tamago was creamy and textured in a way that reminded me of ripe peaches.

I'm a big student of art history. In that field we always talk about the space that sculptures occupy, but more important, we should also talk about the negative space where something isn't. Often, less is more. It's the greatest discipline challenge for chefs. I love young, bold, brash chefs. I love to eat their food. Their experimentation is awesome, but often there are one too many ingredients on the plate. A bold, brave chef who's been around the block a few times yet still harbors that energy and curiosity in the kitchen relies less on gimmicks and needs fewer ingredients. Ingredients, pyrotechnics, and architecture in the kitchen is a great way to cover up lack of skill. Serving a single piece of fish placed on a small mound of vinegar rice is naked cooking. You're on a tightrope without a net. This simplicity and greatness come only from those who understand that all good cooking stems from good shopping.

But Mizutani is more than a shopper. He's disciplined enough to buy only foods at their peak of flavor. He knows the best way to handle and prepare a fish. This passion translates to patrons. He is a master, and that is what he loves the most. It's why he doesn't have twenty seats. It's why he likes to seat people only at his sushi bar. He wants to continue the connection he has with his purveyors, his ingredients, his techniques with the people he's ultimately trying to resonate with. A great chef or restaurateur knows great food doesn't end in the kitchen. It ends on the table. And to think that this type of perfection and artistry sit unassumingly in a basement in Ginza.

Lamb Alley

Dining Nose to Tail in the Djemaa El Fna

Baedeker's antique travel books wax poetic about pulling into a city by boat. I often think of how gorgeous the confluence of waterways must have looked at the site of the ancient city of Constantinople, now Istanbul. How it must have looked to visitors arriving by ship through the Bosphorus, with Asia on one side, present-day Europe on the other, and the Blue Mosque straight ahead. Imagine arriving into Venice hundreds of years ago, when the rest of the world lagged so far behind culturally and architecturally. What a staggering and surprising sight that must have been, or the Canton of a thousand years ago, or sailing up the Thames into eighth-century London when it was traded back and forth among warring tribes of Norsemen on a yearly basis. Modern times don't allow for too many sea-travel opportunities, save mega–cruise ships that lack the certain, romantic *je ne sais quoi* that they used to, and nowadays cruise ships sit in the most unglamorous of ports, shunned from the prime locales mostly for reasons of efficiency. But I think descending through the cloud cover via airplane can be absolutely breathtaking as well.

I've flown over and into Quito's Avenue of Fire. Following a valley of dormant and active volcanoes, we descended into one of the highest elevated capital cities in the world. To see these volcanoes from overhead is intimidating in the extreme and stunning, with the green and gold of the highlands peeking far up to the shoulders of the mountains themselves before giving way to rocky crowns.

As far as man-made sights go, nothing beats landing at New York's La Guardia airport, with its stunning view of the most famous skyline in the world. The shores of Samoa from the air are exquisite; ditto Hawaii. A daytime landing into Tokyo always means a great peek at Mt. Fuji, looking just the way it does on postcards, replete with its white cake-frosting drips of snow running down its face.

I've racked up well over a million frequent-flier miles, and to my mind, landing in Marrakesh, Morocco, still remains one of the most wonderful sights to take in from a plane. A vast, brown hardscrabble desert abruptly morphs into a sprawling city, with thousands of clay-tile-roofed buildings, not one skyscraper in sight. Drying laundry, strung on lazily stretched lines, crawls from small chimneys to iron pipe jutting out of the side of a neighbor's house, crisscrossed and repeated over the whole of the ancient red cityscape. And then there are the satellite dishes, poking out of every single home. And I mean every home. It's an ocean of satellite dishes in the middle of the desert. I found myself absolutely enchanted by this juxtaposition of ancient and modern life. It made me smile all the way through landing and the lengthy immigration process.

Morocco feels like the ultimate food trip. Romantic to say the least, Moroccan cuisine is highly refined, very country-specific—that is to say, unique and delightfully easy to navigate. Chicken, lamb, mint, lemon, chile, cumin, honey, orange, rinse, repeat. As I exited the airport, the sights, sounds, and scents of the city overtook me. Mint tea is to Marrakesh what Starbucks is to New York—you can't go five feet without seeing it up close and personal. Every restaurant, every food stall, and every merchant offers mint tea to any customer or passerby, and the aroma is always lying heavy in the air. The fresh mint mixes with cooking smells, cinnamon, and sour perspiration, which to an ethnocentric Western nose might sound disgusting, but for me it's become a familiar odor I associate with the vibrancy and claustrophobia of northern African life.

By the time we landed in Morocco, I could barely keep my eyes open. I flew all day and night, and arrived smack dab in the middle of the day. It's one o'clock, and all I want to do is sleep for eight hours, which will do nothing but royally mess with your system. I've discovered that a little sunshine, exercise, and a catnap by the pool is the key to combating jet lag. Sitting by a five-star hotel's pool in Morocco is, in many ways, like sitting by any luxury hotel pool . . . except when it comes to the staff. With a ratio of nearly one staff member to each guest, you can't help but be impressed by the graciousness and attentiveness—it almost makes you uncomfortable with its cloying sense of devotion. I appreciate good service, but I loathe endless sycophantic kowtowing to the point where you have to kick somebody out of your hotel room because they are simply overstaying their welcome. Offering to do everything but brush your teeth for you just feels downright awkward.

As I headed from my room to the pool, I had at least fifteen interactions with employees. Each one wanted to escort me somewhere, steer me toward a restaurant, or get me into the gift shop. Half of it is New Age hucksterism, with employees earning a few cents if they can maneuver you into some other part of the hotel where you can be separated from more of your money. I couldn't quite put my finger on why this all seemed to feel so unusual, especially considering that I have been to more than my share of cities with overly pandering hotel staff. They weren't making fun of me, but it seemed there was an inside joke going on that I just couldn't quite figure out.

Want a refresher course on the right way and wrong way to travel? Head to the hotel pool, where you'll stumble upon ugly Americans, ugly Brits, ugly Aussies, ugly Germans, and ugly Italians barking at pool attendants, stuffing their faces with the endless sea of Westernized buffet fare. Hamburgers, lasagna, and pizza—you name it, it's there at any one of the half-dozen hotel restaurants. Here's a travel tip: Moroccan stew, chock-full of lamb innards and brains, served on the street, is one of the safest dishes you can eat in this country. It's fresh, cared for by hand, and battle-tested for generations. What will leave you praying to the porcelain gods are sliced tomatoes at the hotel buffet, or worse, Americanized food cooked by people without the faintest idea of what it's supposed to look or taste like, or how to properly handle the ingredients. Needless to say, the majority of my fellow hotel guests complained of the Moroccan stomach issues by day three, while I bounced around feeling like a million bucks.

As they ate themselves into pathogenic bacterial oblivion, I sipped on light and sweet iced mint teas, knowing the evening would be filled with lots of phenomenal food from one of the world's great food centers. I also snacked on a platter of fruit, which made me fall in love at first bite with fresh Moroccan produce. Lounging poolside that day, I made it my mission to eat as much fresh Moroccan fruit as I could handle.

To my taste, Morocco grows the world's finest fruits and vegetables. The agrarian communities at the base of the Atlas Mountain chain are filled with rich soil, with ample waterfalls streaming down from the highest peaks, transferring decayed, volcanic mulch to the valleys below. Plantless rock formations tower ten thousand feet high, and in the crooks of their arms lie piles of the most fertile soil imaginable. These valleys, often many degrees warmer than the surrounding areas, create microclimates perfect for farming. Driving through the mountains, you see palm trees, plants, and rich vegetation sitting at the bottom of two rock formations, lush and dense like an oasis, and everything ten feet above the tree line is solid rock without even a blade of grass to be found. Odd, but the radiant heat rebounds off those rock faces as well as back into the lush ravines, making it even more beneficial for the growing of fruits and vegetables. In one valley, you find nothing but sweet onions; one mountain over, tomatoes; one more over, oranges. The list goes on and on.

Locals will carry tree-ripened apricots a half mile up from the valley floors to the roads and highways coursing along the mountainside, selling handmade baskets filled with fruit for a few pennies each. One bite of this succulent fruit and there was no turning back. We'd sit in the car snacking on apricots for hours. This fruit was perfect; no blemishes, mealy spots, or bruises—incredible, considering that this fruit is legendary for its instability. I'd pop these tree-ripened apricots into my mouth and spit out the seed in one fell swoop. It was completely addicting, like powering down a bag of peanuts at a baseball game, and I couldn't jam the second apricot in fast enough. This perfection carried over to the tomatoes, pineapples, grapes, melons, and nearly every other food we encountered. The quality is inextricably tied to their fertile soil, as well as their organic, sustainable approach to farming. However, "organic" and "sustainable" aren't buzzwords in Morocco. They don't need to turn down chemicals or make a safe choice about their farming practices; it's just the way things work there, and always have.

Of course, Morocco isn't just about the fruit. After my afternoon lounge fest, I left our hotel that night around five, making my way to the Djemaa El Fna. The Djemaa El Fna serves as the city's bustling market center, complete with snake charmers, street performers, and food vendors. Behind that, you'll find the Souk, a thousand-year-old marketplace reminiscent of something you would see in a dime-store novel illustration or an Indiana Jones movie. Vendors set up daily and are very mobile, so even if you've been there a few times, each visit will be different from the last. It is also a shyster's heaven, and running scams is almost as big a business as hawking wares. The Djemaa El Fna and Souk both attract grifters of the highest order. They can sniff out a sucker like police dogs hot on a fugitive's trail. Women sell tin bracelets at a nearly 1,000 percent price hike to anyone dumb enough to believe it's real silver. Con artists stalk fanny-packed tourists. One false move and bam! There goes your wallet. I've heard stories of locals showing tourists around the market for a few pennies, eventually leading them to their family's shop, where they give some elaborate sob story about an ailing cousin laid up in the hospital. Next thing they know, they're heading back to Orlando with a stunning sixteenth-century rug (often a cheap knockoff) rolled up under their arm. If you spend enough time in the market, you'll see this happen all around you, and while I don't like to laugh too much at others' misfortune, you can easily pick out the most vulnerable tourists and watch the whole thing go down before your eyes.

The Djemaa El Fna is nearly vacant in the late afternoon—when the temperature reaches well into the hundreds. At this point, it's just me, a few juice-cart vendors squeezing all kinds of fresh fruit, and the occasional snake charmer playing their *ghaitahs*, who seem to operate in their own little world. Over the next hour, I watched as hundreds of carts rolled into the square and linked up, cart to cart, to form "streets" of stalls. Vendors set up wooden tables with foot-high stools, essentially serving as mini-restaurants. As vendors finish setting up, wives and kids arrive with wheelbarrows filled with ingredients. Full-service restaurants with twenty or thirty menu items, from fried fish to *bistilla*, the country's justifiably famous pigeon pie, are re-created on a daily basis.

Tourists certainly wander this part of the market, but it's no tourist trap. The majority of patrons are Moroccan and work in and around the Djemaa. In recent years, the surrounding area filled up with hotels, a few restaurants and bars, a couple of shops and drugstores. This modernized shopping and eating environment caters to the out-of-towners, with the locals finding everything they need—from lunch, to a haircut or a dentist—in the Djemaa. Non-Moroccans will feel like an interloper, but experiencing the Djemaa is a must, especially because this is where you'll find some of Marrakesh's best food.

I found one guy cooking up large pieces of boiled lamb and

cow in oversized, bubbling vats. He boils lungs, feet, intestines, and heads, pulls the meat from them, plops it down on a piece of butcher paper, adds a little shake of seasoning (mostly cumin and salt), serves it with a hunk of bread, and you're good to go. Another vendor grilled paper-thin slices of lamb and pig heart marinated in chilies and spices; another placed chopped organs inside pieces of fresh intestine, grilling them like sausages. Then, just down the road, another man grilled small local lake fish rubbed with turmeric and served it with fresh tomato salad and lime. This may have been the most elegant dish that I ate in the city, and it cost no more than a dime.

With every step I took in the Djemaa, I garnered harsh stares. Eyes followed me with every move, in much the same vein I'd experienced at the hotel. I soon realized it wasn't the fact that I'm an American, nor that I'm generally more talkative and animated than the average person. It's because they saw me as one of those "people from around the hotel pool." In the Djemaa, I ate meals with the sons, brothers, and often even the employees who work in those hotels. I'm here to tell you there's a hatred on the Moroccan street about what goes on behind those hotel walls, but tourism drives much of the economy, so they just grit their teeth and bear it. Walking around the Djemaa El Fna, I felt like a character out of a bad Kipling poem, the tension and resentment toward white Europeans and Americans palpable at every turn. Aside from my dealings with the Berbers, who were some of the kindest, most loving people I've encountered anywhere on the road, nearly every interaction I had in Marrakesh was strained. They accept our money, let us stay in their hotels and eat in their restaurants, but they don't like us. There's so much hullabaloo these days about the world's animosity toward Americans, and I know we've made our fair share of enemies, but I've found that people are generally kind and accommodating no matter where you are in the world. Thus far, my experience in Morocco is the first and only time in my life I've felt otherwise.

This didn't stop me from enjoying myself. After three or four dishes in the Djemaa El Fna, I ventured into the Souk. Navigating this series of congested streets and alleys typically feels like stepping into a *Where's Waldo?* book, but at night, many booths and shops are vacant. Visiting the Souk in the evening is something every traveler ought to experience. With most stalls closed for the evening, you can meander down the streets without too much harassment from vendors trying to sell you T-shirts or fake suede handbags. I ventured into a few of the stalls that remained open, purchasing fabulous beaded leather slippers for my wife. I happened upon some incredible dried-fruit vendors, hawking hundreds of varieties of nature's candy: fist-size strawberries, sweet and chewy dates the size of golf balls, raisins and piles of salted nuts, which made for some delicious Moroccan gorp to keep around the hotel room. As I wandered back into the streets, I was smacked in the face by the heavy, mouthwatering scent of roasted lamb. My nose led me through the streets, but I just couldn't find the source. When it comes to food, I'm blessed with a sixth sense. I just know when something is good, and that smell alone compelled me to return to the same spot on the very next day.

I achieved my goal of making it out of the Souk in one piece, with the bonus of finding the next day's mission, so the next morning I marched back to the scene of the scent. The same street that had looked like a ghost town the previous night was now vibrant and alive, with cart after cart serving a different lamb dish. At the top of what I dubbed Lamb Alley, a bread baker turned out loaves of crusty fresh bread, which he in turn sold to the other seven or eight vendors in the alley. There's wheeling and dealing everywhere you turn, with the stalls working together to assemble a well-rounded meal for their patrons, most of whom they share on some level. The guy serving up roast lamb down the alley gets bread from the baker, they both serve tea ferried from a third booth, and so on. Somehow, at the end of the day they have a way to figure out everyone's share of their profits.

I hit up the next vendor in the alley, who serves mashwi, or whole roasted lamb. Mashwi is the most expensive item in the alley, and is literally roasted underneath the stall itself. Underground clay ovens the size of elevator cars are accessed through a narrow hole, which resembles a manhole cover on the street. Fires are lit in the ovens and dozens of lambs, tied to ancient, cured pieces of wood, are lowered into the oven the night beforehand, where they lean away from the fire itself and slowly roast over low heat for twelve to fourteen hours. The meat takes on a dark honey color, without a burn or scorch on it, just perfectly cooked whole lamb. Given that the vendor's family has been in this business for centuries, it's no surprise that they have the process nailed. In fact, many stall operators date their trade back hundreds and hundreds of years, and in some cases nearly a millennium. I asked one olive merchant how long his stall had been there and he pointed up at the mosque tower, which is almost 900 years old, and said, "Since before that."

As you work your way down lamb alley, the cuts at the various stalls progress from luxury to leftover to, finally, gnawed bones. Truly. Store owners, wealthier merchants, as well as a handful of tourists don't even bother making it to the end of the alley. The stuff at the top of the alley was the best. I couldn't resist plowing into the meat, which was devoid of that fatty flavor typically associated with mutton, despite the provenance of the older animal. From the mashwi, we continued on to a stall vending only the braised lamb shanks. Next, there was a stall serving roasted sheep's heads, followed by a stewed lamb tripe merchant. I don't know whether it was the roasting techniques, the heat of the day, or the citrus juice and herbs rubbed on the meat before roasting. Maybe I can chalk it all up to the romance of eating the lamb at the Djemaa El Fna, but I couldn't get enough of anything I found on this little pitch of a roadway buried in the back of the Souk.

By the time we reached the alley's last vendor, I couldn't even imagine what pieces of the lamb I had yet to see. This stall, run by a peasant in rags, this simple humble stall, consisted of only a beat-up wooden card table, no chairs, and a stack of six recycled tin bowls. This man operated his business off the bones left behind at the other stalls by diners as they left, essentially turning garbage into soup. He used pieces of fat, skin, connective tissue, and any other scraps of edible parts—and believe me, every part is edible—boiling them with water, spices, and some type of lentil-like bean I'd never seen before. Since he had only a few bowls and spoons, once a customer finished, he'd dip their bowl and spoon in a pot of dirty water, wipe it clean with a rag that hadn't seen a washing since Churchill ran England, fill it back up with the thin "bone soup," and serve it to the next customer. Local shopkeepers and middle-class regulars ate mashwi, day workers and laborers could cobble together a few pennies for a shank or a bowl of the pluck, but here at the other end of the alley is where all the beggars and the indigent masses could fuel up during the day. It was such a humbling experience watching these men line up for their turn at one of the bowls that I had to try it. I could never forgive myself a year or a month later, sitting in some swanky boite in some modern city leading my spoiled and coddled Western existence, thinking of Lamb Alley, if I never tried the bone soup. So I did. And you know it was indeed thin, and tinny, and tasting of that minerally quality that overcooked bones always provide. It was tough to think about the cleanliness of the dishes that I was slurping out of, but walking back up the alley I didn't feel like one of the "pool loungers" anymore.

If I could pick any place to return to for lunch these days, it would be Lamb Alley. The spirit of the place, the hustle and bustle, the energy and the enthusiasm of the Souk, excites me like nothing else. You need to be aggressive and decisive or else be prepared to get lost in the shuffle—it's kill or be killed in more ways than one. In a way it reminded me of Papaya King or Carnegie Deli in New York—just one of those places where, if you make it to the front of the line and don't know what you want, they'll skip your chance to order and send your sorry ass to the end of the line. I guess it's the New Yorker in me that loves the get-down-to-business-or-get-the-hell-out vibe.

I wandered back into the Souk after that lamb lunch, where I found one of the most horrific foods I have ever encountered. The foundation of k'lia is mystery meat; sometimes it's beef, sometimes horse, and sometimes it's probably so wacky that it's better left a secret. The mystery meat rots, then is sliced thin and slow-cooked in its own fat, much like the making of pork or duck confit. The meat is stored in the fat itself at room temperature, and because the stuff is already spoiled, it lasts for days without any kind of special care or refrigeration. It took two days of traveling around with k'lia in my backpack before I found someone who would cook it for me in its most desired form: sautéed with some fried eggs. I'm usually in the "fried eggs make anything delicious" camp, but no amount of yummy, runny yolk could mask the putrid meat flavor of the k'lia. I think the frying actually heightened the rotten flavor, and not in a good way. That food is not for the faint of heart, but if you want to check it out, the Souk behind the Djemaa El Fna has plenty of vendors eager to help you.

The Djemaa has been a gathering place for all of Morocco for centuries. It's got a sordid past—even as late as the nineteenth century the square was primarily used for beheadings—but every single evening, 365 days a year at five on the dot, the space is transformed from an orange juice vendors paradise to a phenomenal food festival. This is the place to catch a real slice of traditional Moroccan life. It's the best way to see this country and its people. You'll learn more about Morocco spending one night in the Djemaa and the Souk than you will strolling the museums or touring the antiquities by carriage. Trust me, it's a lot more fun than hanging out at the hotel pool.

INGREDIENTS
AND RITUALS

Andrew hunts down some fresh tuna
off the shores of Samoa's Nu'utele Island
before gearing up for the giant fruit bat hunt.

Nature's Candy
The Achachairu

When it comes to global cuisine, I've tasted it all. Whole roasted sparrows in Vietnam, stinky tofu in Taiwan, a glass of warm steer's blood in Uganda, deer penis soup in Singapore. As the Cantonese say, "Anything that walks, swims, crawls, or flies with its back to heaven is edible." I can tell you firsthand, the Cantonese are onto something. Considering the range of crazy foods I've eaten in my lifetime, it might shock you to know that my most memorable food experiences involve fruits. This certainly shocked the hell out of me. I never would have guessed that my most thrilling food moments would come in the form of a juicy bite of fruit. Whether it's rare and exotic or ridiculously plentiful, you can't beat fruit grown in the ideal environment, picked at the right time. It's nature's candy.

Mangosteens were the first exotic fruit that opened up a world of new ideas for me. Often referred to as the queen of all fruits, mangosteens are universally well regarded for their sweet, succulent flavor. It's like eating a sorcerer's blend of honey blossoms and wildflowers ingeniously mated with the sweetest melon. These small, round fruits have a sturdy green stem and a firm, purple, husky exterior. Place the fruit between your hands, making sure to not crush the delicious center to smithereens, press your palms together, and crack the spongy, fibrous shell. Inside, you'll uncover eight or nine misshapen segments around a central core or pit. It's not entirely unlike a snow-white mandarin orange. Sweet and juicy, and once you take a bite, you can't stop. What makes them extra special is their relative scarcity around the world out-side of their growing zones. The small mites that live inside their thick skins make these fruits next to impossible to transport, and attempts to cultivate the fruit in similar climates, like Hawaii, California, and Florida, have failed miserably. While I wish we all had better access to this incredible fruit, there is something to be said for only being able to eat it while in a specific area of the world. Why? Because when it comes to food, I believe in eating with the seasons. Can't enjoy a summer tomato unless you eat beans and stew all winter long. And in the age of the jet plane and in a time when all our lives are built around instant gratification, it's nice to have something to look forward to when you travel.

When you think about perfect fruit-growing climates, an arid, African desert does not come to mind. However, one of the most interesting fruits I've ever tasted hails from Botswana's Kalahari Desert. The marula trees drop yellow, golf ball–size fruit, which sun-ripen (rot, actually) on the ground. Marula, with an extremely tart frontal assault and a sweet finish, is not only a Bushman favorite but popular with the kudu and baboons as well. Unearthing the small bit of fruit is an involved process. First, you bite through the rind, remove the cap, then squeeze the fruit from the end. The marula pops into your mouth like an oversized lychee. Suck out the sweet-sour flesh and spit out the big seed—but don't throw it away. When roasted and dried, this seed can be cracked open and eaten. For thousands of years, marula nuts have been one of the five primary staples of the Bushman's diet. I savor the simple pleasure of walking through the desert, ten marula fruits in hand, snacking on them as juice streams down my face and hands. SweetTarts never tasted so good.

As I ate my first marula fruit, it brought me right back to Santa Cruz, Bolivia, where I first tasted my favorite fruit of all time. For twenty years, I measured everything against the mangosteen. Tree-ripened apricots from the mountains a day's ride outside

Marrakesh, Morocco, placed a close second. That is, until both were trumped by the achachairu.

Compared to the stark, cold, and brown lunar landscapes that sweep most of Bolivia, Santa Cruz is a lush tropical paradise. Serving as the country's gateway to the Amazon, this area teems with amazing produce and wildlife. We headed to Yacapani, an even smaller town in the area that boasts a restaurant whose reputation for serving some of the world's best fish and roasted armadillo reached me all the way back in America. Some people love licorice, beef jerky, or ice cream on road trips, but to me nothing accompanies a long, dusty car ride quite like fresh fruit. I'm always on the lookout for roadside fruit stands. Taking out your penknife and cutting into a fresh papaya, melon, or bunch of bananas on a road trip is my idea of heaven.

The first fruit stand we encountered outside of Santa Cruz was filled with watermelon, avocado, and baskets of a strange citrus fruit. However, the stand looked a little down on its luck. There is nothing more disappointing than fruit that is not up to snuff—I'd rather eat my Puma sneakers than a mealy pear or a flavorless melon. My driver assured me there would be more stands along the road. Sure enough, we pulled over at a gem of a place ten minutes later. Mesh baskets hung from the wooden edge of the lean-to that protected the fruit from the hot noonday sun. At first glance, the baskets looked to be full of small lemons or limes. Upon closer inspection, I realized I'd never seen anything like it: pale orange in color, some almost flaming red, and figlike in appearance, with a harder, leathery skin, much like the marula fruit.

"It's called an achachairu," the vendor explained. "It's a fruit." Sounded more like a sneeze to me, but I purchased a small bag anyhow. I was smitten.

Attacking a foreign fruit can be complicated business. It's very crucial for the neophyte to ask how to eat it. Imagine diving into a coconut, pineapple, or banana without any guidance. Do you bite into it like an apple from the orchard? Peel it like an orange? Like the marula fruit, fresh lychee, and rambutans, achachairu flesh must be opened in order to access the fruit, but instead of a tidbit of white flesh surrounding a large nut, it's the exact opposite. The skin is rather thin compared to its cousins', so slipping the fruit out is a much easier endeavor. Inside, you will find a huge bite of the most delicious floral, sour symphony of flavors, which explodes into your mouth.

Advice to exotic-fruit lovers: Never ever, ever, ever buy a small piece of fruit for a couple of pennies and get back in the car. And don't ever drive away in a hurry—especially when you have yet to sample your purchase. If it's disappointing to your palate, you haven't lost anything. No matter where you taste the purchase, at the curb or an hour's drive away, you're going to dispose of it if you don't like it, or stop eating it, or give it to someone else who is going to enjoy it, probably in reverse order. But if it's new to you and you love it, you're going to want to eat a lot of it. I always sample on the curb.

One bite of achachairu sent me into a frenzy. They came in little one-kilo bags with roughly twenty fruits inside. I bought three bags and finished them within hours. That night, I ventured to the village market, bought three more bags, and brought them back to the room. I pounded those down in a day. On the way back to the airport, I bought five more bags. By this time, I had convinced the crew that maybe they would want to eat some, and over the course of the next couple hours we demolished three of the bags. Just before we headed to the airport, I made a pit stop for a few more bags. My passion for fruit knows no bounds. I ate two more bags in the airport. If I could have taken them back to La Paz, I would have. Sadly, I couldn't buy enough, couldn't hold enough, and couldn't bring enough onto the airplane. I was eating every single piece of achachairu that I could.

Cultural elitism, price, and difficulty in procuring a certain ingredient can give food an artificially heightened sense of scarcity. However, where there is sunshine and water, there is fruit. Fruit is a very egalitarian edible, and obtaining it doesn't require special privilege—just a keen eye in a field if you're foraging, or a few cents if you're shopping in a market. Unless you're after a $200 square watermelon in Tokyo, fruit offers the best bang for the buck when it comes to exciting ingredients. Fruit also teaches us all a lesson in immediacy politics—there's a "carpe diem" quality to eating fruit that other foods don't have. Eat it when it's ripe, or miss your moment forever. And never pass up the fruit stand unless you know something that I don't.

Pleasant Surprises

A Gallimaufry

Falling in love, landing the perfect job, starting a family—the greatest things in life seem to happen when you least expect them. Experiencing food and culture is no different. I see it on the road all the time. Sure, there's huge hype over a lot of the strange things I eat and experience on the road. Paint a thousand pictures and no one ever calls you an artist, but eat one bug on one show and you will forever be labeled the Bug Guy. On the other hand, I will also never forget cooking with Nobu Matsuhisa on two continents or my personal, one-on-one crash course in molecular gastronomy with famed French scientist Herve This. However, I anticipated greatness in these situations. It's the times when my expectations are low that I find the most pleasant surprises.

Since childhood, I've dreamed of seeing the Great Barrier Reef in Cairns, Australia. When I had the opportunity to travel there as an adult, I regressed back to that giddy little kid staring out the window of my New York City apartment, dreaming of the world. Surfing, sharks, amazing snorkeling—what's not to love? Few more incredible natural structures exist than this reef that rims almost the entire northern coast of the Australian landmass.

I was stunned to discover just how far offshore the reef is located. Operators run giant diving barges with semipermanent structures floating above the reef, which support the massive influx of annual visitors ferried in and out. There is no question about it: Pressure on a reef kills it. Activity in the water equals damage. The growth of the shipping lanes and commercial fishing, combined with the environmental circumstances of global warming, have resulted in a less productive and less vibrant reef. That being said, the Great Barrier Reef is one of the top ten attractions in the world, as far as I'm concerned. My palms were sweating as we boarded our boat in Cairns for the two-hour drive to our dive spot.

When it comes to describing Australians, "crazy" seems to be just part of their psychological makeup. Everyone has sort of a screw loose, and I mean that in a really beautiful way. My diving companion was a gentleman named Lurch. He was a crazy Australian if there ever was one, a carefree guy who spent his formative years on the water. His family made their living on the water, and he's stuck with the family business, resulting in days filled with free diving for fish equipped with only a mask, an incredible oversize spear gun in hand, and a pair of flippers. We finally arrived at our diving spot, where Lurch instructed me to start putting on my gear. As I dealt with my equipment, Lurch gave me a fifteen-minute tour of the shark bites and moray eel stings that covered his body (I think this an intimidation technique, which, frankly, kind of worked). However, this was a once-in-a-lifetime experience and I didn't have time to freak out, so over the side we went.

Lurch and I have the same idea of a good time. We spent a couple of hours in the water, pulling up as many shellfish, crustaceans, and mollusks as we could. We headed to a deserted island, fired up the "barbie," and ate. We got a giant coral trout for the grill and a beautiful Spanish mackerel, but the real star of our lunch was a rainbow crayfish—or a proper rainbow crayfish, as Lurch likes to say.

Often referred to as painted lobsters, these creatures are actually members of the crayfish family. When I hear the name "crayfish" I think of some mud bug down in Louisiana, boiled with a mess of corn, potatoes, sausage, garlic, and onions. This is one of my favorite food treats, and I was expecting to experience the Down Under versions with the hundreds of crayfish we were to collect that day. Lurch kept looking under these giant rock over-hangings in about eighteen to twenty feet of water, where most of the hefty ones live. He pulled out the first couple, showed them to me under water, and signaled that they were too small to keep. I was stunned. These crayfish were the length of my arm, with a tail as big as my forearm. These were no mud bugs; they looked like giant tropical lobsters, complete with brilliant blue, red, and orange flanging all along their exoskeletal armor.

I've seen tropical lobsters before, usually in the Caribbean, where they are camouflaged to disguise themselves in the sand and dark rock of their environment. They need to blend in with earth tones and shadow—hence all the brown, black, and some-times sandy orange color displayed on their shells. The rainbow crayfish, however, live in rocky recesses not necessarily all the way down on the ocean floor, but sometimes midway on the reef itself. Consequently, they live in a vibrantly colored environment, their shells becoming a canvas for some of the most beautiful hues in the animal kingdom.

Lurch finally found one big rainbow crayfish, weighing in at about two and a half kilos. This massive beast was lunch. I'm a New England lobster guy and just assumed this lobster was going to be roasted whole. Lurch had another idea. He brought a small pan to put on top of the grill. Next, he dabbed a tablespoon of but-ter in it, twisted off the lobster tail, cut the tip of the tail off the rear fin flaps, pushed this giant two-pound raw lobster steak out of the tube of skeleton that it lives in, chopped it into one-inch chunks, and panfried the meat in browned butter, finishing it off with a generous squirt of lemon.

We sat there on the beach while the Spanish mackerel, the king-fish, and the coral trout cooked. I tolerate warm-water lobster. The North Atlantic *Homarus americanus* is my kind of crustacean. However, the second-best lobster I've ever had is that rainbow crayfish from the Great Barrier Reef. Taxonomists can take issue with this—I know that technically it's a crayfish. But to me, anything that frickin' big, that tastes and looks so much like a lobster, is getting called a lobster.

Rainbow crays are one of those delicious foods that you can find only down in Australia and some of the island countries just north of it. They have them in Indonesia and Okinawa, Japan, but physically plucking them from the Great Barrier Reef with a man who has spent his lifetime diving there is an experience I wish for everyone.

Samoa also offered up some pleasant surprises in the food department. Samoa is a food lover's paradise. People still live very much in an old-fashioned, timeless manner. It's extremely remote, and many of the simple ways of life that have all but vanished in other parts of the world are still alive and kicking in this South Pacific region. Men stroll the towns barefoot, decked in lavalavas, an incredibly comfy island sarong.

No matter how primitive a country, markets are a barometer experience against which you can measure the best aspects of a culture. In Samoa, the markets serve as a place for licensed vendors to set up small booths—no matter how humble; sometimes it's just two stumps of wood and a plank put across them—for them to vend their product. It may be as simple as hawking bananas, but they still pay a license to the Market Co-op setup business. However, there's a time of day at Apia's Maketi Fou Market when anyone can bring their fresh catch and sell it. It's almost like an amateur section of the market where you can find a random assortment of sea creatures.

The Samoan island of Upolu is surrounded by a massive reef that stretches anywhere from a hundred yards to as far as a mile out from the beach. Beyond that, the water quickly drops off. The inland side of the reef reaches a depth of 60 feet tops, whereas the outer side of the reef drops to 400 or 500 feet immediately. Within another quarter mile you're at 1,000 feet, and in another quarter

mile you're at 3,000 feet. The channels around there are just spectacular, and the depth creates a strong current ideal for attracting
big game fish, including tuna.

Samoans head out in small canoes fitted with outriggers and
paddle past the reef through sometimes fifteen- or twenty-foot
seas. Somehow, they manage to use hand lines while dealing with
these incredible currents in a boat thinner than a kayak. They will
put two or three tuna into their boat, sometimes ten-pounders,
sometimes fifty-pounders. If they live in a well-traveled section of
town, they'll hang their catch from the trees near their homes.
Some people will even collect root vegetables or oranges, bananas,
and papayas and set them next to the fish. A ten-pound tuna will
cost you a few dollars; fruit is a quarter apiece. You won't believe
how cheaply you can put together the lunch of your dreams.

For those who don't live in a high-traffic area, hawking fish at
the Maketi Fou is the best option for making a buck. Fishermen
set up in the amateur section of the market, where a few empty
tables are always available. The fishermen stand by their fish,
scribbling the price on a piece of cardboard or the inside of a
matchbook and perching it on the fish itself. Some even write the
price on the fins with a marker. This setup may be bare-bones, but
it's as fresh as it gets. It's the type of tuna that you would pay hundreds of dollars for in a restaurant in New York or Tokyo. Every
Samoan restaurant serves tuna, raw and cooked. It's inescapable.
It's more ubiquitous than the hamburger is in the United States.
For just a couple dollars, you can have platters of freshly sliced
tuna that has never seen the inside of a refrigerator. Giant tuna
schools populate the area surrounding the island, and there is really no formal means to export it. Tuna is sort of the poor man's
food of the island, but one they know the limited population of
visitors really gets excited about—quite a unique system, since in
the rest of the world the tuna economy has turned this fish into
one of the most exclusive ingredients on the planet.

With fishing this great, I couldn't pass up the opportunity to try it myself. We spent the day on the water, where I actually caught three or four yellowfin tuna. We ate them on the boat, which was quite a thrill. It was here I learned of the Samoans' love for tuna eyeballs. They will pluck them out of the head, add a few drops of lime juice, and squeeze the eyeball into their mouth with a pop. It slides right down your throat, sort of like an eyeball shooter.

While in Samoa, I spent most of my evenings sitting underneath the stars at the Apia Yacht Club, gazing at the Southern Cross and eating fish. Before you start envisioning Thurston J. Howell III, I have to explain that the yacht club is more of a dilapidated wooden deck with a smattering of rickety card tables and chairs. The old hut of a building was built about 120 years ago and served as a hangout for the U.K. expats who arrived during the nineteenth century's Robert Lewis Stevenson era. These days, it's basically a place for ten or twenty expats to sit around and drink way too much scotch whiskey. Loneliness and sadness hover like a haze over these civilization escapees, which is a stark contrast from the vibrant generation of young people who've recently come to the island. These groups intermix at this run-down yacht club. They do a fantastic, extremely spicy deviled grilled chicken. However, every meal commences with a platter of tuna oke-oke, the Samoan version of Hawaiian poke.

Bits of onion, coconut milk, lime juice, and minced hot chili are added to a platter of freshly sliced raw tuna. They don't bother to slice it artfully like the Japanese do with sashimi; nor do they attempt to create a miniature masterpiece on a plate the way the Italians do with crudo. Samoan oke-oke is a four-pound chunk of tuna, coarsely cubed and piled on a plate as if it were lumber shavings. Throw eight or nine toothpicks into the massive mound of tuna and serve with some fresh lime juice. There's always a bottle of soy sauce, hot sauce, and vinegar sitting on the table, so dunk the tuna into whatever you like or sprinkle it with some local

Samoan sea salt and have at it. A simple, pleasant surprise—
especially when they come at drive-thru, fast-food prices.

At the end of a long, bountiful summer at home I'm usually
swearing that if I never saw a fresh local tomato again, I'd be okay.
I gorge myself on those things for a month every August and into
September. By the end of this Samoa trip, I harbored those same
sentiments toward tuna. I seriously thought that if I saw one more
plate of raw tuna, I'd spontaneously combust. However, much like
the way I long for a decent tomato in the dead of winter and spring
(all I can find at my local grocery store are mealy, pink tomatoes
grown in a faraway land), by the time I landed back in Minnesota I
thought to myself, *God, I can't wait to get back there.* These days, I
no longer think of Japan as the tuna capital of the world, nor do
I believe the best tuna fishing lies off the shore of America's East
Coast. Samoa takes the cake in both arenas. It's a pure, unadulter-
ated tuna economy.

Speaking of fish, when it comes to seafood destinations, my
favorite might surprise you. Japan certainly comes to mind, as do
lots of places in Southeast Asia, even the East Coast of the United
States. When it comes to seafood, Chile is a force to reckon with.

Interestingly, Chile is probably my favorite destination to recommend to any traveler, whether they are well-seasoned or heading abroad for the first time. Geographically diverse, financially
sound, socially conscious, and certainly a very developed nation,
Chile offers something for everyone. Gorgeous, relaxing beaches?
After Brazil, Chile features the continent's longest coastline.
Bustling cities? Santiago, a modern, pulsing, Latin city, is a great
global hot spot for everything from late-night dining and club-
bing to historical tourism. If hiking and breathing the fresh
mountain air are more your style, head to the Andes Mountains. The best part? All of this can be done on a shoestring of
a budget.

I don't care what anyone says, Chilean wine is right up there
with the best offerings from France and California. As someone

who doesn't drink, I didn't spend a lot of time in Chile's world-renowned wine country, but I stopped in a couple of wineries as we toured and I was really impressed. Anyone who's ever been to Napa knows wine tasting is a waiting game. You wait in line, along with 3,000 of your closest friends, for a tiny swish of mediocre vino from a plastic cup. In Chile there's none of that. Instead of feeling like a teeny speck in a giant herd of tasters, you will be welcomed like a family member. In fact, many vineyards offer great accommodations. The lotus-eaters and the beef-eaters (more on that later) can all find happiness in Chile.

And then there is the seafood. The cold Humboldt Current runs from the Antarctic Ocean along the Chilean coastline, creating a perfect environment for an abundant fishing industry. The quality and variety of the fish boggle the mind. One trip to Mercado Central's Seafood Hall in Santiago will confirm that Chileans are on top of their seafood game—gooseneck barnacles, abalone, pink-lipped angel clams, and loads of fresh fish. Exploring the Mercado Central is a singular experience. This is not one giant market, but several small, specialty markets located within the hustle and bustle of the capital city. Whether you're looking for fresh produce, fine cuts of beef, or the country's best horse meat (yes, *horse* meat), you'll be sure to find it here.

The market's seafood hall is a hub through which the majority of Chile's seafood passes. Giant squid, conger eel, oysters the size of my hand, piles of mussels—you name it, if it swims, you'll find it at Mercado Central. People always ask me about the strangest food I've ever encountered. I think piure takes the cake. Piure is a giant sea squirt about the size of a small piece of luggage, and until this market trip, I'd never even heard of such a thing. If you were to encounter one in the ocean, you'd certainly cruise by it a million times, convinced it's a rock, not food. The best way to eat piure is raw, and the fishmonger slinging the stuff let me try it right there at the market. He took a huge serrated knife—really a sword, it was that huge—and sliced the animal into two giant halves.

Hundreds of pulsing, red, jellyfish, oyster-esque entities live within small nooks and crannies inside the coarse, spongy, rocklike carapace. You simply scoop them out with your fingers, squirt lemon or lime juice on them to both season and coincidentally stun the creatures (which, by the way, are alive and suctioned to your fingers), and pop them into your mouth. These little guys taste like a fish's rear end dipped in iodine. Not surprisingly, after a few bites, I loved it.

As strange as piure is, the item that sticks out most in my mind for sheer hedonistic eating pleasure is picoroco. This tubelike barnacle looks more like a mini volcano than food. Throw these puppies on the grill and they essentially cook in their own shell. Ideally, you can place the shells directly on the coals underneath the grate. Once cooked, poke inside the barnacle and you'll find a white piece of meat that looks like a crab claw but tastes like lobster. You can eat this straight out of the shell, but often picoroco is found in soups. A bowl of cold, tomato gazpacho filled with pieces of steamed picoroco is one of the most refreshing dishes you'll find on a hot day. Word to the wise: Don't hover over the grill too much if you are roasting them fresh—these little treats often become so hot that they explode . . . with seawater, pieces of barnacle, and hot shell spewing all over the place. Dodging a geyser of boiling hot barnacle liquid isn't exactly the most comforting thing in the world, but it adds a sense of danger to the eating experience, which I like.

With access to such fresh and abundant ingredients, it's not surprising Santiago offers incredible dining. The influx of Mapuche Indian and European influences shapes Santiago's highly regarded restaurant scene. From fine dining to street food, this city's got it covered, and I can't recommend a destination as one of my all-time faves without talking about some of my best-loved restaurants. If you ever visit Santiago, please stop at Astrid Y Gaston, a Peruvian restaurant that originated in Lima but opened a branch in Santiago. It is considered one of the best, if not *the* best, restaurants in the city. It has the most amazing ambience paired with delicacies like tuna with spicy honey glaze and crab ravioli—really cool, quirky dishes with bold, fresh flavors. If molecular gastronomy is your thing, Puerto Fuy blew my mind. Each dish that arrives at your table is a work of art, leaving you wondering if you should look at it or eat it. And the lunch I had at Opera, often considered one of the top restaurants in the world, was simply elegant. Now, *there* is a kitchen with an extremely refined skill set.

While I love these world-renowned establishments, none of them really seemed to capture the true heart and soul of Chilean cuisine. Enter Picada Ana Maria, a humble little restaurant off Santiago's beaten path. It started out as a picada—Chile-speak for a restaurant that serves simple, inexpensive meals. But its popularity prompted the owners to break out the tablecloths and open a full-service restaurant. Run by Ana Maria Zuniga, this charming restaurant is located on the first floor of her home. A tiny sign hangs outside the building, telling patrons they must first ring a doorbell to be let in. It feels less like entering a restaurant and more like going to a friend's house for a dinner party.

Ana Maria won't disclose how long she's been cooking, but she's probably in her fifties, looks forty, and refuses to put her kitchen in the hands of anyone else. We ate eight or nine dishes there that were just spectacular. One in particular was the roasted partridge in a rosemary and honey sauce. While Ana serves some fantastic salads and meat dishes, she's earned a reputation for serving incredible seafood, specializing in abalone.

Abalone are giant sea snails that live in thick shells adhered to rocks, usually in cold waters. Harvesting this meal is not an agreeable task. You have to sink into icy water equipped with a heavy iron bar to pry the abalone from the rock. Interestingly, this mollusk doesn't naturally grow in Chile, yet their aquaculture there is rapidly developing as a top industry. Chile is currently the fifth-largest producer of cultured abalone in the world, with 304 tons harvested in 2006.

When it comes to food preparation, abalone is known for its stubbornness and tough texture. Much like octopus, it's a type of dish best eaten raw, or you'll have to cook the heck out of it. Anything in between is inedible. Some chefs will tenderize it first, beating the meat over and over to break the muscle down. You can easily get carried away using a mallet and cutting board to tenderize the abalone, but you risk losing product or damaging the flesh. Ana Maria has developed a unique method I had never encountered before. First, after placing five or six small fist-size pieces of abalone into a rubber tube, one of her prep cooks takes the ends as you'd hold a jump rope and smashes the tube on a cement sidewalk behind the kitchen. It's genius: The abalone doesn't go anywhere, because the centrifugal force keeps the animals in place. The amount of power delivered through the reverberation tenderizes the muscle in just a few smashes. Next, the abalone are cleaned, trimmed, washed, and steamed. I tasted them cold and poached with a homemade lemon mayonnaise. These were easily the most tender abalone I've ever tried—definitely worth the flight to Santiago all on its own.

I also sampled two versions of Ana Maria's pink razor clams. Until this trip, I'd seen them only in Japanese restaurants. Housed in an ovaloid, triangular shell with rounded edges, the clam is a beautiful pale pink color; one corner of the muscle is almost a fiery red, and the hue recedes into a gentle pink as the flesh goes deeper inside the apex of the shell. I ate them raw on the half shell with lemon, olive oil, and a bit of minced vegetable, as well as pan roasted with white wine, garlic, and parsley. A simple, light, and delicious combination.

It's almost impossible to find a bad meal in Chile—with ingredients that fresh, meals need little fooling around with. The country's ultimate seafood spot might be the town of Valparaiso. The actual city is a huge and industrial affair, outfitted with one of the largest port systems in the Southern Hemisphere. However, a short drive outside the city brings you to little fishing villages like Quintay, where you can watch boats coming into sleepy little coves carrying their seafood to local restaurants. Luckily, in Valparaiso, there are many young chefs who pride themselves on their commitment to local food. The best conger eel I ate the whole week came from a little restaurant there called Café Urriola. Six seats, one chef, huge props. I've said it before, and I will certainly say it again: If seafood is your thing, Chile has got to be your country.

I am nearly as wild about pork as I am seafood. To me, pork preparation is an art form. However, with something so widely consumed around the world, it's hard to say that one bite of pig is any better than another.

I've experienced some really special porky goodness on a global scale, and it seems there is no shortage of ways to prepare this delicious creature. In Cuba, I enjoyed a pig finished with palmiche, the little fruits of the royal palm tree. I've dined on suckling pigs roasted to perfection in a 300-year-old Madrid restaurant. I gorged myself on wild boar hunted down by Samoan tribesmen and buried with hot rocks covered with scraps of lamb fat for basting. The memory of whole roasted Kahlua pigs, cooked at a traditional Hawaiian luau underneath giant hot lava rocks, and pulpy pounded roots of coconut palms could never be wiped from my mind. These huge globs of vegetal matter dripped their sugary sap onto the heated rocks, which in turn gave the meat a sweet caramel flavor that has never been replicated in my book.

Pork barbecue occupies a whole different realm in the annals of swine artistry. So many cities are renowned for their special style of barbecue. The Memphis in May Barbecue Championship is the United States' pinnacle 'cue event, a time when the whole city becomes ground zero for the world's greatest barbecue talent. Kansas City may be considered the barbecue capital of the world, with biggies like Danny's Eat-It and Beat-It, Earl's Quick, Gates', Arthur Bryant's, and Jack's Stack, to name a few of my faves, all fighting for top honors in a city built on pork and beef BBQ.

However, not one of these incredible experiences will ever measure up to my personal favorite. It didn't come from Hawaii, Samoa, Vietnam, Spain, or any of the swine-centric hot spots around the globe. Surprisingly enough, it's the Puerto Ricans who make all other pork-worshiping cultures seem tame by comparison.

The Puerto Rican hillside village of Guavate serves as an epicenter of pork meals. Located an hour-and-a-half drive outside of San Juan on PR-184, known colloquially as the Pork Highway, Guavate is a great example of my theory that venturing out to the last stop on the subway is the best way to find the best foods, leaving the tourist traps in the dust and opening your mind to a more honest and authentic experience. Most of the time the reward is just a better meal, some smug satisfaction, and a better story when you get back home—at a minimum. In Guavate I expected a little neighborhood with a couple of restaurants. Instead, I discovered a Puerto Rican village that lives and breathes lechon asado, roasted whole pig. On a Sunday afternoon, you share the pilgrimage to this pork mecca with hundreds of Puerto Ricans and clued-in tourists alike, who dine on the area's specialty and dance away the afternoon and evening to live salsa music.

Guavate restaurateurs are evangelical when it comes to the pig. In no place was this more evident than at El Rancho Original. This lechoneria has spent generations perfecting the lechon asado process. They finish the pigs on an orange, nut, and fruit diet. Once the animals are slaughtered, they are placed on giant wood-fired and wood-assist rotisseries, then turned for hours until every single piece of the animal is perfectly cooked. Back in the day, the restaurant's reputation caused quite a stir throughout Puerto Rico and other Guavate restaurateurs cashed in, opening their own eateries along the same dusty little main street.

Today, about a dozen lechonerias line the street, serving food cafeteria-style. Grab a tray and select a cut: pork belly, pork ribs, pork shoulder, pork chops, cheeks, ears, tails, hocks, and cracklings. The quality of the meat is fantastic—sweet, succulent, sticky, and fatty. The availability of so many different parts of the pig was the most exciting aspect of the meal. Any pig part is fair game, and you can pick a little bit of everything if sample platters are to your liking. The chefs simply place pig quarters on wooden chopping blocks. All you have to do is point to the piece you want. If they're running low, no sweat, they'll just grab another hog from the back. They are cooking them nonstop in a hell-bent pig-heaven tribute to your waistline expansion. As fast as people can line up and fill their tray, the BBQers just keep cooking up and slicing pig. In fact, at Christmastime, some of the restaurants have been known to go through nearly seventy pigs in a single day, each weighing in at roughly 100 pounds. Of course, no Latin meal would be complete without fresh and plentiful sides. Beans, rice, cooked greens, yucca with garlic mojo, fried plantains—you name it, you get it alongside your pork.

Pick a spot under an open, breezy shelter created to protect diners from rain or the blazing sun, and plant yourself with your tray. Grab a napkin and dig in. On Saturdays and Sundays, salsa bands perform while people eat, dance, and chat the day away. As rich and filling as the lechon asado is, the dancing certainly helps burn it off. Take a few bites of pork shoulder, get up and dance three or four numbers, sit back down, splash a little more chili sauce onto your barbecued pig, take a few more bites, and repeat. Oddly, while there are dozens of lechonerias to choose from, everyone is at El Rancho. You would think the competition is fierce, but it's a one-horse town as far as I am concerned.

Unless you're eating a whole little baby pig suckling by yourself, you'll never have the opportunity to sample so many flavors on one plate. The rich and fatty belly is so much more toothsome than the leaner, luxury cuts like the chops. Compare that to the earthiness of the legs or to the way-too-rich-for-your-own-good cheeks. There's no doubt in my mind—if I had to eat pork in one place, it would be in the little hillside town of Guavate, Puerto Rico.

Beverages often provide a pleasant surprise. In Bolivia, I sampled peanut juice for the first time, something that I don't recommend to anybody. I've sipped aloe tonic in Otavalo, Ecuador, and went through a struggle of grand proportions to keep that down in my system. It's a nasty, bitter liquid filled with six ounces of jelly scraped from giant reeds of aloe root. I couldn't even get it down. At one point I had a sticky, goo-like strand that attached from the pit of my stomach into a glass that held the elixir. At that point, I almost lost it. I politely explained to the lovely aloe vendor that her drink must be an acquired taste, then quickly pawned it off on an elderly woman, who chugged the entire glass down in a matter of seconds. I don't know what fraternity taught her that skill, but this grandma earned major points in my book.

I love kvass, a drink they practically give away on the streets of St. Petersburg. Called baby beer by the locals, this near-nonalcoholic beer is made with rye bread, and everyone from kids to the eighty-year-old nanas drink it. The Russians have a very strange relationship with alcohol. Public drunkenness is not socially unacceptable; in fact, it seems to be encouraged, considering the number of times booze is brought to the table in bottles for all to enjoy. Kvass seems to be like booze with training wheels for the Russians.

I've had more types of chicha poured into a cup and thrown my way than I could ever begin to count. It seems every Latin American, South American, Caribbean, and many African countries make their own version. Chicha is essentially a puree of water and some type of root vegetable, usually cassava or yucca. The drink is mildly alcoholic because it sits and ferments, maybe one one-thousandth of a percent, and is extremely fortifying, supplying a lot of healthful benefits from a probiotic standpoint. From a psychological standpoint, I find a lot of these drinks challenging. I've seen families literally chew two or three pounds of root vegetables, spitting the wet, mashed, masticated by-product into a giant pot of water where it begins to slowly ferment. Families graciously offer you a glass of their homemade brew. At the end of a long, hot day, downing a glass of this stuff sounds like the last thing I want to do. However, no one ever said sharing food and experiencing culture is automatically easy, and with each brain-cramp-inducing gulp, I just chalk it up to a hard day at the office.

Despite some less-than-ideal beverage experiences, every once in a while I come across a drink that just flips my trigger. Usually, it's the simplest stuff. The coffee in Nicaragua or Ethiopia and Taiwan's tea are arguably the best in the world. I lost my mind over Ethiopia's mango smoothies—no ice cream, yogurt, or ice, just a puree of massive, juicy, fiber-free mangoes. Served chilled with a glass and a straw, this is a tremendous drinking pleasure. And I can't forget drinking fresh coconut water straight from the shell in the Philippines, which quenched my thirst like no other. Skyr shakes in Iceland, avocado shakes in Chile—you name it, every country has some killer quaffables.

However, when it comes to satisfying drinks, I'm a self-proclaimed soda pop junkie. As someone who doesn't drink alcohol anymore, what do I have left? So despite all these natural, one-of-a-kind experiences, I recall a bottled commercial soda pop beverage as being my all-time favorite. On the road, especially in hot climates, I down water like it's going out of style. There's always that *stay hydrated, stay hydrated* mantra replaying in my brain. At the end of my first day in Tanzania, I was just thirstier than all get-out and way over drinking more water. In the afternoon we settled in at a small café in Arusha, and a waiter asked me if I wanted a Stoney. I'd never heard of such a thing. He looked at me and asked, "You've never heard of a Stoney Tangawizi?"

With that, I demanded a Stoney immediately, if for no other

reason than it had the most fun name I've ever heard. This large, oversize brown bottle, which looked like the old-school 7-Up bottles, soon sat on the table in front of me. The curvy bottle stood fourteen inches high, the thick glass sanded down around the outer edges, worn from being racked and cleaned so many times and rebottled. And there on the label, in beautiful yellow enameled writing, it said "Stoney Tangawizi."

Most folks opt to sip straight from the bottle, often with a straw. I like to pour it in a glass over ice, or chug it straight. It's a perfect blend of ginger beer, ginger ale, and a very unfruity 7-Up, with a nutty, sweet aftertaste. It has almost a sarsaparilla or root beer quality in the finish. If you're really thirsty and you're powering down a whole Stoney, the four flavors play in your mouth like a quartette. I would kill for an ice-cold bottle of Stoney right now; it's definitely my favorite drink in the world. While I did find some Stoney in cans in South Africa, the version that hails from the Coca-Cola bottling plant in Tanzania does it the best. And just my luck, you can't find it anywhere else in the world.

The other bottled beverage that I am just nuts about is Cuba's Tu-Kola. The Cuban government isn't fond of most American products, although they do import a few. For the most part, Cubans are self-sustaining and derive a sense of honor and pride from producing almost everything on their own. Coke products aren't sold anywhere, save a handful of hotels, where they stock one or two cans in the minibars. Instead, the whole country drinks the state-owned beverage company's product, which is Tu-Kola. They make a lemon-lime version, they make a Tu-Kola Light, which is their diet cola, and they make a conventional Tu-Kola—it rocks.

I remember RC Cola with fondness. Slightly sweeter, less robust and acidic than its rival Coca-Cola, this soda was a hit on the East Coast during my childhood. RC Cola tried to compete with Pepsi and Coke but never really made it. I'm not big on conspiracy theories, but I think whoever created RC Cola was smuggled into Cuba to create Tu-Kola. Slightly more acidic and lemony than RC, this cola is made with natural cane sugar, which gives it a level of sweetness and a balance that you don't find in the domestic Coca-Cola. After spending the day in a hot '57 Oldsmobile exploring Havana, there is just something simple and rewarding about popping open a bottle of Fidel's finest cola.

I love pleasant surprises. Often they are the familiar food memories that come to me when I'm out of country rather than the shocking surprises or the anticipated foods. As much as I love Peking duck at Quan Jude in Beijing, I expected it to be good. When I was seventeen years old, my friend Toby and I spent much of the summer on the Cycladic island of Sifnos, in Greece. We lived with a family on the island, and almost every day we ate at the local pizza parlor. Keep in mind that the Greek and Italian varieties of pizza hail from completely different families. The pizza we found in Sifnos started with a cooked piece of round dough, brushed with crushed tomatoes, salty Greek goat's cheese, and oregano, and drizzled with olive oil as it left the oven. It's more like a seasoned focaccia than anything else. As a born-and-bred New Yorker, I'd like to think I'm an authority on great pizza, and I've thought about that delicious Sifnos pizza at least once a month for the last thirty years. One day I will get back there. Nothing would be a more pleasant surprise than discovering that more than three decades later, that Sifnos pizza joint is still putting out their simple, unexpected culinary gems.

Sweat, Tears, and Blood
Rituals Around the World

Taking part in ceremonies and rituals makes for magical adventures. Often people believe you must travel to the ends of the earth for these types of experiences, but I can tell you, there are some odd experiences to be had in the United States. Ask anybody who has experienced the crowning of Princess Kay of the Milky Way at the Minnesota State Fair in Minnesota—which is celebrated by carving a bust of her likeness out of a giant block of butter. Visit a New Age shaman in Sedona, Arizona, where experiencing a sacred Navajo sunrise ceremony conducted by a mystical healer will leave you feeling like you've just retuned from another planet.

My feeling is that diving into another culture face-first gives me the most bang for my buck. There is no better way to gain a unique perspective than to share a meal or participate in a native ceremony or ritual. It's these sometimes challenging and often humorous experiences that make up my favorite travel memories. Since it combines both food and formal socializing mechanism (ritual), the odd sauna-meets-barbecue restaurant experience just outside Seoul, Korea, is at the top of my list of crazy travel stories.

The Chamsutgama Restaurant sits in a suburb of Seoul and features some of the country's most traditional cuisines: barbecue. Pork belly is one of the "it" girls of the moment when it comes to ingredients in fancy American kitchens, but Koreans have been cooking up the stuff for ages. This cut works especially well for barbecue because of its high fat content. When cooked low and slow, it melts in your mouth. Chamsutgama serves some of the best examples of this classic meal, scorching the belly in a 2,000-degree kiln. The meat is then sliced, placed back on the grill, and slid into that oven for just a few seconds. The strips are cut with scissors and served to you tableside with platters of vegetables and loads of ban chan—cups of delicious pickled dishes that Koreans are famous for, especially as accompaniments to their barbecue. Patrons dine in an outdoor pavilion, where tables are outfitted with small grills in the center, perfect for crisping up little pieces of the pork belly.

Despite the fact that Chamsutgama serves some of the best barbecue in the country, the place is known better for premeal rituals than the food itself. You don't walk into Chamsutgama, grab a table, and start eating. First, you have to walk through a locker room and register for a sauna. While breaking a sweat before dining isn't required, the restaurant strongly encourages it. So instead of telling your hostess, "Zimmern, party of four," you grab a locker key and dress up in orange cotton pajamas that look like a cross between a tae kwon do dobok and a prison uniform, with big black stenciled letters on the back stating: DO NOT REMOVE FROM PREMISES—in Korean characters, of course. I learned what the letters translated to in English as I was walking out the door with my pj's clutched under my arm. Someday I will have to learn how to stop stealing orange pajamas from Korean barbecue restaurants.

Once you are dressed in your outfit, an orange napkin is placed on your head. Little ladies prowl the area just outside the men's locker room, being sure to correctly tie the napkin, twisting the edges, then tucking them in and under the headdress, giving you a handsome Princess Leah–style look. It might not be all that attractive, but it keeps the sweat out of your eyes. A long wooden walkway connects the locker rooms to fantastic twenty-foot-high domed edifices made of clay and brick. These kilns house giant bonfires that are connected to a number of similar domes through a pipe system. Saunas vary in temperature—from "damn, that's pretty hot" to "holy crap, I think my face is melting" hot. What can I say? There is a temperature for every taste when it comes to the Chamsutgama.

The experience of sweating to the point of exhaustion is uniquely Korean. Referred to as Han Jeung Mak, Koreans have implemented this practice for the past five centuries. It's meant to draw sickness out of the body, just like any other type of sweating ritual. However, I've never seen this ritual tied to a meal before. Profuse sweating before dinner isn't something I'd ever considered, but I liked it. I was exhausted and spent when I crawled out of my sauna, I drank a ton of water, and twenty minutes later, I was reregulated physically, and boy was I hungry. Best of all, I didn't have to change out of my pj's to go eat!

Of course, food rituals can be a lot more serious. One of the most beautiful and poignant ones that I've ever experienced was in Bolivia on the shores of Lake Titicaca. Regarded by the Incas as the birthplace of their civilization, Lake Titicaca is the highest navigable lake in the world. I headed to this sacred site to take part in something called an apthapi, local lingo for a traditional Andean potluck picnic.

We ventured to a farmer's home to help a family prepare their contribution to this community-wide picnic. Families sit on blankets knitted in the style of their region or their tribal division. Cholitas, or Bolivian women who wear traditional bowler hats, colorful skirts, and sashes, bring a different dish to share with the group. It's more or less their version of a Minnesota potluck, minus the green bean hot dish.

The meal took place at the farmhouse we visited. The home was very small, and our meal preparation spilled from the kitchen into the sleeping quarters. To get anywhere, you had to step over people prepping their dishes on the dirt floor. My favorite dish to prepare and eat was the quinoa dumplings. In recent years, this grain has garnered a lot of attention as a superfood in the United States, but I'd yet to see the traditional Bolivian preparation. Cholitas sit on the floor, grinding the quinoa grain on large stones. Eventually, they create dumplings by combining the ground grain with water. The thumb-size dumplings are rolled out by hand, then stamped with a thumbprint on the ends. Next, they are steamed in hand-woven wicker baskets placed over pots of boiling water. The sweet, nutty flavor reminded me of an earthy bran flake and served as the perfect accompaniment to the rest of the meal. I especially loved it with the homemade farmer's cheese and pan-broiled llama.

Of course, with that many cooks in the kitchen, there was no room to eat inside. We had perfect weather for our apthapi: a thirty-three-degree, icy rainstorm, complete with hail. But everyone pressed on. At this traditional meal, the food is eaten off the ground, literally spilled out of the pots onto woven blankets. I first tried Lake Titicaca trout at the apthapi, a freshwater fish that comes from an absolutely pristine body of water, making its meat sweet and pale white. We also had Ispis, a snack food of the area's indigenous people. Ispis are tiny fish, fried whole, salted, and served with all sorts of different goodies. I ate it with steamed root vegetables, dumplings made of ground quinoa, homemade cheese, broiled llama meat, and chunos—putrefied, rotten, steamed black potatoes. We dined on all these goodies al fresco, but I couldn't resist pulling some of the fish out of the frying pan in the cooking hut. Dee-lish.

I guess a word of explanation about chunos is probably in order. Here's a random piece of knowledge to throw into your *Jeopardy!* file—did you know the potato originated in the Andes? It's true, although we rarely see Bolivian potatoes in our produce sections. Bolivia's Alto Plano region, the high area above La Paz at the foothills of the Andes, is known for its perfect potato-growing climate. However, given its high altitude, most nights dip below freezing, even in the summer. When it's especially chilly, farmers will actually freeze-dry their potatoes. Eventually, these tubers are rehydrated in soups or through steaming, and the end result is fairly edible. Chunos, however, are a different ball of wax. Farmers spread out these potatoes on the hillsides that face the sun. At night, they freeze. During the day, they defrost. After nearly a week of this cycle, the potatoes rot and turn black. Trapped in their frozen, dried phase, they can last for as long as twenty-five years—and trust me, every single one I ate tasted like it. Just before I headed to the apthapi, I spent time with another farmer, who showed me part of the chuno-making process. Stomping on a pile of them with your feet was certainly the most fun. It's actually less of a stomp and more of a rolling technique used to slip the skins off the rotting potatoes. I did one batch myself, so somewhere in Bolivia in the next twenty-five years, someone will eat rotted potatoes that have seen the bottoms of my feet—just hope it isn't you.

Usually, having a hand in creating a dish builds up my excitement toward actually eating it. Not the case with chunos. After rolling up my pants and stomping potatoes in a field filled with snowy runoff, cow poop, and sheep shit, I was ecstatic to leave that farmer's house with just a piece of my dignity intact.

Anyhow, back to the apthapi. The meal concluded with a shaman burning a llama fetus and saying a couple of prayers. His homily was stirring, including his two cents about how Mother Nature treated them that year and a request for better weather in the next one. When the shaman wrapped up his speechifying, the sun came out and the rain stopped. Coincidence? I think not.

After the meal, the elders sit around eating fistfuls of cocoa leaves and dance to live music until the point of exhaustion after eating one of the most delicious meals you could possibly imagine. An Andean barbecue at Lake Titicaca, with an offering up to the Earth Goddess of a llama fetus, followed by a shamanistically influenced weather anomaly, was about as cool an experience as I've ever had.

This fetus-burning ritual is a special form of a traditional ceremony called a limpia, which is Spanish for cleansing or cleaning. This Lake Titicaca festival was both a limpia, in the sense that we were cleaning the farm of evil spirits, as well as an offering to Mother Earth. Bolivians live in an incredibly superstitious society, and limpia ceremonies are quite common. In fact, the majority of homes, new and old, have a burned llama fetus buried somewhere in their foundations to ward off evil. The indigenous Bolivian culture still believes in both black and white magic, so if you're looking to stock up on supplies for your next ritual, there is no better place to be than the Mercado De Las Brujas, the city's witch market. Need to cure an illness? A dried toucan beak will cure what ails you. Empty bank account? According to traditional folklore, placing a cigarette in a dead frog's mouth will increase your chances of rolling in the dough. Whether you're looking for llama fetuses, gold and silver foil, waxed candles, or incense and coca leaves, you'll surely find the vendor hawking it at this market.

For our next limpia ceremony, our fixer had a llama fetus hookup, so there was no need to buy one. We arranged to meet a group of guys who performed traditional limpias in an area called El Alto. Currently, the most rapidly growing neighborhood in South America, El Alto, is essentially a giant slum sitting on the hilltop high above La Paz. I adore Bolivia, but like many South American countries, the gap between the wealthy and impoverished there is overwhelming. Hundreds of thousands of European Bolivians live in the city's relative splendor, while a million indigenous Bolivians, the first people of that country, live in a horrifically depressing slum. Very few houses have electricity or running water, leaving most people in an absolutely depressed condition. There are no movie theaters, no museums or arts institutions, nothing but row after row of threadbare housing, nickel shops for foodstuffs and bars. When it comes to class division, tensions run hot. The physical separation of the poor, indigenous Bolivians from the rest of the city is downright shocking. I can imagine these people looking down, day after day, at the jewel-like old city of La Paz and eventually snapping. I picture them equipped, Frankenstein mob scene–style, with torches and wooden clubs, running down there one day and kicking all of the Valley Dwellers out.

That next limpia ceremony took place at the top of an abandoned four-story building. We discovered that this place was chosen not because of some spiritual significance but because there were no other options. It seemed counterintuitive to get cleansed in such a scary environment, filled with a horde of dicey characters wandering around smoking cigarettes and swilling cheap hooch, but I wasn't about to piss off any gods, spirits, or thugs by leaving. Our hosts built a fire on a table on the floor of this abandoned place, burned their llama fetus, drank a half case of beer each, and ate fistfuls of coca leaf, which more or less has the same effects as snorting cocaine when chewed with the right resinous sap to make the drug's active ingredients water-soluble and processable by the body. Delirious, drunk, and wired simultaneously while managing a fire set to a rotting piece of llama flesh—you can imagine that the scenario just oozed with spirituality. In their drunken stupor, our host mumbled prayers in my direction, most likely because I'd purchased the beer and coca leaf for them, then exited as fast as they could, leaving me and my crew to navigate back to the hotel on our own. It might be the only limpia ceremony in which, when it was all said and done, I felt exponentially dirtier.

The cleansing ceremony that has stuck with me the most took place in the highlands of the Andes. Otavalo, Ecuador, is home to the largest outdoor market in the continent. It's really more of a huge merchandise mart or county fair than anything else. After a day of shooting, a "friend" suggested I see a yachac, Ecuador's traditional witch doctor. Given that the Ecuadorians take their spiritual healing rather seriously—all shamans must be certified by a medical board—I figured this was the place to get the most bang for my buck.

Boy, did I ever. Armed with only a five-dollar bill and a live guinea pig, I met my doctor in his closet-size office. Despite the fact that the outside temperature was a chilly forty-five degrees, this windowless room was stifling hot. Daniel, my yachac, sat opposite me at a desk loaded with trinkets, chain-smoking unfiltered cigarettes as he poked and prodded me. He graciously took my money, fired off a few questions, and then asked me to take off my clothes. In retrospect, I'm unsure why I answered so quickly, but next thing you know, I'm stripped down to my boxers in a strange man's office.

He wrapped my head in a towel and proceeded to blow huge puffs of cigarette smoke on me for about twenty minutes, which didn't exactly feel like the pinnacle of health and cleanliness. Next, he took the guinea pig and, holding its front legs in one hand and rear legs in the other, he beat my body mercilessly until the guinea pig died. He tossed the guinea pig into the pile of cigarette butts in the corner.

You'd think we were about to wrap this whole ritual up, but apparently, we were just beginning. Daniel then spat up all over me. I'm not talking saliva. This was phlegm cleared from the depths of his black lungs and throat. Then he took a few swigs of homemade Everclear and sprayed it from his mouth at my eyes, ears, chest, back . . . everywhere. He followed up by rubbing three hard-boiled eggs, which are said to represent the earth, all over me from the bottoms of my feet to the top of my head.

I completely lost it when he began beating me with poisonous leaves that burned my skin and caused me to break out in hives. If you've seen that episode of my old show *Bizarre Foods*, I'm seriously on the verge of a mental breakdown. I'm done with this healing shit. I'm pulling the plug. Daniel somehow convinced me to soldier on, reassuring me via interpreter that the hives would dissipate after an hour or so. He then filled his mouth with more grain alcohol, held a lighter up to his lips, and blew fire all over me. Our session concluded with Daniel setting fire to the branches, cigarette butts, the bottle of booze, and the dead guinea pig. The evil spirits trapped in my body were passed along to these inanimate objects. The flames then destroyed that bad juju, leaving me free and clear of negative spirits.

At the time, I considered this hour one of the most abusive, torturous experiences I'd had in the past twenty years. However, the next twelve months were probably the best of my life. My wife and I adopted our amazing son, Noah. *Bizarre Foods,* which I'd been shopping around for years, became a smash hit on the Travel Channel. I need to send Daniel a big *gracias* for that.

While all these experiences hold a special place in my heart, they pale in comparison to the Ball Snipping Spring Testicle Festival that I attended in Temuco, Chile. I've mentioned before that Chile is one of my favorite destinations. It's the California of South America, but it's often overlooked. The country is never more than 220 miles wide, so you can go from ocean to highlands to Andes Mountains in less than three hours. The coastline extends 2,700 miles, stretching through a variety of temperate zones and climates. It has the world's driest desert; it has lush expanses of forests and highlands, glaciers, fjords, active volcanoes; it has big cities and rural villages.

Chileans are predominantly mestizos, the result of marriages between the country's indigenous people, most notably the Mapuche Indians, and those of European descent, predominantly the Spanish. The country does house some isolated pockets of pure-blooded Mapuche; however, these populations are quickly disappearing.

If you want to brush against the Mapuche culture, head to Temuco, a city of about 200,000 people. The city is the cultural center of the Mapuche Indians, who make up almost 15 percent of the population. It's in southern Chile and it sits in the heart of the Lake District. It is stunningly beautiful—bold, with growth forests, rolling hillsides, and snowcapped volcanic peaks on the horizon. Most of the activity there is agricultural: oats, wheat, barley, timber, and lots of hard fruits, like apples and pears.

The other appealing thing about the city is that it's the heart and soul of the country's beef industry. While Argentina and Brazil get the hubbub about their phenomenal beef-eating culture, I was really impressed with all the beef that I ate in Chile. I visited parilladas, the traditional Chilean steakhouses, where they bring a grill to your table piled high with every different cut of the cow imaginable—from udders and cheeks to filet. You rotate the meat around the grill's hot spots, charring it on the outside. If you're a wine drinker, nothing will quite wash this carnivore's haven down like a fantastic glass of Chilean red wine.

It seemed that every time I sat down for a steak dinner, the beef originated in the Lake District. This got the dusty sprockets turning in my head. The Lake District: home of the Mapuche Indians *and* the best beef in the country. Why not kill two birds with one stone? My friend's friend Mauricio agreed to arrange a visit with his friends, Moises Velasco and Cristina Doty, owners of Fondo Collanco, a 10,000-acre cattle ranch a few hours outside of Temuco. Fortunately, my trip coincided with a springtime ritual every culinary fanatic should witness at least once in their life.

In the ranching world, spring castration is an extremely important process. When the nuts go, they take the bull's aggression along with it. Additionally, the steer will yield a tastier, more tender meat. Fondo Collanco, lying in the shadow of the Llama Volcano, castrates between twenty and thirty bulls a day, leaving one of every twenty-five bulls still intact for the beef-replication market, which I'm sure is a lot of fun for those chosen few.

As we pulled into the ranch, I felt an air of excitement. The quality of the red meat in Chile far exceeds what I'm accustomed to seeing in the States, and I eagerly awaited watching the meat go from farm to table. The cattle pens teemed with activity and commotion, which intrigued me from a distance.

The castration process is not taken lightly. Moises always has an experienced veterinarian perform the procedure, along with twenty of his Mapuche ranch hands helping out. These workers come from families who have worked on the Velasco farm for generations; their fathers worked there for Moises' father before them, and so on. Little about the actual castration freaked me out. The whole process is sterile and safe, and not messy in the least. Everybody cares for the animals. They have to—it's the lifeblood of their personal economy. The farmhands herd the bulls into a corral. They take one at a time, tie their feet together, and gently tip them over. The veterinarian places a giant hedging shear around the testicles, snips them off, and immediately sprays the wound with an industrial-strength vaccine/disinfectant to prevent disease and infection. This snipping noise, which sounds a lot like snapping a tree branch, was the only thing that caused me to cross my legs in phantom pain. The criadillas, or testicles, are tossed into one bucket; the capullo, or scrotal sac, is placed on a separate tray where it will be skinned or peeled off the hide. These were big balls, much larger than ones I've seen commercially available in Europe or the States.

I couldn't believe how quickly these bulls recovered. The process took all of five minutes, and after the light medicinal spray, they hopped up as if nothing had happened. Later, Moises, Cristina, Mauricio, and I took a brief horse ride to explore the ranch. The newly minted steers lay in the grassy pastures, relaxing and resting very naturally, gathering back their strength again. I'm happy to report that after two or three hours, all of them were up and prancing around, and they were all free-ranging and drinking and eating, which is a sign of good health. I was in way more pain after having my wisdom teeth pulled. Castration is the ultimate outpatient surgery.

Then we retired to the barn, where everyone, from the Velasco family to the ranch hands, gathered for a celebratory feast. Different pieces of cooking equipment were set up all around the barn.

In an odd turn of events, the vet skinned the scrotal sacs, rinsed them off, and began to sauté the "meat" with onions and chilies over a wood-burning fire. He continually added pieces of the capullo, tomatoes, and copious amounts of white wine and covered the pot. The pot was moved to a less intense spot on the fire, where it simmered three hours.

When it comes to eating balls, I'm a seasoned veteran. Deer penis, rocky mountain oysters, even tuna sperm—I've tried almost everything in that buffet line. But up until this trip to Chile, I'd never eaten an animal's scrotum. Everyone was excited for me to try it, which made me excited to do it as well. Long ago, I learned that a large population of satisfied customers can't be wrong.

The testicles were peeled and cut into slices. The farmers took an old plowshare, a long, sloping, triangular piece of metal about the size of a kitchen table, and suspended it over a fire in the barn. Once this troughlike grill was ready, the vet-turned-chef added a generous pour of olive oil, twenty garlic cloves, and a handful of dried red chilies. Once the garlic and chilies were sufficiently scorched, he added hundreds of sliced testicles, which quickly seared on the plowshare. The testicles, now browned on both sides, were moved to a lower heat, where they cooked for a few more minutes. Seasoned with salt and pepper and placed on homemade rolls, we ate traditional Pil-Pil-style sandwiches as we waited for the capullo to finish.

The capullo had a few more hours to go, and I was confused about what we would do and eat in the meantime. I watched as a few women brought avocado, tomato, and onion salads and other side dishes to the table, along with popping open a few bottles of red and white. Something was going down, to which I was not privy. The Mapuche take the spiritual side of the spring castration week seriously, to ensure that they respectfully usher in the new growing season. No start of spring is complete without a traditional niache ceremony.

The ceremony commenced with two beautiful, fat spring lambs being led into the barn and hoisted up by their hind legs. The Machupe farmhands placed a sling around their necks, bent them to the side, and slit their throats by driving a knife out from behind their trachea. The blood flowed quickly, pooling into two pans where it was immediately seasoned with dried chili, salt, pepper, fresh cilantro, lemon juice, and minced onion. Within two minutes, the lemon juice, salt, and herbs caused the blood to congeal to the consistency of firm pudding.

The European Chileans watched from the sidelines, but you know me—I dove right in. We passed around the pans, taking a spoonful of this red blood pudding. They love that mineraly, tinny flavor of blood. Flavorwise, it reminds me of biting into a copper roof on a hot summer's day. We've all nicked a finger and shoved it into our mouth. Whether it's blood from a paper cut or blood from a spring lamb, it more or less all tastes the same, except this time it had the added bonus of lemon juice, cilantro, and the chili pepper, which sort of negated the richness.

The problem with consuming blood dishes, especially fresh blood dishes, is the effect on your body temperature. Eating whale blubber causes the body to behave similarly. While I toured the western village of Bethel, Alaska, I ate a lot of blubber with the locals. Within minutes, your body temperature rises two or three degrees. Even in a cold room, you're compelled to start stripping down; the sweaters and outer layers disappear pretty damn fast. The same thing happened at this niache ceremony. Interestingly, the Mapuche swear that niache works as a powerful aphrodisiac, although I did not find that to be the case.

After bleeding out, the lambs were immediately skinned, quartered, trimmed, and placed on rotisseries, which were turned by hand over a wood-burning fire. After about an hour and a half the lamb was ready, which coincided perfectly with the capullo finishing—the scrotum-sac stew was coming off the stove on the wood-burning oven—and we sat down to eat.

The spread teemed with fabulous comfort food. We passed platters of fresh avocado, tomato and onion salads, roasted potatoes, and loaves of crusty bread. The fire-roasted lamb and the bowls of capullo were incredible. If you like bone marrow, capullo is right up your alley. Rich and fatty, the inch-size pieces of scrotum literally melt in your mouth. They look like big square yellow cubes of Turkish Delight. They have a translucent quality to them but remain opaque in the center. The wine reduction around them added the perfect amount of acid. Initially, I thought the amount of wine added to the dish was overkill, but simmering for three hours on an open fire caused the excess to evaporate, leaving an intense, winey concentrated sauce.

The capullo is so filling, you can't eat large amounts of it. We toasted our newfound friends and paused for a traditional Mapuche blessing from the elders. The spring harvest holds a lot of significance for these indigenous people. It celebrates the planting of the crops, the castration of the animals, the sacrificing of the spring lamb, and the blessing for a successful farming season. More than a celebration of the agricultural year to come, it's one of the last remaining rituals that the Mapuche regularly celebrate.

What is fantastic and quite unusual is how the Mapuche share this ceremony with mestizos. The Mapuche are some of the kindest and friendliest people in the world, and they feel that the circumstances of their life are just as they should be. There is no hostility. They don't feel like second-class citizens, nor are they treated that way. To this day, they serve as a powerful group in the Lake District. The meal felt like a family celebrating together, despite their differences. For me, that's what sharing food and culture is all about.

Ritual Royalty

The Kalahari Trance Dance of the Bushmen

Rituals usually fall into some fairly predictable categories. There is the created modern ritual, like toasting business partners at a celebratory dinner after closing a big deal. It's the kind of custom rooted in the ancient world. It's been done for thousands of years, but every generation shapes it, creating a new cultural footprint.

Then we find marketed experiences. These are not re-creations; rather, they are combinations of traditional cultural experiences married with modern need and efficiency, like the Korean Barbecue and Sauna Restaurant. There is nothing ginned-up about it; the experience is authentic. Independently, Koreans adore the sauna and barbecue. It's just the goofy marriage of the restaurant and the sauna that makes this experience distinctly modern. The Santeria ceremony I experienced in Cuba is much of the same, melding the modern with elements of traditional African religious practices. While these customs have filtered through generations, deep-seated rituals that accompanied African slaves to Cuba 500 years ago have stuck around in a big way. The Santeria practice of loving worship is still relevant and practical in the twenty-first century. It's a combination platter of old and new.

I've experienced a lot of indigenous, first people's shamanistic practices, most notably in South America. In Ecuador, Bolivia, and Chile, I participated in—or was the subject of—cleansing rituals performed by shamans, healers, or yachac, that lovely Ecuadorian medicine man. These experiences took place in small villages or in towns. Despite the stark contrast to the way you and I probably live, it's next to impossible to travel to many of these places. It's quite strange to visit someone practicing ancient traditions with your feet planted in the here and now of the twenty-first century.

But the most amazing traditional first people's ritual that I ever participated in was the Trance Dance ceremony I sat in on in Botswana.

A few weeks ago, I flew into Maun, Botswana, a pocket-size airport: one gate serviced by a couple of flights a day from Gabarone, Francis Town, and Johannesburg. Botswana Airways runs two or three forty-eight-seat propeller planes in and out of there. Despite the almost antique airfield qualities to the infrastructure there, it's one of the busiest small-plane hubs in the entire Southern Hemisphere. And here's why: If you want to experience safari life, and it's extremely popular these days for the people who can afford it, you fly into Maun. Safari and expedition companies set up offices or headquarters in this tiny town. Safari-bound tourists deplane and stroll into this little terminal in the middle of the Kalahari Desert. Every plane is met by a dozen or more guides from different camps spread out all across the Kalahari in southern Africa. They basically pick up their charges at the gate and take them away on the adventure of a lifetime. Maun is ground zero for bush plane activity. A handful of adventurers pile their brood into customized Range Rovers and Land Cruisers modified to handle eight to a dozen passengers in open seating, like a small double-decker bus in London, and drive to their camps. The vast majority of travelers board two- and four-seater planes that carry them to the camps by bush pilots, making Maun quite the bustling hub. Planes buzz in and out of there like mosquitoes.

Our bush pilots took us on a ninety-minute ride past the Okavango Delta, the world's largest inland delta. We circled over the water, which teemed with wildlife. Huge numbers of elephants and giraffes grazed in and along the delta as the sun set. This southward-tilting water system irrigates the desert as best it can until eventually it gets sucked down by the sand. The Okavango in Botswana is probably one of the last great animal paradises left on our planet that doesn't feel like a zoo. Leopards, crocodiles, hippos, lions, giraffes, elephants, elands, and kudus flock there in tremendous numbers. As we bypassed the delta, I felt a pang in my heart. My assignment was to meet up with the legendary Bushmen of the Kalahari, but missing this once-in-a-lifetime animal experience bummed me out. I soon discovered skipping the delta wasn't going to be such a big deal.

We landed on a grass airfield a couple hundred miles to the west in the small town of Xai Xai, a teeny cluster of homes built around one of the most famous watering holes in the world. Between flights, pilots spend most of their time filling in gopher holes on the landing strip for the next incoming flight, which are often weeks apart. Occasionally, geology companies that are reconnoitering the area for mineral exploration will visit, but it's thrilling to land on this grassy airfield while the entire town of 100 people turns out to greet you.

The entire history of human civilization might not exist if it wasn't for Xai Xai's watering hole. The Bushmen of the Kalahari are one of the oldest civilizations in the world, with ancestry reaching back 35,000 years. The watering hole served as the hub of their activity, allowing them to survive there for all those years. Since the best theory of human growth tells us that all men are thought to have walked out of the Kalahari many years back, then we're all potentially descendants of the Bushmen, which makes this watering hole one of the most culturally, historically, anthropologically, and sociologically important sites in the entire world. It's not like Chichén Itzá in Mexico or the pyramids in Egypt. There are no lines, no tourists—it's just a muddy hole in the ground, surrounded by a rickety old fence made up of twigs and sticks so the children and animals don't fall in. You can gaze down into the somewhat fetid water, now used mostly by animals. It's arguably the most important physical site of any kind in the world, and there's no signage and very few even know it. I got goose bumps just standing nearby.

On this trip my goal was simple. I wanted to discover what life would be like living with a San tribe known as the Ju/'hoansi. It's important to mention that the Bushmen of the Kalahari speak dialects within the Khoisan language family based on five or six clicking and whistling sounds. There is no written version of the language. But I can tell you that Ju/'hoansi (pronounced *junt-wazee)* is the Western rendering of the tribe's name. The Ju/'hoansi tribe spend the majority of their time still living the way their ancestors did 30,000 years ago. No stores, no restaurants, nothing but a cluster of homes that some Bushmen take refuge in during the cold season when the desert is the least hospitable, when foraging and hunting are at their nadir.

Gaining access to the Ju/'hoansi was an extremely difficult feat. After months of lobbying with the Botswana government, we finally were permitted to meet these folks. It's no wonder the government takes their custodial role of this tribe seriously. They've often been abused. Outsiders have often depicted them—through movies, photographs, articles— with a message that's not necessarily on target socially. One company even tried to use some of the women in an adult film. However, the government also understands that documenting this tribe's history is of utmost importance. But once we were finally allowed in, we needed an entrée to these people. There was not a better choice than Ralph Bousfield.

Ralph's great-grandfather relocated to Botswana from England in the middle part of the nineteenth century. He was an adventurer and explorer, and every generation of Ralph's family followed in his footsteps, each with a seemingly more exotic story than the last. Ralph's father, Jack Bousfield, is one of the most legendary hunters and safari specialists to have ever worked in southern Africa. To this day, he holds the Guinness world record for crocodile kills. During the fifties, Jack supplied the entire European couture handbag, luggage, and clothing houses with the most valuable crocodile skins.

In the fifties, crocodiles were in such great numbers that few questioned the harvesting of these animals. These reptiles from the delta, with their silk-soft bellies, were almost blemish-free and in stunning condition. Jack Bousfield killed more than 53,000 crocodiles in his lifetime. The number could have been much greater, but he was also way ahead of his time as a conservationist. His ecological sensitivity and desire to preserve the biodiversity of Botswana prompted him to change courses. In the sixties, he abandoned crocodile hunting altogether and set up a safari camp, with the intention of preserving the Botswana he loved, and today that camp is known as Jack's, established in the Makgadikgadi Salt Pan.

Ralph took over the family business that Jack established in the sixties, called it Uncharted Africa, and developed it into a business. The company now leads tours to four locales: Jack's Camp, San Camp, Kalahari Camp, and Planet Baobab, the last named after the legendarily fantastic-looking trees that grow in the desert. Jack's Camp and the San Camp are the only permanent camps to offer a chance to explore and understand the Kalahari. There are buildings at Planet Baobab and Kalahari Camp, but that's a pretty generous term to throw around. Uncharted Africa also specializes in roving, tented safari camps, giving Ralph the ability to lead safari enthusiasts straight to the action. He knows the best stuff to see in Africa and how to find it, making this the trip of a lifetime for anyone fortunate enough to run with an Uncharted Africa tour, rated as the best safari camp on the continent.

With the number of tourists drawn to Africa to see the animals, game-preserve management is a very important aspect of tourism departments. It's a necessary component to preserving the land itself and all the animals that live there, and not just the Big Five—

lions, elephants, leopards, rhinos, and buffalo—but the baboons, go-away birds, honey birds, insects, scorpions, hedgehogs, porcupines, and pigmy antelopes as well. It's just as important to be mindful of the animals that you don't see as it is the Big Five. Tourism supplies so much money here, and has actually benefited the preservation of these animals in such big ways, that tourism management has taken on new problems for Africa. How do you manage the expectations of the experience, and what should the biggest take-away be? What message matters most?

Ralph's ability to find the Big Five is not what makes his company special. Instead, it's his ties to the indigenous people of the Kalahari that separates him from the pack. Ralph Bousfield—and his father to a great degree before him—were the first to pick up on the idea of having archaeologists, zoologists, psychologists, and biologists accompany guests into the most remote regions of Botswana to experience the people and the culture firsthand. Along the way, you see some animals. Conventional visitors get entire days in the delta to observe wildlife if they like, but Ralph realized early on that it's not about taking pictures of hippos. Africa is about people. And I agree.

A little side note. I've visited many different game preserves in Africa. One day I saw a six-day-old giraffe being taught how to feed by its parents, and I was told by my guides—this was about three hours outside of Johannesburg—that this was the first giraffe born in that preserve in more than fifty years. The safari guides and the hunting guides who work that preserve were ecstatic; they were still beaming days later from what that birth represented to them. They had managed the land so well and they had restored so much of that part of Africa to the way it was 1,000 years ago, or 500 years ago or even 200 years ago, that some real firsts were being achieved. So much of the hunting in the nineteenth and early part of the twentieth centuries decimated some animal populations almost to the point of extinction, and it's the land management that has been responsible for returning some of those populations in great numbers. So believe me, I know animal management works in Africa.

But in Botswana, I spent no time looking for animals; I spent all of my time with the Ju/'hoansi, a small group of twenty-four or twenty-five Bushmen living in grass and twig huts in the middle of the desert, which is not sand so much as fine red sand-dust populated with impenetrable thorny scrub. The people who live here lead a very simple life. They rise at the crack of dawn to hunt and gather, but the tribe spends only about 30 percent of their time hunting and gathering. The remainder of their day revolves around enjoying life and taking part in daily rituals such as beading, creating crude equipment, cooking, and other chores—all while telling stories and laughing. It's quite a modern existence in terms of their social structure. I am so grateful for Uncharted Africa and Ralph Bousfield, one of the most charismatic and intelligent and committed individuals I've ever met, for understanding that the Bushmen's extraordinary story must be seen and their stories told so that their culture can be preserved. It's the story of a people who are disappearing faster than the animals. The Kalahari Desert is a vast, harsh place. Life there is hard. It's amazing to think that the Ju/'hoansi still hunt, eat, worship, and celebrate in exactly the same way their ancestors did tens of thousands of years ago.

After spending a week with them, it really makes me question our definition of "modern." These people seem to have skill sets that we've long since forgotten and now attribute to supermen. The Ju/'hoansi can outrun antelope. They literally run them down for hours on end until the antelope are exhausted and collapse before being killed. Astonishingly, they can hunt and run all day in the hot desert without drinking liquid. I was told not to travel with less than 120 ounces of water on my person, carried on my back, just to make sure I stayed properly hydrated. Men, especially in the older generation, are slight, about five and a half feet tall, weighing no more than 100 to 110 pounds. I met men in their seventies and eighties who worked and hunted all day long and never seemed to tire. The younger generation is growing a little taller because of the healthy protein additions to their diet (they have access to beef, and trading routes for food have improved), and the government has stepped in to help feed and house tribe members when needed. The Botswanan government has also now mandated education for tribe children, which is another reason that villages like Xai Xai have sprung up and become a little more developed, complete with schools.

The tribe elders are jacks-of-all-trades. They serve as shamans and healers, and can set bones, perform operations, cure illness, and act as pharmacist, internist, and surgeon. They track animals at night or during the day. They can tell you within fifteen minutes or as much as a week ago what kind of animal has passed, what it was eating, and whether it's a male or female. Anthropologists tested their ancient tracking skills, placing collars on animals and charting their course, every move, over two or three days. They then asked the Ju/'hoansi to follow their trail as well. When comparing timelines, the Bushmen were spot-on, even more accurate than a GPS system in some cases.

The daily life of these people is extremely simple. They hunt in the morning. They can go all day if they are on an animal, but in the heat of the day they like to come back to camp and take a nap. That is, unless the excitement is brought back to camp with them. One afternoon during my stay, a Black Mamba snake slithered into camp. Known as Africa's deadliest snake, this creature is colloquially called the "five-step snake." If it bites you, you can take five steps, then fall down dead. I was two days away from a hospital, and frankly, seeing this territorial man-hunting beast in the camp was petrifying.

While I scrambled, figuring out if I needed to run for my life, the tribespeople, barefoot and in loincloths, took off after the snake—all of them, women and children included. Their goal was simple: kill the snake no matter what, or how long it took. They eventually cornered it up in a tree and brought it down with a small slingshot fired by Xao's son. He hit it from forty or fifty feet away with his slingshot, facing into the sun, landing three out of four shots right on the snake's head. The head of a Black Mamba, despite this one being seven feet long, is only about the size of a golf ball. It was an amazing display of marksmanship.

As I walked into the camp every morning, women cracked marula and mongongo nuts, two of the most important foods to the tribe. I saw them eat mostly nuts for breakfast, maybe some small pieces of leftover meat. Xao, the eldest shaman, the de facto leader of the tribe (technically, there are no leaders, but no one made any big decisions without consulting Xao), took small wooden oval discs made from a very special tree and threw them on the ground. This act of throwing the bones told the tribe which direction the ancestors wanted them to hunt on that particular morning.

I joined them on a few hunts, tracking and hunting animals, laying snares for birds, foraging for roots both for medicine and for consumption. They dig false potatoes and desert turnips out of the ground, placing these bulbous root systems into their antelope-skin clothing, keeping different foods in the folds of their capes. Some men carry small kits with a bow, poison-dipped arrows, and fire-starting sticks. Their one vice is smoking, and every couple of hours, they pause to smoke a crude local tobacco from their pipes. They snack on berries, nuts, and fruits, and when possible, they eat hoodia, a plant some Westerners use to suppress their appetite and lose weight.

Before the hunt's end, if you're lucky, they will have killed a small antelope, porcupine, or bird captured in their snares and bring it back to camp. This type of hunting takes a lot of patience. One day, we followed a honey bird, which led the tribe to a tree buzzing with activity. You can imagine how rare and delicious sweet honey is to the Bushmen, so when they see or hear honey birds, everybody joins in the hunt, sometimes walking or running for miles. Of course, the honey hives are populated by deadly African bees, but the tribe lights a fire, burns certain types of woods, and blows the smoke into the tree, essentially anesthetizing the bees. Then, using sharp-edged instruments, they hack away at the trees and retrieve gobs of honey. It's regarded as a precious resource.

The Ju/'hoansi, a small tribe, avoid hunting big animals like elephants, despite their technical ability to accomplish the task, because it would be selfish to do so. They only take from their habitat as much as is needed, and an elephant would be overkill, literally. In fact, the tribesmen sometimes won't even bother to track larger antelope if they are a small family. If a small eland or kudo crossed our path, great. That's dinner. However, they'd let the larger ones carry on. More interesting to them, and certainly more interesting to me, was the rare wild giant African porcupine, which we ended up successfully hunting one evening. After the thick, rock-solid, and needle-sharp quills are removed, the meat is set aside. Trust me, it takes a lot of muscle to pull out a porcupine's bristles, especially these giant spikes that were about a foot long. All that elbow grease was worth it—this was one of the most exotic meals I've ever eaten in my life. Under the quills you'll find a carpet of fat and muscle, which is grilled first, along with the heart and liver. If you like pork belly, that fatty, meaty, melt-in-your-mouth sort of food that's become the darling of chefs these days, you'd love porcupine skin—trust me. No part of the animal goes to waste. They make soup out of the bones. They even roast the feet, throwing them into a fire, gnawing away after the fur has singed off. It's quite a treat.

The porcupine was the gift that kept on giving. It served as a big lunch and then the soup for an early dinner that night around four or five o'clock. There was much celebrating, the mood was very festive, and that night the shamans decided they were going to do a Trance Dance and asked if we wanted to join in.

For thousands of years, shamans in the Ju/'hoansi tribe have believed their ancestors are all around them. In fact, if a tribe member becomes sick, breaks a bone, even loses a digging stick, they believe that their ancestors are behind it. If something bad befalls you, it's really your ancestors trying to pull you over to their side of the spirit world. The shamans serve as a way to communicate with the dead. The tribe trusts the shamans to bring them back onto the living side of the equation by communicating with the ancestors. It boils down to ancestors missing their loved ones—they create sickness and misfortune within the living tribe, hoping they will finally pass over and be reunited. Ancestors aren't always out to harm the living. According to the Ju/'hoansi, ancestors know and see valuable things that hold great value for the tribe, which is why tribes roll the bones prior to a hunt. Every important activity begins with the simple rolling of the bones. And tonight the bones said, *Let's dance.*

Contrary to what you're probably thinking, the ceremony has nothing to do with drugs. The process begins in the early evening, with the women (and only the women) singing and dancing for hours. Over time, the rhythmic singing and dancing become more and more of a steady call and less of a fun entertainment. As the sun begins to set, the song and dance propel the men to begin dancing as well. For hours, they chant and dance, stamping their feet around a fire. Once the sun sets, and the moon begins to rise and the stars come out, the fire is built bigger. This is a group dead set against wasting resources, so normally they will build the fire only for as much light or warmth as they need. During the Trance Dance, they built it up higher than any other night I'd ever seen. It wasn't a bonfire; rather, it looked more like a large fireplace in a northeastern hunting lodge. Slowly but surely, with the women encouraging the men with certain songs, rhythmic clapping, and sometimes physical assistance in order to help the elder shamans dance in a certain way around the fire, the men eventually fall into serious trance. For this particular ceremony, the three principal healers—Xaxe, Bom, and Xao—along with two older male healers and several of the other young members enduring the mental and physical anguish of training to be a shaman, all went into trance at the same time. Ralph explained he had experienced a trance as large as this, in terms of numbers of men "in trance," on only a handful of occasions in his forty-odd years of being with these people.

Anthropologists have documented that these ceremonies, and particularly this tribe, exhibit three levels of trance. Level one is achieved when the men reach a meditative state, where they access the spirit world and begin to experience visions.

Once they hit level two, the shamans and healers have out-of-body experiences and astrally project themselves into other places. It's been documented that when these men come out of the trances, they can describe things that have taken place many miles away, like a sick person in another camp or physical anomalies. Xao is one of the few men who anthropologists claim can actually achieve a level-three trance, whereby someone transforms him- or herself into an animal and experiences that life for a while.

I sat near the fire, feeling the heartbeat of the desert. The men shuffled around me as the women continued to chant. Occasionally, a woman danced with the men to get them going a little more. As the men fell into trance they would get very hot. They'd scream and shout, experiencing real physical torture, with their muscles just about to burst from their chest. You could visibly watch their bodies tense up until they could no longer take it, throwing themselves into the sand to cool off. When they became too cold, they propelled themselves into the fire, often leaping over it. I witnessed Kao pick a golf-ball-size, white-hot coal out of the fire with his hand, roll it in his palms, and eat it to warm himself, with absolutely no ill effects once he came out of the trance the following day.

I saw these men crying and screaming. I saw blood and phlegm dripping from their noses—the same physical manifestation depicted in 20,000-year-old cave paintings discovered in other parts of Botswana. This tradition has continued on, essentially unchanged, for tens of thousands of years.

The healers lay hands on individual tribe members. They check a person's physical health in almost the same way a Western doctor performs a rudimentary exploration, listening to your heart and lungs or looking into your eyes and ears. However, by laying their hands on you, the Ju/'hoansi project a part of themselves into you and explore your spiritual health as well.

Several of the men laid hands on me. I felt an incredible energy sitting around the fire that night—not necessarily electric, but you could feel the intense amount of energy coming from within them. It felt like they were connecting with something very powerful inside you. And they would lay hands on you for anywhere from thirty seconds to a minute and a half, sing over you, then hug you and move on to the next person. They'd focus on four or five people, then move on to twenty minutes of dancing, chanting, spasming, eating coals, and diving into the sand. At times, they were so exhausted that they collapsed for as long as a half hour, almost passing out. The women attended to them, cradling the men's heads in their laps and holding their hands until they were able to stand again, still in trance, and continue to walk around the fire.

This trance work was incredibly intense to experience as a spectator—and I can't even imagine what actually entering the meditative state would be like. For the Bushmen, this ritual is necessary. The men are said to remember everything that happens during their trance experience. If they have an out-of-body experience, they can document it. If they discover someone is sick, they will relay the message, ensuring proper care is taken.

Toward what I believed to be the end of the evening, Xaxe, a great hunter, healer, and shaman, laid hands on me. Things got very different very quickly. By that point, I'd had hands laid on me two or three times by each of five men. Each time, I tried to quiet my head, breathe, and shut my eyes so that any access they wanted to have would be as unfettered as possible. However, the last time Xaxe laid his hands on me, it felt as if a defibrillator got strapped on my chest and back. They grip you sideways, one hand palm inward on your chest, fingers spread, and one on your back. I felt the energy, his energy, surge through my body. He had his hands on me for about twenty-five or thirty seconds, but it felt like he had only touched me for a split second. Time stood still. I literally had a short out-of-body experience. I could see him touching me from just above my body, almost like I was floating six feet off the ground, watching myself. All of a sudden, I was back in my body observing an image of him thumbing through the book that contained all the pictures and moments in my life. I saw images of my childhood I hadn't remembered in years, pictures of my mother and me walking on a beach and shelling, very strong images. At the time, both during his touch and immediately afterward, I described it as him flipping through the pages of my life. I felt he was curious and wanted to see what I was all about. In true Bushmen form, the only way to achieve that was to plumb my mind for images and stories, because our ability to communicate with each other was limited. (We did have translators with us, so holding conversation was possible but remained fairly simple.)

Later the next morning, I spoke with Xaxe about the trance dance. He told me he wanted access to me in a way that was not possible through a translator. The other men attempted to do the same thing, but it took hours until I achieved a meditative state myself that allowed me to feel them rummaging around in my head. Apparently, they had been going into my head and my body the entire night, but I just hadn't been able to feel it.

Xaxe's curiosity was such a caring, loving gesture. It didn't feel intrusive or strange at all. He wasn't treating me like a museum piece; he really wanted to understand me better. When he detached from me, I felt like someone was unplugging a lamp from a wall socket. As he let go of me and continued to dance around the fire, I spontaneously burst into uncontrollable tears. Not because of the beauty or his curiosity—simply put, I had been stripped to my emotional core, completely stunned by what I had just witnessed so up close and personal.

At that point, it was about midnight and I'd been at the fire for more than four hours. Exhausted, I headed back to my tent and collapsed into bed. The sounds of them singing and dancing in the desert lulled me to sleep. They have rattles on their feet that make this incredibly rhythmic noise, and the clapping, the singing, the rattling, the stomping combine to make a perfect sound to sleep to. When I woke at six in the morning, as the sun started to break the dawn, they were still at it. Still dancing, still singing, still clapping, one or two of them still in trance. Eventually, the ceremony ended, and nearly everyone slept through most of the day and evening.

The next afternoon, I sat down with Xaxe, Bom, and Xao and some of the other shamans to get their take on the Trance Dance. At the end of our conversation, Xaxe took my hand in his and, through our translator, told me to always respect people as I went out into the world. He explained that the most important thing a man can do is respect all people and love all people. He said it simply and very matter-of-factly. These are words that I've heard my whole life, but sitting there in the desert around the fire, they touched me in a unique way. I realized that I have a very unique set of circumstances working in my life, one that allows me to tell stories in written form and on television, and when I'm interviewed on radio or in a blog. I have an audience to which I can communicate the stories that make up the fabric of our global life. I have the power to bring down boundaries that separate people so we can legitimately spend more time talking and celebrating the things we have in common, rather than arguing about our differences. Xaxe saw that and wanted me to be sure to focus on the right message.

I changed in many ways on that trip, and I saw many things that illustrate our overdeveloped disposable cultural zeitgeist. The

Ju/'hoansi make sizable ropes out of a small plant that looks like an aloe plant. First, they squeeze all the water out of it, which is used for ear medicine. Then they scrape away the pulp and extract the fibers out of the plant. Men and women alike work on creating this rope; they grease their hands, wet them with saliva, then braid the fibers by rolling them in the palms of their hands and knitting them together. They make both short and long ropes; three or four two-foot-long sections were rolled one day, and we were able to make little nooses out of them and affix them to the end of trip snares, which they set up using small sticks that we found on site in an area where large birds would come to feed on little nuts and berries in the ground. The bird takes the berry, trips the snare, the noose comes up, and the bird is caught.

As we returned from a hunt one day, we discovered a hawk bill dead in one of the snares, its neck snapped. We weren't allowed to eat it that night, because if you eat the bird at night, the bird's spirit will go out into the rest of the world and tell the other birds to avoid the snares. The Ju/'hoansi have lots of myths about this kind of thing. But when we found the bird in the snare, I immediately took out my bush knife and unfolded it. I was trying to be helpful and offered to cut the rope. The Ju/'hoansi looked at me as though I were crazy, asking the translator why I would cut the rope. They need the rope. They made that rope. No need to cut it—just loosen the rope and remove it from the bird and reuse it.

I realized at that point, like a sledgehammer being taken to my head, how wastefully and thoughtlessly I proceed through my life as a Westerner. I don't live a life based on necessity and need. When it comes to taking twine out of the kitchen drawer to perform a task, I don't think twice about tossing the used twine into the garbage. Unknot and fold the string away—that's what crazy old people do, right? Don't save little balls of string. You need new string. I'm the product of the modern American consumer culture of the twentieth and twenty-first centuries. We're the most wasteful society on earth, but we have the ability and curiosity to see things in the world and learn from them. That's what is special about these types of experiences: taking away the moments that touch and change you forever. I am no longer a rope-tossing fool.

It took a visit to a place 7,000 miles away from my home to be reminded—by somebody else's grandfather—that life is meant to be based on love and respect for other people, not love and respect for self. Love and respect for self will come only by loving and respecting other people in the world around you, which makes the Ju/'hoansi the most highly developed people on the planet. Love and respect is in all their hearts. There's not a selfish bone in them. They have no personal possessions. The extended family, group, or tribe owns everything. These people are some of the last truly pure sprits on earth. Meeting and spending time with them is more important than spending time in the back of a safari vehicle in some national park, looking at elephants.

SMALL
WORLD,
BIG ISSUE

A Santero drips the blood from a freshly
slaughtered rooster over Andrew's head during
a traditional Santerian initiation ritual in Cuba.

¡Viva Cuba!

The recent thaw in Cuban-American relations coincided with my recent trip there last spring. Travel can be transformative. One person, from one country, representing their own blend of culture and experience, meets another citizen of the world on their home turf. This is what makes what I do for a living such a powerful force for growth and change in the world. People often see me as the bug-eating guy, but I have only eaten bugs a handful of times in a few memorable minutes in hundreds of hours sprinkled across my television career. I see myself as creating a powerful voice for globalism and international understanding, for the idea that by sharing food we experience another culture in unique, personal ways, by breaking bread with real people, in truly local haunts, eating honest and authentic cuisine. You'll never get the full picture clinging close to a hotel lobby. By focusing on our commonalities like our mutual love of food, we can really share life with people we just met in lands far away. We forget our differences, and the matters of our daily life that can only lead to conflict and misunderstanding. Cross the first barrier, share a meal, and the next conversation can safely be had. Trust me on this. I spent a week in Chile last year. It wasn't until I shared a meal in a Chilean home that I finally got the real story about the struggles of dissidents, changes in national identity, and personal experience with both. Try learning that by shoving a microphone in someone's face. It has happened for me in China, Vietnam, France, and Italy, even Tennessee. It was here that a young woman confided her personal story in me. We sat quietly in a corner and I listened, eating possum neck and dunking my corn bread in pot liquor from the greens. Just a Jew from New York and a mountain girl from rural Appalachia trusting each other because we were sharing a meal.

Look what happened when the Berlin Wall fell, or in 1971 when the U.S. State Department lifted the ban on travel to China, leading up to the presidential visit there in '73 that birthed "the week that changed the world." A lot happened over dinner and dumplings, I can assure you. Mutual distrust with Russia and China, Vietnam, and other formerly closed worlds replaced by an advancing understanding and ongoing free exchange of ideas. Opportunity feeds relationships. I am of the mind that if it can happen with those countries it can happen now with Cuba, a country ninety miles from our back door. And I believe that cultural and political osmosis begins with a meal. I went to Cuba with an open mind and an open heart. I spent time in Havana, lounged at the Nacional, stayed in Frank Sinatra's old room, prowled the music clubs, danced to the salsa beat, visited with world-famous artists, and strolled the storied ancient cobblestone streets of Vieja Habana. I saw for myself the beauty, inside and out, of this amazing country, and I believe more than ever that restrictions and barriers do nothing but foment misunderstanding and make life tougher on citizens of both our countries.

We are all richer for a free-flowing exchange of ideas, and the people of Cuba feel the same way. I asked. We have a rare opportunity here to see a country on our doorstep redevelop in many ways, and the stagnating isolation of the last fifty years has been our loss. Canadians and Europeans, South Americans and Africans all travel safely to Cuba every day. They are the richer for it. We are the losers here, and I can proudly say we have a lot to offer Cuba. I ache to see walls removed, not created. I believe travel is a game changer for remaking our world in a more positive way, and I can safely tell you that Cuba is a once-in-a-lifetime travel experience.

The country isn't diluted or polluted by the corrosive aspects of culture that prevent our seeing what a people are really like or how they live. In some cases, Cuba is a paradise-prison. Ninety-nine percent of Cubans can't get on a boat (even to go fishing), beef is considered contraband, and markets are sparsely stocked despite many resources.

However, the country is changing at breakneck speed, and the sooner you see it for yourself the better. Once the Palm Curtain rises, the country is changed forever, for good and for bad. The doors to Cuba will open soon, and trust me, once they do, it will transform at a rapid rate. Look what happened in Eastern Europe. Estonia, for example, carried on in a style more like the Bronze Age than the Modern Age for hundreds of years. The moment the borders opened up, they experienced a Western technology boom, bypassed hundreds of years of development, and eased into the twenty-first century overnight. In Estonia, you can pay for a bus, a movie, or a parking meter with your cell phone. Estonia entered the modern era at warp speed.

It certainly would not surprise me to see a similar change in Cuba. I'm sure they'll devalue one of their two currencies—the Cuban peso, which is the official currency used by the citizenry, and the Cuban convertible peso, or CUC, which is typically used by tourists and was created to take foreign currency out of circulation—and the rush will be on. Take one nighttime stroll in Havana, one of the most glamorous cities in the world, and you'll quickly discover the intoxicating sights, smells, and sounds of this sexy, caliente-hot environment. The old Russian buildings serving as state-run hotels in some of the most beautiful parts of the country will be demolished; most are empty anyhow, but they will finally be nudged out of the market by grand five-star resorts. The Four Seasons in Trinidad, Cuba, is not far from becoming a reality. Giant tourism companies offering too-good-to-be-true packages, cruise ships overtaking the harbors. Katy, bar the door! This place is going to be crowded in a hurry. My advice? Get down there while you can, because when the Palm Curtain does rise (or is it proper to say it will fall?), it'll only be a few years before you are looking at Nassau, Jamaica, theme parks, or, maybe even worse, the Dominican, a country where barbed wire surrounds the great resorts to keep the "locals" and the guests from intermingling, unless you count the towel attendant at your cabana. Talk about a place that's ripe for a revolution.

I flew from Minnesota to Toronto, then on to Havana's José Martí Airport, armed only with some elemental credentials for the Cuban government. The issue for Americans is in returning and in finding external travel help in booking reservations. Domestic travel businesses won't even talk to you about Cuba. American travel to Cuba isn't illegal per se, but the U.S. government prohibits Americans from spending money there. Our production company made the necessary arrangements working through a British company doing business in Cuba. I was nervous, even jittery, leaving Toronto. I've never been harassed or felt like I was in danger from any official representative; I figured the worst that could happen is having to spend the night in the airport and head right back home the next morning. But things went smoothly going in. I landed, breezed through immigration, and met our fixers, who took me to get my official credentials at the Cuban Press Association's office in Havana. I continued on to our hotel, the Parc Central, located on the edge of the historic old city. Our stay coincided with the International Conference of Non-Aligned Nations, with every crackpot, two-bit dictator, and his delegates flooding the hotel. This made for great people-watching—if observing awkward security shakedowns and marveling at the audacity of snotty teenaged diplobrats is your idea of a fun time. The events of the conference made for more traffic, crowded eateries and cultural events, and increased security at every hotel in town. It also meant getting bumped from my room at the Nacional, where I had been booked for months. No matter, the PC was a great hotel, and ironically, the rooms were a lot nicer. New hotel, foreign owner/partners means nicer everything. Even with international heads of state around, the Cubans can't quite get it together enough to serve anything other than tinned imported ham on the breakfast buffet line at the Nacional, where I did manage to stay my last two days in country.

The Nacional is one of the great hotels in the world from a historical and cultural standpoint. This was the place to see and be seen in the decades leading up to La Revolución. In its current condition, I felt I was visiting an ailing legend on its deathbed. Think Gloria Swanson in *Sunset Boulevard*. The food is terrible, the service bottomed out, the grounds unkempt. The cleanliness factor appeared to have reached an all-time low. Despite the hotel's condition, I found my stay thrilling in the extreme. Sipping a virgin mojito in the same spot as Churchill, taking in the view of the ocean beyond the Malecón, was simply surreal. I stood on the same space occupied by every legendary gangster, international jet-setter, president, and king who lived in the first half of the twentieth century. I even slept in the Frank Sinatra and Ava Gardner honeymoon suite. Not the luxurious accommodations I'd expected: dingy, oddly small, located on the second floor with an average view, and offering no amenities at all. I'm no dilettante, but this room didn't strike me as the way Frank would roll; I did sleep in the bed he schtupped the lovely Ms. Gardner in, and that was enough for me. The Nacional is rich with stories and history— everything from the visible shell marks on the outer walls of the hotel from the 1933 Sergeants' Coup, to the incredible smoking lounges where kings and princes sat enjoying a late-night cigar and a glass of aged rum, makes the hotel as romantic and classic a spot as you'll ever find. The famous Parisian Nightclub, though not as big and swanky as the Tropicana, remains one of the greatest locations to see a show in Cuba.

Cuba teems with fabulous nightlife. Discovering phenomenal food proved more difficult. The majority of restaurants are state-run, and these restaurants are trash. Restaurateurs must purchase their food from the state, must adhere to the portion control administered by the state, use only the recipes mandated by the state. The servers, many of whom have never even eaten in a restaurant before, come from state-run service schools and are expected to give tourists Western-style service. With a few exceptions, which I will get to later, avoid government-run restaurants like the plague.

Instead, try eating at one of the many paladares—or privately owned, family-run restaurants—in town. This type of eatery, fairly new to Cuba, emerged on the food scene in the nineties when Castro relaxed tourism requirements. The resulting curiosity boom led to a huge demand in eateries. The government remains very involved in the business. Paladares are one of the only Cuban businesses that pay a hefty tax to the government, essentially profit sharing, and they must adhere to a strict code of conduct. For instance, a paladar cannot have more than twelve seats and must serve rustic, Cuban food. I did discover that rules are often bent, wildly and fantastically bent, but if caught, owners can face serious jail time.

My first Cuban food adventure took place at La Guarida, an old mansion where the Spanish film *Strawberry and Chocolate* was made. This faded, crumbling, 200-year-old building with marble balustrades and classical statuary was once a large, single-family home. Currently, it houses over a hundred people, some who live in squalor, sharing teeny rooms way in the back of the building. I crept all over the old palazzo and saw some shocking, sordid things, most having to do with deplorable living conditions. But many other Cubans live in beautiful rooms up front, in what I found out was a crazy sort of first-come, first-served basis. If Cubans want to move (they can), they have to trade spaces with someone else. Good if you live in a nice spot already, bad if you don't. But on the building's third floor, you'll find one of the country's best paladares.

Since La Guarida is privately owned, paying huge license fees and "taxes," you can eat like a king. The Cuban chef Enrique Nuñez del Valle was tight-lipped about how he'd managed to check out food around the world, but it was clear that he had had some serious training; nothing rustic here. We ate a sautéed, grilled piece of tuna skewered on sugarcane over a lobster salad that was just stunningly plated, with a real eye for modern plating style. We ate an eggplant and goat's cheese timbale (they called it a tart), layered with paper-thin slices of roasted vegetables. Their eggplant terrine was as good as anything I've ever had in Europe or San Francisco; the octopus salad at La Guarida rivals that of any seafood restaurant in Spain or California. And clearly they are cooking for Europeans, using local ingredients for a discerning crowd: European-style food, European-style decor with crazy little antiques everywhere, piled high like you would imagine Auntie Mame's house would look. The pictures on their hallway wall featured every icon you could imagine, everyone from Benicio del Toro to Rob Schneider to Steven Spielberg. It's like the Cuban Carnegie Deli.

On the way home, I swung by La Floridita—best known as Ernest Hemingway's favorite haunt, as well as the place that put the daiquiri on the map. This bar is as faded as everything in Cuba, despite the fact that it's one of the most visited spots in the country. Tourists are compelled to down at least one drink at La Floridita, myself included. As I drank my juice, I took in my surroundings. Here is a 100-year-old room in dire need of a renovation. The vinyl-upholstered banquettes are ripped and falling apart, the velvet curtains faded and dusty, void of their original luxury. You'd think the government would be interested in maintaining this legendary destination, but that's not how Cuba works. The country has been working with the same goods for fifty years. Occasionally, they get an infusion of product from a particular country—but remember that for decades the Russians ran this place, and free trade (if you can call it that) has been going on here for only about fifteen years. Oddly enough, we ran into some Canadians one night who freaked out because the school buses from their hometown were rolling through the city, the signs calling out stops in the city of Montreal still in the front windows. For fifty years, the Cubans have existed on secondhand goods from all over the world, but not from us. And they still make it work.

The next day, we took a carriage ride around Old Havana, a UNESCO World Heritage site. Now, here's a model for renovation and reclamation projects in any ancient town in any country in the world. The ancient Governor's Residence and all the old, private homes have been meticulously restored. The Plaza De Catedral, dating back to the eighteenth century, and the Plaza D'Armas, constructed in the sixteenth century, are two of the most stunning public squares in the world. This is a wonderful spot for tourists to check out—rich in history, architecturally stunning. You can still buy used books, pillaged from the houses fifty years ago when the Fidelistas came through. You can buy first-edition books on the street, often in Spanish, sometimes in English, for pennies on the dollar. Smoke a great hand-rolled cigar, sip a fresh OJ, and check out some of the only stores in Havana that sell real merchandise. Walking through the old town is a lot of fun, and since they do not allow cars in the area, I did it by carriage ride.

I am a sports nut and insisted we check out a local boxing gymnasium. Cuba's sporting life is immense, mainly because few activities here are anything more than homespun distractions. Life is simple and slow, so everyone dances, plays instruments, is religious about playing one or several sports. With only a couple local radio and television stations that repeat the same propaganda and stale telenovelas, Cubans swap plopping on a couch and eating Doritos for painting, or whatever they are inclined to do. And of course, they play sports. I've never seen such incredible talent exhibited in any culture I have ever spent time in. During my stay, I saw nearly 100 pickup baseball games. These were just little kids mostly, between eleven and fourteen years of age, and I guarantee that most of them could make any college team in the States. That's how good these kids are. I saw them using secondhand equipment and hand-me-downs; I even saw kids playing with homemade cardboard and masking-tape gloves. I saw kids boxing at the gym (open air, by the way, with no changing rooms) in street shoes and work clothes. Some kids donned forty-year-old baseball cleats in the ring, the metal weathered down to the rims. Cubans typically do well internationally in sports not only because of natural athleticism, but also because they work so hard at it and are graced with a lifestyle that allows them to train extensively at whatever they find interesting. It was awe-inspiring.

Next, we headed to El Morro, the picturesque fortress built to guard the entrance to Havana Bay in 1598. El Morro Cabaña was added to the site in 1763, when the Spanish took back occupation of Cuba from the British in exchange for Florida, at the time a smart move for Spain. In the eighteenth century, Cuba's GDP was six times that of Spain. Havana was home to more ill-gotten pirate booty than almost anywhere else on the globe. It was the global capital for the sugar and seafaring trading industries. Spice farms, citrus groves, and mining opportunities made Cuba an international powerhouse. By the way, you can also see a display of missiles at Morro Cabaña, some newer than others, still aimed toward the States. You can walk among scud missiles and check out the wing from the infamous U-2 spy plane that went down in the 1960s there.

I wanted more insight into how life functions in this complicated country, so I met up with my friend Toby Brocklehurst over lunch. Toby is a British expat who has called Cuba one of his homes for many years. He lives in an old apartment on the edge of Miramar, overlooking the western end of the Malecón. He'd invited us over for chicken salad, which I thought was rather thoughtful of him—who doesn't love a good chicken salad? You can imagine my surprise when I showed up and discovered a lobster feast instead. Toby procured thirty lobsters, steamed them, and had his housekeeper pull the meat from the shell. His neighbors joined us for lunch, which also featured huge platters of fresh, sliced sun-ripened tomatoes, baskets of warm bread, and bowls of homemade mayonnaise seasoned with curry. This might sound like a special-occasion lunch to most Americans—I can't remember the last time I had lobster for lunch. However, despite its cheap cost here, it's actually illegal to eat lobster in Cuba. But Toby knows some people who know some people, and trading food and favors in Havana is practically the local sport. It's never printed on a menu, save a few restaurants frequented by foreigners and okayed by the state. At La Guarida, my favorite paladar, they acquired it from the black market. When I asked the manager about the lobster on my plate, I received only a blank stare and some ugly silence in return. Kids on the Malecón dive for lobsters when the weather is suitable, and everywhere you go you see them being eaten. But no one will talk about it. I asked again at Toby's house for lunch about this crazy setup, and I was quickly convinced to drop the subject after our Cuban friends shot me some very strange looks.

I've discovered the more strict a nation's governing body, the more vibrant its art scene. Cuba is not an exception to the rule. Havana Rakatan is a dance group that melds Afro-Cuban rhythms, country-inspired campesino story lines, and contemporary Latin dance styles. This is a group that's mastered the rumba, cha-cha, and salsa, and performs with a live band who accompany them as they rehearse and tour all over Europe and Australia. These dances stem from Africa—specifically, from slaves brought to Cuba to work on sugarcane farms. With them came the food, dance, religion, and music that influence the entire Caribbean culture and birthed not only the great Cubano dance styles but the amazing music of Cuba as well. Heard of Son? This is where it was born, and the Buena Vista Social Club is just the tip of the iceberg, my friends.

I admit that my dance skills need a little work, and what better place to get a refresher than Cuba. Nelda Guerra, one of the most famous choreographers in all of Cuba and the "creative force" of this dance company, offered me a private lesson. You can't imagine how grateful I was for her help, because as the trip progressed, I found a lot of use for those moves. The lessons were awkward. I was on stage in an old run-down (go figure) theater in Miramar, surrounded by a group of world-class dancers, all of whom I had been watching for almost two hours, mesmerized as they rehearsed for their upcoming world tour. The artistry and athleticism of these dancers was impressive, so when Nelda took my hand and pulled me on stage I almost peed myself. I'm old, fat, out of shape, and extremely clumsy. But Nelda had me shimmying away. In no time she even allowed me to lead, which was less embarrassing than her leading—trust me on this. Nelda swayed around me, pulling me into her hips to music provided by Turquino, one of the most famous and accomplished bands in the country. I was swept away by it all, which is good when it comes to dancing, so I'm told.

One of the most famous Cuban artists in the world is a gentleman named Fuster. Yes, he is like Cher or Bono—one name. We met up with him at his home, which he built and designed himself. The exterior is covered with millions of little ceramic tiles, each one hand fired and glazed. This design motif extends throughout his neighborhood, where he's spent the last seventeen years transforming his surroundings into a wild, outrageous, and bawdy pop art display. Fuster is also realpolitik communism in action, in the best sense of the word. He travels the globe, selling paintings and art installations for small fortunes, and disburses the money in his neighborhood so that everyone can enjoy a better life. He is a Cuban of Privilege, or COP, and COPs are a part of the local hierarchy here. They are popular if they give back, and almost all do. The reality on the street is that there are gorgeous mansions with palatial grounds in Cuba, and some privileged few get to live in them, mostly politicians and the like. Fuster lives in a beautiful, loft-style home that reminds me of the funky places in Venice Beach. Everyone in his neighborhood owns an air conditioner. The streets are clean. He puts people to work building new houses and working on his art projects. He does it for the love of his country and the love of his people. Seeing the results of these selfless acts is extraordinary.

Transportation is one of the most culture-shocking experiences for an American in Cuba. There are only eight cars per thousand citizens in Cuba, and therefore, hitchhiking is most people's transport of choice. Much like bus stops, hitchhiking stations line Cuba's empty three-lane highways. Picking up hitchhikers is a national obligation. Even if you're in a private taxi, chances are your cabdriver will stop and give someone a ride as long as they are going your way and a seat is empty. There is nothing scary or dangerous about it. It's just the way Cuba moves her people. Communism in action, one hand helping the other in a very practical sense.

Cars are probably the most valued luxury item in Cuba. First of all, it's difficult to get your hands on one. Before the revolution in 1959, roughly 150,000 cars existed in Cuba. Since the United States' embargo, American auto giants have been prohibited from selling cars to the country—and it's estimated that only 60,000 pre-1960 cars roam Cuba's streets. Without the ability to trade with the States, it's nearly impossible to find auto parts on the island, and engines are cobbled together. Like a Frankenstein automobile creation, cars are patched up with Russian, Czech, German, Japanese, and Swedish parts. Open up the hoods of some of these cars and you wouldn't even recognize them. It's almost as if lawn mower engines are powering some these vehicles. Last year, modern Chinese flexi-buses hit Cuba for the first time, replacing some of the oldest and most dilapidated camels on the city streets. The Havana Police finally have a few new cars, courtesy of Škoda, and they were able to retire some of the thirty-year-old Ladas they had run into the ground. We drove all around the town one day in a 1952 Oldsmobile, touring Miramar, the Malecón, and the other drivable parts of the city, eventually meeting up with Enrique, a mechanic who's essentially Cuba's most famous car surgeon. He fixes motorcycles, cars—really anything with an engine. This man is a mechanical genius who will go as far as engineering and machining his own parts when he can't find the right one. I peered under the hood of a few of his current patients and was stunned by the mess of unconventional materials he implements. The man has resorted to using old surgical tubing for some of the hoses in his Willy's Jeepsters.

Housing is almost as strange as the transportation. I visited the home of Damian Ruiz, one of the most famous painters in Cuba. He, his wife Pamela, and their son Bastian live in a crumbling, 300-year-old palazzo in Miramar. This house must have been something in its day, but now it looks almost condemnable. Honestly, I couldn't believe they lived there. But when we stepped inside, I was dumbfounded by this gorgeously restored Spanish villa, complete with an incredible inner courtyard, giant rooms, twenty-five-foot-high ceilings, and floor-to-ceiling French doors. It's very common to rehab only a home's interior, keeping the outside in shambles to remain inconspicuous. And when it comes to buying or selling property, forget it. Remember that houses are exchanged. Like a house? Approach the current owners about trading. The Ruiz family lives here because the former owners couldn't afford to fix it up. When Pamela approached them about a trade, they jumped at it.

I really enjoyed my time with the Ruiz family that morning. I missed my son and it was fun to hang out with Bastian, who watches my show with his friends on pirated satellite cable television, and we decided to take them to lunch. They suggested El Ajibre, yet another state-run restaurant. At this point in the trip, I'd lost my patience for state-run places. However, I was pleasantly surprised with El Ajibre. The restaurant opened about eighty years ago, and since its inception, they've specialized in one item: roast chicken. It comes with five or six different side dishes, rice and beans, plantains . . . the usual suspects. But the miracle of El Ajibre is their lemony pan sauce drizzled on these golden rotisseried beauties. I asked one of our Cuban fixers how this restaurant is able to maintain its quality compared to the other state-run, crap-tastic restaurants. Apparently, El Ajibre ranked highly with the upper classes in the old days but was snatched away from the family who ran it during the 1959 revolution. People were so outraged, post-revolution, over the decrease in quality that the government struck up a side deal with the original owners, which is how things work in a benevolent dictatorship. El Ajibre is the exception to the rule. It's a state-run restaurant with extremely high-quality product. I guess everyone needs a good must-go-to place for roast chicken.

That night, we drove to Vinales, another UNESCO World Heritage site. This place is breathtakingly gorgeous, like Vietnam's Ha Long Bay without the water. Giant granite pillars rise up from a flat valley high above the central Cuban hillside. This area, with its ideal volcanic soil, perfect growing climate, and local population—everything is done by hand—makes Vinales ground zero for what is regarded as the world's best tobacco.

Tobacco holds a special place in Cuban history. Historically, it was used as medicine, food, for social rites and religious ceremonies, and as offerings or gifts. People believe the crop has miraculous powers, which is an interesting viewpoint as seen from the States, where tobacco use is chastised. However, it seems even smoking's biggest opponents find merit in handcrafted Cuban cigars. They truly are of unparalleled quality, and considering the skill that goes into creating these stogies, it's easy to understand why they reign supreme. Cuba still implements traditional technique when it comes to agricultural production. Farmers work with oxen and homemade tills fashioned on anvils and attached to wooden frames. It's a completely different way of life. I spent a day picking tobacco, racking it in the field on cured split timber, then helped lay it into the aging house, where it would dry for up to a year. After that, the tobacco is fermented or cured—what the locals call The Fever, because during this process the leaves are usually spritzed with liquid (often rum) and covered with special tarps for several days. If you lay your hands on the pile during this process, it is actually a few degrees warmer than the rest of the barn due to the bacteriological process. After the curing, and some more aging if need be, the leaves are trimmed of large stems and the tobacco shipped to the famous Havana factories, where the stuff is graded, smaller veins and stems are removed, and leaves are classified according to color, texture, and leaf type. I had the privilege of enjoying a smoke in the Cifuentes family's renowned Partagás factory, in the VIP lounge no less, with Ganselmo, who works as the head catador, or quality-control expert. This man is responsible for the consistency and quality found in the world's greatest cigars—from Cohiba to Partagás, he creates them all. He typically tests between three and five cigars a day. It works a lot like wine tasting—he smokes only a small portion of each cigar before rating each one, drinking only unsweetened black tea to cleanse his palate between tests. I witnessed the whole cigar-making process, from stem to stern, even the rolling, which is an incredible experience. Cuban cigar rollers, called torcedores, spend nearly two and a half years perfecting their skills. Achieving master roller status may take upward of twenty years. An experienced torcedor will roll anywhere from 60 to 150 nearly identical cigars a day. I never in my wildest dreams thought I would ever get there to see it actually happen in front of my eyes. The aged Partagás Series 4 Ganselmo selected from his private humidor of rare, vintage smokes was amazing, but the rustic, rolled-up cheroots farmers smoke in the fields as they work are made with tobacco so good it doesn't leave the farm. I smoked three that day. Put that in your mouth and smoke it!

Vinales offers a lot more than just tobacco farming, so we decided to stay for a day and a half. Our crew met up with Dago and Omar, a pair of crazy brothers who took us jutia hunting. Jutia are these giant jungle rats that can be skinned and eaten whole, like small pigs. The process was pretty simple. We laid some traps one night, then hit the sack. The next morning, we collected our jutia and headed to lunch at Dago's friends' farm on Vinales's valley floor. We dined on our freshly caught rodents, as well as crayfish as big as my arm from a local river and two massive red snappers, all grilled. We also ate roasted pig, and finished with palmichas, small dates harvested from royal palm trees. I was thankful for my salsa lesson from Nelda, because when a local band showed up to get the party started, I danced up a storm, played a little guitar, and had a good ol' time with my hosts.

We'd arranged to stay at a bed-and-breakfast that evening, which was very rustic. We were way out in the country, without electricity or many modern conveniences. I'd anticipated skipping dinner, since it didn't appear there was much to eat. Instead, we experienced one of the most memorable meals of the trip at a paladar in the woods called, of course, Paladares del Bosque. Toby had dined there once before and swore up and down it was a gem, but we were out in the middle of nowhere and it was 11 at night. We parked our car on a dirt road, then walked through a forested ravine past about a hundred angry barking dogs. Outfitted with a bougainvillea-and-wildflower-covered deck, here was a little house on stilts perched on the side of a mountain. Food in Cuban homes is extraordinary from a visitor's perspective; it is everything that the restaurants aren't. We dined on fresh grilled tuna, rice, beans, yucca with garlic mojo, roasted pork, chicken with olives, cucumber and tomato salad straight from the garden—easily the best tomatoes that I have eaten outside of Morocco. Spring tomatoes in Cuba are just beyond words. The chicken was incredible, freshly butchered and simply thrown on the grill with oil and garlic, finished with an olive-spiked tomato Creole sauce. Slow-roasted pork from pigs pulled out of the pen, starved for a couple of days, and then fed more of those rare palm fruits, dates, orange rinds, and coconut husks for days before butchering, made for another sweet and succulent course. This is food the way it should be.

It seems my show's ratings spike whenever I'm subjected to some form of bizarre physical ritual. And as long as viewers like it and I find it culturally significant, I'm going to keep doing it. Santería is a system of beliefs that merges the Yoruba religion with Roman Catholic and Native American traditions; it was developed by slaves brought from Africa to work the Caribbean sugar plantations. I grew up in a Jewish household in New York City, so the idea of Santería itself is rather foreign to me. I met up with Gonsalo, a Cuban expat who moved to Miami but returned after a few years. I'm not sure how he swung that, but maybe it has something to do with his status as a Santero, an exalted position in the culture. He is very high up in the Santería food chain, and invited me to the house of a Babalao named Rafael, basically a Santero priest who holds ceremonies in his house. Their goal? To cleanse me of evil spirits so that I could access the spirit world through their saints as I moved through my daily life. I went through the process with eight or nine other locals from the neighborhood who were already Santería practitioners. Since I was the new guy, they took extra care to ensure I received a thorough blessing, saying a couple prayers over me at every opportunity. An essential aspect of Santería involves the use of herbs, roots, flowers, and plants as well as sacrificial birds and other animals. They sacrificed a few pigeons for the first part of the ritual and proceeded to rub them all over my body in order to transfer the evil spirits in me to the bird. Next, they rolled coconut pieces on the floor to ensure that everything was cool (like rolling bones or dice). Once I was clean, they hooked me up with Yarusha, one of the Saints through which you communicate to the other side of the world in the Santería religion.

Next, they pulled me into another room, where I knelt on the floor. They killed a rooster by slicing open its neck with a ceremonial knife, pouring the blood over my head and letting it drip down my skull into a little cup, threw some feathers in the cup, and wiped my head clean with a special cloth. The whole thing took about forty-five minutes, all done to call and response prayers and ritual drumming. The ceremony concluded with Rafael leading me to the foot of a sacred Saba tree at a park near his house. I laid my bloody clothes and the rag used to wash my head at the tree's roots, making sure I clutched the tree and said some prayers with him. Rafael explained that I needed to pursue a better relationship with the God of my understanding. He sensed that at one time in my life I was more connected. Tears formed at the corners of my eyes as he spoke, reminding me that it didn't matter what I believed in as long as it wasn't me. He was right. About everything. Life is hectic, and the worldly clamors have overtaken mine, to be sure. My spiritual condition is not what it once was. I couldn't believe how simple and intrinsically caring and tender the whole morning had been, despite the animal sacrifice. Santería for me had always been on par with voodoo. I simply was ignorant and had practiced contempt prior to investigation. Ouch. One of the most wonderful aspects of my life is the ongoing enlightenment I feel every time I experience another world religion or spiritual practice. It makes a day seeing the sights on a tour bus pale in comparison.

While I'd been a little stressed about going to Cuba for legal reasons, once we arrived, I felt fairly comfortable all the time, save one incident. Our crew traveled five hours to the colonial city of Trinidad, founded by the Spanish in 1514. Hoping to shoot a fishing trip, we discovered that the Marina Trinidad had a handful of state-run boats. Remember, Cubans are prohibited from being on boats at sea. Local fishermen work from tiny rowboats they can only take a few feet offshore. Alternatively, some take old truck tire inner tubes or large blocks of Styrofoam and propel themselves out to sea with flippers, using hand lines to catch giant-size fish. It's a wonder they have any fishing industry at all here, given the inherent dangers. A small number of captains get variances so that they may take some privileged guests out on the water, but that's about it.

Now, I'm not perfect. Never said I was. In fact, I spent a fair amount of my adolescent years bending the law. However, never have I attempted to experiment in human trafficking. That is, until I went to Cuba. We were shooting on a boat, after all, and we needed sound. Our sound girl, Sheyla, was Cuban. She was willing to take the risk, we were willing to take the risk, so we smuggled her on board. The whole thing seems asinine looking back on it. It's easy to lose sight of the fact that despite the amazing beauty, the resilience of the people, their willingness to share their lives with you, the cultural pride, the amazing talent pool of smarts and savvy, you're in a country with restrictive, horrific rules that prohibit some of the basic privileges we take for granted—like spending time on a boat. For the most part, a big part, I fell in love with Cuba. Everyone here has an incredible level of acceptance and pride for their country, even when it involves restrictions or limitations—yet I could see the happiness in Sheyla's eyes as she went out on the water for the very first time. Let's face it: Cuba is in many ways a paradise, but it's also a prison. The Cubans know it in their heart of hearts, I think, and they see change coming. Fast.

Anyway, our day played out perfectly. We set out twenty miles offshore to a string of little islands called the Queen's Gardens, Gardenia de la Reina, which is a set of roughly 400 islands, some no more than an acre in size, sitting just inside the massive reef system that rings the Cuban side of the Caribbean coastline. We dove for lobsters off Callo Coca. We caught mackerel, pouring rum down their gills to put them to sleep before filleting them. We smoked five-year-old vintage Churchill cigars that were actually rolled by the very fellow who used to roll them for Churchill himself. We putt-putted a couple more miles over to Callo Macho and sat in the tree line, surrounded by a score of wild iguanas and a few very curious jutias. We went bone fishing with some fly rods; we feasted on boiled lobster on the beach and had a grand old time, right up until it was time to head back.

As we headed back to Cuba proper, our engines died, one by one, about five minutes apart. As luck would have it, an unexpected rainstorm blew in as well. So there we were, stranded at sea in the middle of our experiment in human trafficking. A lonely boat on a giant, empty ocean that never looked bigger. I've been scared shitless at sea by bad weather, rickety boats, unskilled captains, lack of radios or life jackets, but this was a new level of petrified. What would happen if the police or the navy showed up? Under any other circumstance, there is no one I would have wanted to see more, but in this instance I might have just been asked to leave the country, or worse. Proceed to airport . . . or a Cuban prison, do not pass go. "Say, Andrew, you brought a Cuban national on board a boat, twenty miles off the coast. Really!?" People just don't do that. Out of nowhere, a catamaran with some drunken British tourists sailed by and towed us back to the marina before the authorities caught wind of our operation. Thank you, Yarusha, who I am sure was looking out for me.

We drove that evening to Raul and Rosa's house, two friends of our Cuban production team. They expected us at noon, and we rolled in at 7 P.M. Rosa prepared a giant crab, some roasted goat, and a grilled snapper dinner, along with her famous tamarind and sugar candies. Raul is an old-world soul, a real campesino, with no need for cash. He is one of those guys who occasionally take a rubber inner tube out into the water fishing for snapper, sea crabs, and lobster in addition to raising goats, selling goat milk, and taking care of his family's needs by himself. He built his house overlooking the sea and works off the land. In our dog-eat-dog Western world, this type of life might seem too simple, too boring, and way too full of unnecessary challenges. But these were some of the happiest people I had ever met in my life.

After dinner, they brought me to the Casa del Musica, which is in the Trinidad town center, smack dab in the middle of the perfectly restored and mostly preserved seventeenth-century city. We danced the salsa, listened to live music, and met Pablo, the guy who runs the outdoor nightclub on the steps of the ancient cathedral. There is no better setting for a music club that I have ever seen. This wasn't a state-run spot designed for tourists; this was the real thing. Great music and dancing in an unpretentious way, designed for locals, attended by them in droves. Clued-in visitors were made to feel welcome. As I said before, there are so few outlets for Cuban citizens; movie theaters are scarce, and people don't really watch television (few have them), play video games (ditto), or surf the Web (hahahaha). Instead, Cuba as a country goes out at night, listens to music, and dances. They are still excited about most of the simple things the rest of the world has lost sight of, which says more about us than about them.

And just when I'm all wrapped up in this wonderful culture, just when I've forgotten about Cuba's strained political scene, we spot policemen arresting a man in the country. Which begged the question *Why?* No one knew and we didn't ask, but under Cuban law, killing a cow can pack a heavier fine than murder, with cow killers facing between four and twenty-five years in prison, depending on whom you talk to. However, with the country's strict food rationing, often a desperate farmer is forced to tie cows to the railroad tracks, which they refer to as "cow suicide." These incidents must be reported to the police. The farmer typically gives the policemen a piece of meat, which helps them look the other way when it comes to writing an angry report. Of course, this process can get rather messy and complicated, so sometimes a farmer will opt to kill the cow in a barn. This is risky, because Cuba's vultures, notorious for smelling blood miles away, often lead country cops traveling on horseback right to the scene of the crime. Watching the cops aggressively shaking someone down leaves you with a sickening feeling in the pit of your stomach, especially if you come from a society where more beef is thrown away than Cubans eat in an entire lifetime.

We motored back into Havana and ate lunch at the Sociedad Gastropol—a quasi-state-run, private eating club on the third floor of a decrepit apartment building. The owner, Hector, operates a simple little restaurant in an amazing setting, with a handful of tables inside and eight or nine tables on a balcony overlooking the Malecón and the ocean. We ate plateloads of real Cuban food, from fresh escabeche of snapper and shrimp ceviche, to a ham-and-potato frittata. But the most interesting dish was a massive grilled lobster tail, pounded out between two pieces of wax paper to roughly a half-inch thick. The tails were about two pounds each, simply huge. They marinate the meat overnight in garlic, lime juice, olive oil, and salt and pepper, then grill it over charcoal and serve it with fresh, paper-thin slices of pineapple and local tomatoes. With this incredible fresh food and a classical guitarist playing in the background, it was a perfect last lunch in Havana.

We spent the rest of the day walking around the Capitolio and the old National Ballet Theater, then headed back to Hotel Nacional for some needed rest. That evening, I sipped on another virgin mojito and watched the sun set over the Gulf of Mexico. Evening plans involved catching yet another meal at a state-run place called El Emperador with Toby. With its close proximity to the Nacional, this restaurant gets a lot of traffic from the international diplomatic and business community. What's more, years ago, El Emperador was Chilean president Salvador Allende's favorite restaurant. Castro invited him to the twentieth anniversary of the attack on Moncada Garrison in the summer of 1973. When he returned on what was to be his last trip to Havana, after not being there for twenty years, he remarked to Castro that he was very excited to finally return to El Emperador. At this point, the place had been closed for years. In one of the great Cuban tales the locals love to tell about their dear, beloved Fidel, Castro allegedly made one phone call and declared the restaurant back open. The original kitchen team was reassembled, they spruced up the joint, filled it with food, trained some waiters, and *voilà*: El Emperador has been up and running ever since. The atmosphere is very cozy, with light provided by candles. I can see why Allende loved the place. In this dimly lit environment, I noticed the guy at our neighboring table chowing down on a very good-looking steak. I already knew beef was on the no-no list, as was selling it or importing it, so I was baffled. And I still can't understand or explain the lobster rules, so I was perplexed. My friends explained that in high-end, foreigner-driven restaurants, steak is sort of a business within a business. They have some Cuban beef on the menu, but they also bring in some frozen Argentine, Aussie, and Brazilian beef. If you're an expat living in Havana, or a well-connected Cuban, and you know a chef in a restaurant who is willing to trade, you can get some frozen Australian racks of lamb or an Argentine tenderloin. So you get some high-quality frozen Argentine or Brazilian beef from your chef friend for cash or some other favor, he leaves you an indiscreet bag by your seat as you leave, and then he just offers some black-market suicide cow meat on his menu for the next couple of weeks so the state inspectors don't see a discrepancy in the ordering. There is an element of this classically Cuban, "one for all and all for one" sense. It's very entrepreneurial, yet very much an every-man-for-himself kind of deal. This is one of the things that make Cuba charming in the extreme when it comes to trying to find durable or disposable goods. There's always a way to find a car part or an exotic piece of food. You just need patience and the ability to go at a moment's notice to fetch what you need, but it's also a mañana, mañana culture, so you've always got lots of time on your hands.

Our departure coincided with Cuba's May Day celebration. I arose from my bed at Hotel Nacional to the sounds of the holiday masses assembling in the streets. People flooded the city, with literally a million Cubans gathering at the José Martí Memorial in Plaza de la Revolución. Another million-plus were marching through the streets. I joined them briefly at nine in the morning, marching for a couple of miles, taking pictures and absorbing the scene. Right before I needed to leave for the airport, who should come sauntering by but Teofilo Stevenson, Cuba's Babe Ruth and Muhammad Ali, all rolled into one. A three-time gold medal–winning Olympic boxer, Stevenson is a living legend—and not just in Cuba, but all over the world. This amazing cultural icon was surrounded by a couple of quasi-assistants and friends who I am guessing spend their time looking after him. It's thought that had Stevenson not been Cuban, he would have dominated the heavyweight boxing world for years, and of course would be living in Vegas in a huge house with a nineteen-year-old girlfriend. I was absolutely starstuck by this man, a superstar whose every televised Olympic bout I was glued to growing up in New York City. I walked up, shook his hand, and wished him a happy May Day. I'm such a complete sports geek, I turn into a little child in front of all those sports heroes. Teofilo Stevenson is the one guy I wanted to meet in Cuba—besides Fidel, of course.

¡Viva Cuba!

Final Thought

So what is the Bizarre Truth? It's lots of things, I think. It's the ugly mass of humanity of metro Manila that masks the incredible hospitality and kindness of the Filipino people. It's the fierce nationalistic pride of Catalonia. I landed in Barcelona once and a cabbie asked me how I was enjoying myself. I told him I loved Spain, and he replied, "Dees eeez not Spain, eeez Barthelona!" It's the desolate beauty of Alaska that is best seen being pulled behind a team of world-class sled dogs. It's standing in line at Kuznechny Market in St. Petersburg with a history teacher who is crying because he can remember as he stares at hundreds of cold cuts behind the deli counter that just a few years before he waited for two days for a portion of canned Danish ham. It's the impact that precolonial cuisine has on Mexican food, even today. It's the disappearing rain forest, the destroyed fishing grounds, the first peoples of the world who are driven from their homes by governments who don't realize the catastrophic nature of their decision making. This truth is real, and it's not going to end.

The Bizarre Truth is also the generosity that the least fortunate people in the world (by ethnocentric Western standards) have afforded me in their homes on a moment's notice. I am often asked how I can stomach some of the food I am offered, as if it is somehow "less than" because it's not a luxury cut of beef in a fancy restaurant. That question pisses me off. I am always grateful for a meal, any meal, and often I am served sitting next to someone's mom who cooked it. How can you not smile and say thank you? I was once invited to lunch at the home of Donaldo, one of my native guides in the Amazon jungle, and he was so proud of his two-room home on stilts on the banks of the Pilchi River. We sat in the cooking room, on the floor, eating fried coconut grubs served on leaves, along with small steamed tubers from his garden. He ate one grub, giving me two on my leaf, and also giving two to each of his three kids who were there that day; the oldest one was six. Nine grubs and a few root vegetables were all they were going to get to eat that day. How do you explain kindness and generosity like that? How can you be anything other than grateful and humbled by that experience?

The Bizarre Truth is that there are good people and bad people everywhere, and let's face it, simplicity is often overlooked as the most important contributing factor to happiness. I have spent a lot of time sharing food and experiencing culture, and along the way I realized that my own curiosity is fulfilled by a life devoted to continued learning and becoming more open to the idea that there are many different ways of living a complete and useful life—not just mine. In fact, the lives we lead ourselves might be the least important way, regardless of who you are or where you live, because it's the one you are most familiar with and the one you use as a crutch most of the time.

At the end of the day, my curiosity is the driving force in making my life complete, and the Bizarre Truth is that a simple meal with friends, regardless of where I am, connects me to others and in turn to their purpose, dreams, and desires. Those connections and binding tissues are the most important elements of what I think is the fabric of a useful life.

When I was a little kid in New York, I would look at public-television documentaries about tribal Africa and think to myself how better off I was, how sophisticated our big-city culture seemed to be. How superior and smug I felt. What a little snot I was—well, actually, I was just inexperienced and untraveled. So forty years later I am in Botswana, and I realize I have finally changed my core way of thinking and feeling when Xaxe leans over and quietly tells me in the simplest terms what the Bizarre Truth really is— that despite all the messages to the contrary, despite the obsessions we all have with ourselves and our own problems and our own egos . . . in the end, the Bizarre Truth is that the secret to happiness is simply the ability to "love and respect other people." Thanks, my friend.

Acknowledgments

The list of people who helped me get this book off the ground and into your hands is voluminous in the extreme. Naming them all is no easy task, and any omissions (of which I am sure there are many) should be apologized for at the outset.

When you win a Webby for excellence in online media you are allowed five words of thanks. This is not a Webby and brevity is not my strong suit.

Most important, I would like to thank my parents, Robert and Caren Zimmern, and my stepdad, Andre Laporte, who have always been there for me in every way imaginable, even when I did my best to make that job an impossible one. My in-laws Bill and Joenie Haas and their families, without whose support my career would have fizzled long ago. There are also many families who, for a variety of reasons, adopted me as their own many years ago and must be deservedly credited with making me the eater, traveler, and experience junkie that I am today. The Wakabayashis, the Vales, the Macks, the Salks, the Salkes, the Saltzmans, and the Jaffes all need to take a big bow. My friends from East Hampton and Amagansett, my college cronies, my coworkers at all the restaurants over the years, and many teachers and mentors should be on that list as well.

My extended family in Minnesota deserves special mention. I was lifted out of a horrific hellhole in NYC on January 28, 1992, and woke up days later in Center City, Minnesota, at Hazelden, and for the next six months was under their continuum of care. Over the last seventeen-plus years my life has gotten better and sweeter, one day at a time, and I owe it all to Jim L, Bob B, Aaron M,

ACKNOWLEDGMENTS

Mike and Norm A, John C, Craig L, dozens of young men who shared themselves with me, and millions of others around the world with whom I share a very unique and beautiful relationship. Anyone looking to make a difference in someone's life can contribute to the Rishia and Andrew Zimmern Scholarship Fund at The Retreat in Wayzata, MN (www.theretreat.org). The Retreat provides low-cost recovery services to those seeking help with their alcoholism and chemical dependency.

Professionally, Elio Guatalini and Anne Isaak gave me a chance to do things at a young age that I will never be able to adequately thank them for. Steve Hanson taught me the value of hard work and allowed me to succeed well beyond my capabilities. Steven Kalt and Ken Frydman helped me grow a business and then saved my life by asking me to leave it. Michael Morse, Lee Lynch, and Terry Saario gave me places to show up each day for work that I looked forward to every day, a rarity in any business. Thomas Keller and Anne Rosenzweig taught me there is actually a best way to do everything. Rebecca Kolls, Greg Mack, the Fox 9 News team, the gang at FM 107—especially Dan Seeman, Christopher Gabriel, Doug Westerman, Mary Ellen Pinkham, and many others—all helped me do the best job I was capable of doing at various times in my life, and I am thankful to have worked with them all.

Carrie Paetow, Leah Bolfing, and Kate Kunkel worked tirelessly in my office before all the hoopla, often for no gold or glory, and without whom I would have been lost. Molly Mogren deserves special mention for both her role on my current team in creating andrewzimmern.com and for her collaboration with me on this book, the best parts of which are due to her tenacious dedication, and the mistakes are all mine. Dusti Kugler is my right hand, right foot, and right side of my brain; she is simply the best there is. John Levy, Tom Wiese, Stephanie Unterberger, Natalie Burns, and John Larson handle all my affairs, and doing what they tell me to do is something I have always benefited from. I should remember that more often. Larson and Wiese deserve a special place in Valhalla; they are Norse Warriors of the highest order.

The Tremendous Entertainment team is the best there is, and Colleen Steward believed in me at a time that no one else did and continues to make my television life a dream job. My field producers and videographers, with whom I spend more time each year than I do with my wife and son, inspire me more than I ever let them know. I am in awe of Pat Younge and all the folks at Travel Channel Media (past and present) who handed me a thoroughbred horse and let me ride. I am indebted to them for all they do for me day after day, and a special thank-you to David Gerber for steering the ship that was *Bizarre Foods* and is *Bizarre World*. Ditto to Marjorie Hall, James Ashurst, Kwin Mosby, Karen Hansen, Eliza Booth, and Sarah Rooney.

Thanks to the BEET team at MSN.com, Reveille, Toyota, and EyeBoogie for creating the Web-based series *Appetite for Life* and letting me do my thing online for such a huge audience.

Connie Mayer taught me to write. Adam Platt taught me how to be a writer, and a huge nod goes to Deb Hopp, Gary Johnson, Brian Anderson, Jayne Haugen Olson, and all the folks at *Minneapolis-St. Paul* magazine and *Delta Sky* magazine for letting me grow that side of my career.

Charlie Conrad, Jenna Ciongoli, and the team at Random House went through hell to see this book through; their patience, tolerance, and understanding were limitless, and without their persistence and faith there would be no book. Charlie especially, and every first-time author should be so lucky.

Finally, I would like to thank my wife Rishia and my son Noah, to whom *The Bizarre Truth* is dedicated. Without them none of this—not the book, the shows, the magazine columns, none of it—is worth doing. They are my world, and they are always there for me despite the fact that they have to share me with so many, so often. . . .

Minneapolis, MN ~ June 2009

About the Author

Andrew Zimmern is a food writer, dining critic, chef, and co-creator, host, and coproducer of the Travel Channel series *Bizarre Foods* and *Bizarre Worlds with Andrew Zimmern*. Zimmern is the founder and Editor-in-Chief of www.andrewzimmern.com, writes monthly for *Delta Sky* magazine and *Minneapolis-St. Paul* magazine, and lives in Minneapolis with his wife and son.